THE
SECRET
CHAIN

SUNY SERIES IN PHILOSOPHY AND BIOLOGY
David Edward Shaner, Editor

THE
SECRET
CHAIN

Evolution
and
Ethics

Michael Bradie

STATE UNIVERSITY OF NEW YORK PRESS

Published by
State University of New York Press, Albany

© 1994   State University of New York

For information, address State University of New York Press,
State University Plaza, Albany, N.Y., 12246

Production by Christina S. Tartaglia
Marketing by Theresa Abad Swierzowski

Library of Congress Cataloging-in-Publication Data

Bradie, Michael.
    The secret chain : evolution and ethics / by Michael Bradie.
        p.   cm. — (SUNY series in philosophy & biology)
    Includes bibliographical references (p.   ) and index.
    ISBN 0–7914–2105–8 (hard : acid-free) — ISBN
    0–7914–2106–6 (pbk. : acid-free)
    1. Ethics, Evolutionary—History. 2. Evolution (Biology)—Moral
    and ethical aspects.   I. Title.   II. Series: SUNY series in
    philosophy and biology.
    BJ1298.B73   1994
    171'.7—dc20   93–47679
                                                                          CIP

10 9 8 7 6 5 4 3 2 1

For my father

Contents

Preface

This study is the outgrowth of a convergence of interests in evolutionary theory and the role of models and metaphors in science. I first became interested in Popper's use of natural selection as a model for scientific change. This led me to an exploration of the scope and limits of an evolutionary approach to epistemology. There are certain obvious affinities between ethics and epistemology, and I wondered how far these affinities could be drawn. This book is the result.

Several themes run through the book. First, a historical argument shows the connection between the arguments of the eighteenth century British moral theorists and the development of evolutionary treatments of ethics in the nineteenth and twentieth centuries. These issues are the main focus of Chapters 2 and 3. Chapter 1 explores the parallels between evolutionary approaches to espistemology and evolutionary approaches to ethics. Second, the import of evolution for ethics rests on the claim that our conception of human nature is substantially altered by our appreciation of the impact of the forces of evolution in shaping it. The relevance of appeals to human nature for ethics faces two major challenges. Insofar as conceptions of human nature are normative as well as descriptive, any attempts to draw ethical conclusions from an analysis of human nature appear to be circular. Also, the very concept of human nature smacks of "essentialism," the idea that human beings have fixed and unchangeable natures. One philosophical offshoot of Darwinism is a challenge to essentialism. It has been argued that Darwinism undermines any appeals to human nature for the explanation of anything. These concerns are taken up in Chapter 4. Chapter 5 discusses several recent attempts to use an evolutionary perspective to draw substantial conclusions about the nature of ethics, the justification of ethical principles, and specific moral issues. The sociobiologists are not the only ones to make such attempts. An assessment of some arguments for expanding the moral circle to include nonhuman animals based on evolutionary considerations is the focus of Chapter 6.

In the eighteenth century, Francis Hutcheson argued that a "secret chain" linked benevolence and self-interest. This secret chain that Hutcheson saw as underlying the human ethical condition was given a special twist by Darwin and the nineteenth century evolutionary moral theorists. These chains persist, albeit in altered forms, in the efforts by contemporary moral theorists to reflect the relevance of biology for ethics. In the chains we shall examine, some of the links are weak and problematic but others have a certain strength to them. From a broadly naturalistic perspective, which I endorse, human biology and human evolutionary history contribute significantly to our general understanding of the human condition. The evolutionary analysis of specific moral practices and principles is somewhat more problematic. A final chapter presents summary conclusions and reflections about the future for evolutionary treatments of ethics.

I shall argue that evolutionary analyses do provide valuable insights into moral phenomena. The claims of moral autonomists that biology can have no special relevance for ethics are rejected. The claims of other sociobiologists that biology provides the basis for a complete analysis of ethics are also rejected. The immediate challenge is to forge together the resources of workers in diverse interested disciplines such as biology, philosophy, anthropology, and psychology to create a multidisciplinary basis for the analysis of the relevance of evolutionary considerations to the development of human moral systems.

A note about my understanding of the term *moral* and its derivatives. Part of the problem in attempting to assess the relevance of evolutionary biology for morality is that the term *moral* is used by different moral theorists in radically different ways. Constructing a theory or account of moral phenomena is unlike the problem of constructing a theory of planetary motion. In the latter case, most theoreticians will agree on what relevant data needs to be explained. Not so when it comes to moral behavior, moral judgments, and moral rules. No general agreement among moral theorists (whether they be philosophers or scientists) exists as to what to count under the moral domain. Indeed, the Australian philosopher Mary Maxwell has recently suggested that, from a biological point of view, what is comprised under the heading of "morals" is liable to turn out to be a very mixed bag with disparate evolutionary pedigrees. Rather than try to sort through this morass here, I will qualify as "moral" any aspect of human behavior for which the application of standards of right and wrong or good and bad is appropriate.

The beginning of my serious efforts in this direction can be traced to a productive semester spent in Dick Lewontin's lab during the spring of 1984 and his offhand query, "You're a philosopher. Why aren't you doing ethics?" This excursion into moral theory and the history of moral thought represents a significant departure from my prior work and interests. I have had a lot of help along the way both from students and colleagues. In this regard, I wish to acknowledge the help, in particular, of John Beatty, Michael Ruse, Pat Williams, Barbara Horan, R. D. Alexander, John Collier, John Paul Scott, Chris Morris, Robert Ham, Carrie-Ann Lynch, Pytor Boltuc, Bill Kline, Jana Craig, and my students in various classes on ethics and evolution. Special thanks go to Kathy Hicks, Mark Gromko (for the biology, as usual), and R. G. Frey. I am grateful to Gene Torisky for his critical reading of the manuscript and proofs and preparation of the index. My treatment of the British moralists is indebted to my colleague R. G. Frey, who was unstinting in his criticism of my efforts to understand this tradition and, from time to time, contributed materially as well as intellectually to the completion of this work. The Faculty Research Committee at Bowling Green State University provided me with several summer research grants, and the final touches were added while I was a visiting fellow at the Center for the Philosophy of Science at the University of Pittsburgh.

Acknowledgments

Some of the material in Chapters 5 and 6 has appeared in earlier versions, in the following places, and is reprinted here with permission.

"Ethics and Evolution," *Inquiry* 36:199–217 © Scandinavian University Press.

"Darwin's Legacy," *Biology & Philosophy* 7 (1992): 111–126, and "Darwinism and the Moral Status of Animals," in D. Prawitz and D. Westerstaahl, eds., *Logic and Philosophy of Science in Uppsala: Papers from the Ninth International Congress of Logic, Methodology and Philosophy of Science,* Synthese Library, vol. 236, pp. 499–509, © Kluwer Academic Publishers, 1994.

Chapter 1

Ethics and Evolution

THE SECRET CHAIN

Francis Hutcheson, in *An Inquiry Concerning the Original of Our Ideas of Virtue or Moral Good*, wrote "[i]t is true indeed, that the actions we approve in others, are generally imagin'd to tend to the natural good of Mankind, or that of some Parts of it. But whence this secret chain between each person and mankind? How is my interest connected with the most distant parts of it?" (Hutcheson, 1969, p. 111). The secret chain that Hutcheson had in mind was the chain that links private interest and universal benevolence. The metaphor captures one of the central problems faced by the eighteenth century British moralists. It was a problem that captured the imagination of Darwin when he rejected the providential solution endorsed by his kinsman Sir James Mackintosh. It is an appropriate metaphor for the interconnected themes of this book. In addition to Hutcheson's chain there is the chain that allegedly links biology and evolution to ethics, the chain that links views of human nature to the explanation and justification of moral theories, and the moral echo of the chain of being that details the phylogenetic development of the moral sense.

What, if anything, can we learn about ethics or morality from the theory of evolution and the fact that human beings have evolved from ancestral forms? This topic has been controversial since the publication of Darwin's *Origin of Species* (in 1859) and *The Descent of Man* (in 1871). Darwin argued that evolutionary theory could throw some light on what was known in the eighteenth and nineteenth centuries as the *moral sense*. Darwin's "bulldog," T. H. Huxley, argued that nature was violent, competitive and the antithesis of morality. Human morality, he thought, arose in opposition to the evolutionary tendencies of nature. Herbert Spencer, their contemporary and an evolutionist before Darwin, argued that biological evolution, social evolution and the evolution of morality were all

1

part of a single process—a single cosmic evolution. Spencer, unlike Darwin (in his more cautious moments) or Huxley, was a progressionist, who believed that evolution tended toward the better. Kropotkin took exception to Huxley's reading of evolutionary theory as portraying nature as "red in tooth and claw" and emphasized what he saw as natural tendencies toward cooperation and sociality.

A philosophical reaction against drawing any ethical consequences from evolutionary theory was started by the English moral philosopher Henry Sidgwick (in the 1870s) and crystallized in G. E. Moore's (1903) claim that evolutionary ethics committed what he called the *Naturalistic Fallacy*. The alleged fallacy was related to a cautionary note sounded by Hume with respect to the tendency of some writers on ethics to glibly slide from expressions of the form "X is . . . " to expressions of the form "X ought. . . . " Moore did not mention Hume in his analysis, and his view that *good* is indefinable rests on a number of dubious and contentious metaphysical assumptions. With respect to the evolutionary ethicists of the nineteenth century in general, and Herbert Spencer in particular, Moore was concerned with the implied identification of claims of the form "X has evolved" with "X is good" and "X is more evolved than Y" with "X is better than Y." In any case, any reasoning from the facts of nature to conclusions about the good or what ought to be done has come to be labeled as *committing a naturalistic fallacy*.

For a time the ethical implications of evolutionary theory became a nonissue. Then, in the early 1940s, Julian Huxley, the grandson of T. H. Huxley, reexamined his grandfather's arguments and claimed that granddad got it wrong. Nature and ethics were in harmony not in opposition. Still, nothing much happened until the advent of sociobiology in the early 1970s. All of a sudden, ethics and evolution became respectable again, at least in some quarters. Critics of sociobiology were quick to point to the "fallacy" committed by inferring ethical conclusions from scientific or factual premises or by construing biological altruism as related in any significant way to ethical altruism, for example. Several philosophers and biologists, such as E. O. Wilson, Michael Ruse, and Robert Richards, have tried in the past several years to construct versions of evolutionary ethics that outflank the naturalistic fallacy or otherwise defuse the criticisms directed against sociobiological analyses of ethics. In 1989, Princeton University Press reissued T. H. Huxley's *Ethics and Evolution*, with a historical introduction and an afterword by a leading sociobiologist, G. C. Williams. Williams argues, in effect, that not only did Huxley get it *right*—nature is evil, as his recent paper entitled *Mother Nature is a Wicked Old Witch* has it—we now have the sociobiological arguments to prove it.

Other considerations in addition to sociobiology justify a reexamination of the philosophical relevance of evolutionary theory. In recent years, there has been a resurgence of interest in various naturalistic approaches to philosophical issues. In particular, there is a large and growing literature in what is called *evolutionary epistemology*.[1] There are obvious parallels between epistemology and ethics, and it would seem that if a case can be made for an evolutionary approach to epistemology, it is possible that a parallel case could be made for an evolutionary approach to ethics as well.

EPISTEMOLOGY FROM AN EVOLUTIONARY POINT OF VIEW

Epistemology is the study of the foundations and nature of knowledge. The traditional approach beginning with Plato and developed in its modern form by Descartes is that epistemological questions have to be answered in ways that do not presuppose any particular knowledge. Such approaches might be termed *transcendental* insofar as the appeal to knowledge to answer these questions is rejected as question begging. The Darwinian revolution of the nineteenth century suggested an alternative approach, first explored by Dewey and the pragmatists. Human beings, as the products of evolutionary development, are natural beings. Their capacities for knowledge and belief are also honed by evolutionary considerations. As such there is reason to suspect that knowing, as a natural activity, should be treated and analyzed along lines compatible with its status, that is, by the methods of science. In this view, no sharp division of labor is made between science and epistemology. In particular, the results of particular sciences such as evolutionary theory and cognitive psychology are deemed relevant to the solution of epistemological problems. Such approaches, in general, are called *naturalistic epistemologies*, whether they are directly motivated by evolutionary considerations or not. Those that are directly motivated by evolutionary considerations and argue that the growth of knowledge follows the pattern of evolution in biology are called *evolutionary epistemologies*. Three distinctions need to be made.

The first distinction concerns two interrelated but distinct programs that go by the name *evolutionary epistemology*. One is the attempt to account for the characteristics of cognitive mechanisms in animals and humans by a straightforward extension of the biological theory of evolution to those aspects or traits of animals that are the biological substrates of cognitive activity; for example, their brains, sensory systems, and motor systems. The other program attempts to account for the evolution of ideas, scientific theories, and culture in general, by using models and metaphors drawn from evolutionary biology. Both programs have their roots in nineteenth century biology and social philosophy, in the work of Darwin, Spencer, James, and others. There have been a number of attempts in the intervening years to develop the programs in detail (see bibliography and review in Campbell, 1974a). Much of the contemporary work in evolutionary epistemology derives from the work of Konrad Lorenz (1977, 1982), Donald Campbell (1960, 1974a, 1974b), Karl Popper (1968, 1972, 1976, 1978, 1984), and Stephen Toulmin (1967, 1972, 1974, 1981). I have labeled these two programs *EEM* (evolution of epistemological mechanisms) and *EET* (evolution of epistemological theories). (Bradie, 1986) *EEM* is the label for the program that attempts to provide an evolutionary account of the development of cognitive structures. *EET* is the label for the program that attempts to analyze the development of human knowledge and epistemological norms by appealing to relevant biological considerations. Some of these attempts involve analyzing the growth of human knowledge in terms of evolutionary (selectionist) models and metaphors (e.g., Popper, 1968, 1972; Toulmin, 1972; Hull, 1988). Others (e.g., Ruse, 1986; Rescher, 1977, 1990b) argue for a biological grounding of epistemological norms and methodologies but eschew selectionist models of the growth of human knowledge as such.

A second distinction concerns ontogeny versus phylogeny. Biological development involves both ontogenetic and phylogenetic considerations. Thus, the development of specific traits, such as the opposable thumb in humans, can be viewed both from the point of view of the development of that trait in individual organisms (ontogeny) and the development of that trait in the human lineage (phylogeny). The development of knowledge and knowing mechanisms exhibits a parallel distinction. Therefore, we can study the growth of knowledge from either the ontogenetic point of view of the development of knowledge and epistemic norms in individuals or the phylogenetic point of view of the development of knowledge and epistemic norms across generations. Similarly, we can study the ontogenetic development of brains in individuals or the phylogenetic development of brains in the human lineage. The EEM/EET programs cut across this distinction because we may be concerned either with the ontogenetic or phylogenetic development of, say, the brain or norms and knowledge corpora. One might expect that, because current orthodoxy maintains that biological processes of ontogenesis proceed differently from the biological processes of phylogenesis, evolutionary epistemologies would reflect this difference. For the most part they do not, curiously enough.

A third distinction concerns descriptive versus prescriptive approaches to epistemology and the growth of human knowledge. Many have argued that neither the EEM program nor the EET program has anything at all to do with epistemology as traditionally understood. The basis for this contention is that epistemology, properly understood, is a normative discipline, whereas the EEM and EET programs are concerned with the construction of causal and genetic (factual) models. No such models, it is alleged, can have anything important to contribute to normative epistemology. To the extent that this is true, it casts some doubt on the plausibility of related efforts in evolutionary ethics.

Traditional epistemology is in large part a normative discipline. Evolutionary epistemologies in particular, and naturalistic epistemologies in general, insofar as they construe epistemology as continuous with science, would seem to be purely descriptive. Can such enterprises deal with normative questions? How one approaches this question depends upon how one construes the relationship of evolutionary epistemology to traditional epistemology. If evolutionary epistemology is seen as a "successor" discipline to traditional epistemology, then one may well be prepared to write off many of the traditional questions that epistemology set for itself. Other naturalized theories of knowledge, for example, Laudan's, involve reinterpreting normative claims in terms of empirical hypotheticals (Laudan, 1984, 1990). Quine (1990) also argues that naturalizing epistemology does not lead to a rejection of norms; "normative epistemology gets naturalized into a chapter of engineering: the technology of anticipating sensory stimulation" (Quine, 1990, p. 19). Campbell argues that evolutionary epistemology is the descriptive complement to traditional epistemology. As such, it begs some of the traditional normative questions of epistemology, such as "How is knowledge possible?" (Campbell 1974b).

Deriving epistemological norms from the facts of human knowledge acquisition would seem to commit some version of the naturalistic fallacy. It is open to evolutionary epistemologists to challenge the contention that the naturalistic fallacy (or at least any attempt to base norms on facts) is a fallacy. An argument of this form can be found in Richards (1987) with respect to the naturalistic fallacy in ethics. Richards argues that not all derivations of moral norms from facts are fallacious. The general idea is that norms need to be calibrated against intuitively clear cases. If some evolutionary account is forthcoming regarding why we are inclined to argue in certain ways with respect to morality (or logic or epistemology) then we can ground our normative principles in these evolutionary considerations. Richards's argument is complex and perhaps not completely successful, but it is not unpromising. It is analyzed in some detail in Chapter 5. A similar argument should be constructible for epistemological norms (cf. Vollmer, 1987; Munz, 1985; Bartley, 1987; Bradie, 1989a). In any case, even if some evolutionary account of the emergence of epistemological norms is forthcoming, it is very unlikely that specific norms are going to be derivable or justifiable from biological or genetic considerations alone. The specific form of the epistemological norms that are accepted by communities of cognizers will most certainly reflect local cultural contingencies in much the same way that specific moral codes reflect local cultural contingencies.

ETHICS FROM AN EVOLUTIONARY POINT OF VIEW

Can a parallel case be made for an evolutionary approach to ethics? Given that both ethics and epistemology are normative disciplines, one might expect that the possibilities for and difficulties inherent in an evolutionary treatment are the same for both. We must proceed with caution, however, because the parallels are not exact.

Campbell (1974a, p. 1109) rejects the obvious criticisms by Flew (1967), Quillian (1945), and others, that evolutionary ethics fails to provide grounds for normative ethics. For Campbell, the evolutionary ethicist is interested in what Campbell calls *descriptive ethics*. Descriptive ethics portrays the moral and ethical standards that various past and present cultures employ and would aim at the formulation of "hypothetically descriptive laws of social organization, including optional modes of individual behavior for optimizing collective goals." Such an enterprise could rightly be called a *science of ethics*. Given that some goal G has been adopted by a group, the science of ethics could "provide sets of derived, mediational values, which if adhered to would further the achievement of the chosen ultimate values." It may also serve as a predictive, though not justificatory instrument, in that it should be able to predict "which ultimate values animals such as social humankind are likely to choose." The parallels between Campbell's conception of descriptive ethics and its relation to normative ethics, on the one hand, and his conception of descriptive epistemology and analytic epistemology, on the other, are obvious. It remains to be seen whether "descriptive ethics," so characterized, is not merely ethics "in name only." It is interesting to note, however, a certain parallel between descriptive ethics and what the eighteenth century ethical theorists called *moral psychology*. There is a sense in which the post-Hobbesian British moral theorists who set the stage for the problem of morality that Darwin tried to address were more akin to empirical psychologists describing the moral behavior of human beings than they are to moral philosophers as we understand them. It is, of course, a well-known fact that the distinction between philosophy and science as we construe it was not clearly drawn by the eighteenth century thinkers. In one sense, normative ethics is the late complement to a descriptive tradition in contrast to descriptive epistemology which is a late complement to a prescriptive tradition.

One can distinguish two approaches to evolutionary ethics corresponding to the EEM and EET programs in epistemology. The one, which we might label *EMM* (evolution of moral mechanisms), focuses on the evolutionary considerations that are relevant for understanding the phylogenetic development of the capacity of organisms to be ethical. Possibly no one today seriously disputes that the capacity to engage in practices for which ethical judgments are appropriate, as well as the capacity to make moral judgments, have evolved. That is, no one disputes this except perhaps some religious fundamentalists and biblical literalists. A certain degree of intellectual ability, including the power to remember and reflect on one's actions, is a prerequisite for that capacity. Darwin was of the opinion that any sufficiently advanced social species would involve some ethical sense. Even so, it is a program with more promise than product because we do not know how the specific biological structures that make us "ethicizing animals" came to be or, in fact, which ones they are. The other, which we might label *EMT* (evolution of moral theses) can be construed either narrowly or broadly as contending that particular ethical systems or maxims or practices are capable of being explained or even justified in terms of some evolutionary or natural selection model.[2] Most of the arguments examined in this book deal with one or another aspect of the EMT program.

Just as there are three possible configurations of the relationship between evolutionary epistemology and traditional epistemology, there are three possible configurations of the relationship between evolutionary ethics and traditional ethics.

1. Evolutionary ethics is a competitor to traditional ethics. In this view, evolutionary ethics provides alternative answers to the traditional ethical questions, including those dealing with the evaluation and justification of norms. Herbert Spencer's *Principles of Ethics* and Julian Huxley's *Evolution and Ethics* are historical examples of this approach. More recently, Robert Richards has proposed such an approach in *Darwin and the Emergence of Evolutionary Theories of Mind and Behavior*.

2. Evolutionary ethics is complementary to traditional ethics. Evolutionary ethics, in this view, is a descriptive and explanatory account of the rise and development of ethical views. It complements the concerns of traditional ethics with normative issues. As noted earlier, Campbell has endorsed this point of view. Westermarck's monumental *The Origin and Development of Moral Ideas* is the classic here. Darwin's treatment of morality in *The Descent of Man* falls roughly into this category.

3. Evolutionary ethics might be construed as a successor discipline to traditional ethics. In this view, traditional ethics, with its focus on the justification of prescriptions, is to be rejected in favor of accounts that describe and explain how human beings come to have the moral beliefs and attitudes that they hold. Views that use evolutionary arguments to attack traditional normative accounts of ethics would fall into this category. Wilson (1979), Ruse (1986), and Ruse and Wilson (1986) would seem to fall here.

The distinction between phylogenetic and ontogenetic development carries over to evolutionary ethics as well. I do not have much to say about the ontogenetic development of ethics in this book, but following in the tradition of Piaget, Kohlberg, his students, and critics have addressed these issues at length. (See Kohlberg, 1981, 1984; Gilligan, 1982; and Wren, 1990.)

The parallels between ethics and epistemology are not exact. Allegiance to different ethical norms seems to shift more radically and more quickly than allegiance to epistemological norms. The extent to which this is true depends on the level of analysis. If goodness is the moral equivalent of truth, then moral norms appear to be more stable. Specific ethical maxims shift from culture to culture and era to era, but if they are analogous to specific epistemological methodologies or theories in science, then these latter do so as well.

Taking Darwin seriously in ethics means at least that we reconsider what it means to be human and an ethical being in the light of all the evidence that suggests we are not the privileged agents in a divinely created universe as we once thought. The challenge of Darwin and evolutionary theory is to reconsider, in the light of that evidence, what it is to be a human being or biological organism who can make moral judgments and what it is that we know about the universe in the light of that fact.

MORALS AND MODELS

The eighteenth century British moralists who set the agenda for Darwin's sketchy treatment of the subject did not make a sharp distinction between science and philosophy. Much of what they had to say about human morals then was as much a contribution to moral psychology as it was to moral philosophy as we understand that term today. It is characteristic of science to produce models of the phenomena to be understood. Scientific theories employ models as the theoretical tools investigators use to predict and explain. The models serve as templates for the organization and codification of information about the behavior of the natural systems, for which they are primarily descriptive. Moral theories are putatively different in that they focus on prescriptions rather than descriptions. However, it will be useful to consider the extent to which moral theories can be construed as models, which are theoretical devices to help explain why human beings behave as they do and to provide some rationale for arguing that certain modes of behavior are preferable to others. Moral theories rest, either implicitly or explicitly, on theories of human nature. These theories or models contain both descriptive and prescriptive elements. The differences between Hobbes, Shaftesbury, Hutcheson, Hume, Butler, Smith, and Darwin on the nature and characterization of morality can be attributed, in part, to differences between the models of human nature each employs.

A close examination of these underlying models will lead to a better understanding of the moral systems themselves and the role of appeals to human nature in shaping those moral systems.

I adopt a method of analysis characteristic of the descriptive sciences and use it to analyze the moral models of the eighteenth century moral theorists who contributed to the set of problems concerning moral motivation inherited by Darwin. The idea that the difference between physics and morality was not as great as we conceive it to be today was a common assumption of the period captured in the phrase *a science of morals*. The differences between descriptive and prescriptive utterances were not as sharply demarcated as they are today, and the moral models of the period more or less imperfectly reflected these two elements.

In the physical sciences, we distinguish between the phenomenon to be explained (e.g., an elephant sliding down a steep hill) and a theoretical model or representation of the phenomenon which we use to try to understand it (Galileo's equations or an idealized model of a weight on an inclined plane). We can use a similar approach for understanding moral phenomena. It is important to distinguish between the phenomenon to be explained (e.g., a moral action of some sort, such as, Mother Theresa ministering to the poor of India) and a theoretical model we might employ to try to understand or evaluate that phenomenon (e.g., in terms of egoistic or benevolent considerations). I shall use the term *moral phenomenology* to characterize the range of phenomena that moral theories, so construed, are attempts to explain and justify. The models, typically, will be models of human nature that incorporate both descriptive and prescriptive principles. The need to incorporate prescriptive elements into the moral models marks a significant difference between moral and physical models, and it is an open question whether the need to do so disqualifies this approach from any chance of success.

Having made the distinction between moral phenomena and moral models we need to distinguish several issues:

1. What the model says. This will consist of an articulation of several principles of action based on empirical assumptions, usually concerning human nature, and normative assumptions.
2. What the phenomena to be understood are. This constitutes the moral phenomenology and consists in a catalogue of features that the author deems to be "moral," either in the broad sense in which any action or agent is capable of being characterized as good or bad, or right or wrong, or in the narrow sense in which the moral actions and agents are those we would call the *good* or *right* ones.

3. Whether the model is a "good" model of the phenomena. Here, the standard criteria of model fit would seem to apply. We want our models to be both descriptively adequate and prescriptively adequate. Prescriptive adequacy means that the model in question delivers the same moral judgments that are revealed in the moral phenomenology, at least with respect to central cases. The world being as it is, our models will not be perfect reflections of our moral experience. Some adjustments will have to be made. Whether we are led to revise our phenomenological characterizations or our models is something that needs to be decided on a case-by-case basis. But the situation is no different in the physical sciences.

4. What the implications of the model are. The implications of the model are those descriptive and normative consequences that follow from the fundamental assumptions of the model. The relationship between them and the considerations in 3 is this. To the extent that the fit between model and phenomena is a good one, the implications of the model, which are theoretical predictions, will be identifiable with some appropriate piece of the phenomenology.

In many cases the distinction between 1 and 2 will not be clearly drawn. Thus, in the eighteenth century literature, *principles of self-love* must sometimes be read to refer to aspects of the situation to be understood and at other times to be elements of the explaining model. The fact that the same terms may be used in these two different senses is an unfortunate complication. A parallel is to be found in Hempel's analysis of the relationship between pure and physical geometry. The distinction cannot be made clear until one recognizes that crucial terms such as *straight line* can be used either to refer to elements of the physical world or components of a mathematical system (Hempel, 1949). These complications are endemic to the use of models in both science and morals. I am not implying that the eighteenth century moral theorists were consciously trying to construct such systems, although given their fascination with Newtonian methods, it is not beyond the realm of reason to construe their activity in this way. Adam Smith, who was an astute methodologist as well as an economist and moral theorist, saw one difference between science and morality in that scientific theories, which were accepted at one time, could be thought afterwards to be outrageous, whereas no moral theory that appeared could, in retrospect, lose all sense of plausibility[3] (Smith, 1982, p. 313). But this rests on the questionable assumption that human beings are in such close contact with their sentiments and wills that they could not be long fooled about their true motivations. The Freudian revolution and its aftermath should give us pause here. More recently, the attempt by some sociobiologists to argue that we are in fact mistaken about the nature of our motivations provides a contemporary example of the attempt to construct a theoretical moral model with which to interpret, understand, and evaluate human moral behavior.

The conflation of model descriptions with phenomenological descriptions may lead to a confusion between what are facts of moral phenomenology and what should properly be regarded as model assumptions, and vice versa. For instance, two authors may well agree that human beings have certain passions or appetites, from the phenomenological point of view, and yet disagree about whether for every such passion or appetite there is a corresponding element in the model. This feature of the situation is often obscured in arguments between reductionists and their opponents. Therefore, Hobbes is construed as a reductionist because he takes all passions and tries to reduce them to one. If self-interest is understood as an element in a model rather than as an element in the phenomenology, then this view is not subject to the criticism that human beings who act from other motives, or so claim to, are either self-deceived or duplicitous. Whatever the truth about Hobbes's view may or may not be, the reductionist account is not undermined by the observation that the passions of self-interest and benevolence are introspectively equally genuine.

The Darwinian legacy demands that the models of human nature or of our moral nature that form the basis of our characterization of moral phenomena must be situated within an evolutionary framework.

EVOLUTION AND ETHICS

The rationale for thinking that evolutionary biology has something interesting to say about ethics lies in the empirical fact that human beings have evolved to become what they are through the influence of natural selection and other factors. Thus, human nature, to the extent that such is compatible with an evolutionary way of thinking, has been shaped to no small extent by evolutionary and natural forces. All ethical systems, naturalistic or not, rest, either explicitly or implicitly, on a conception of human nature. The very foundation of ethical thinking would then seem to be rooted in biology.

At one level none of this is controversial. If ethics is rooted in human nature, and human nature is rooted in our biology, then it would seem that ethics should be rooted in biology as well. What is controversial is the claim that evolutionary biology has anything of *significance* to contribute to our understanding of ethics. There are three distinct but interrelated areas in ethics about which one might think biological considerations were relevant. These are, broadly speaking, particular moral issues, ethical theory, and meta-ethics.

The scope of particular moral issues can include issues faced by individuals on a day-to-day basis as well as questions about particular classes of moral actions. The former include such questions as, "Should I share this pie? Should I steal that apple? Should I have an abortion?" The latter include questions such as the rights and wrongs of abortion, capital punishment, equal rights for women, animal experimentation, and the like. There is little reason to suppose that an appeal to evolution will be especially relevant either to the explanation or the justification of particular decisions by particular individuals that are made on a day-to-day basis. The plasticity of human behavior would seem to preclude such appeals. There is some reason, and some have so argued, to think that an appeal to evolutionary considerations can explain the adoption or abandoning of particular norms. Whether such norms can be justified by appeal to evolutionary considerations is another thing entirely.

The relevance of evolutionary biology for ethical theory hinges on whether or not a case can be made for arguing that evolutionary considerations can explain why consequentialist or deontological analyses of morality are more or less appropriate.

Finally, there are issues in what is called *meta-ethics*. Meta-ethics deals with questions concerning the status of moral claims. Are they capable of being true or false or are they merely conventions or expressions of approval or disapproval? Are there any moral facts? If so, are they reducible to "natural" facts or are they sui generis? I employ the term *meta-ethics* in a broad sense to include not only these traditional questions of justification, objectivity, and meaning, but also questions about the origin, function, and development of morality. Many philosophers and biologists have claimed that evolutionary theory and the facts of human evolution are relevant for answering questions in one or more of these three areas.

Michael Ruse suggests that "a fuller understanding of the causes of morality will surely have fairly direct implications for the bounds which we draw to moral behavior" (Ruse, 1979, p. 198). A precondition for morality is the possibility of choice. Some human behaviors are not voluntary. Some exonerating reasons can and do rest on genetic causes. Ruse concludes that, in the light of this, "there are times when, because of a person's genes, we are less inclined to say that they are responsible for their actions." The bottom line for Ruse is that sociobiological research may well lead to a resetting of the limits on responsible human action. A "reverse" implication concerns the impact of ethics on evolution. Technological developments in gene manipulation procedures hold open the possibility of fulfilling the dream of the eugenics movement to control and direct the course of evolution in the future (Ruse, 1979, p. 81). On a less technological but no less sophisticated level, problems of ecological manipulation raise delicate issues of the interrelationship of ethics and evolution. The greater our understanding of the processes underlying ecological change, the greater is our chance of successfully shaping the environment to our heart's desire.

To the extent that the resources of evolutionary biology can be tapped to provide an evolutionary account of the development of the capacity for making moral judgments, and perhaps for the development of moral visions as well, "moral philosophy, uninformed by contemporary breakthroughs in biology, can no longer be taken as the last word on subjects so central to the human social order" (Maxwell, 1984, p. 230).

According to Dewey, the significance of evolutionary theory for ethics lies in the emphasis it places on the "continuity of change." The evolutionary message is not progress but the fact of open possibilities that need to be addressed and readdressed. No static, finalistic vision of ethics is possible in a world with evolutionary possibilities (Dewey, 1957, p. 262).[4]

The bottom line for judging the relevance of evolutionary biology for ethics must rest on the answer to the following question: Would our ethical views or the analysis and support we offer for them be different if our evolutionary history had been different? If the answer is no, then we can effectively dismiss the claim that evolutionary biology has any bearing on ethics. The message of this book is that we cannot dismiss the relevance of evolutionary biology for ethics. Determining exactly how these evolutionary considerations do and should shape our ethical consciousness is a more delicate question for which the final answer is not yet known.

NOTES

1. See, e.g., Campbell (1974a, 1974b), Popper (1976, 1978, 1984), Bradie (1986), Ruse (1986), Callebaut (1974), and Wuketits (1990).

2. Whereas identifying survival value with truth value may be passé among evolutionary epistemologists, identifying moral virtue with survival value still has supporters among evolutionary ethicists (e.g., Wilson, 1978). For an attempt to show that an evolutionary model can justify as well as explain moral practices, see Richards, 1987, and Chapter 5 later.

3. For Smith's views on scientific methodology and the growth of scientific knowledge, see his essay "The History of Astronomy," in Smith, 1980.

4. Cf. Höffding (1909, p. 457): "All knowledge is systematic, in so far as it strives to put phenomena in quite definite relations, one to another. But the systematization can never be complete. And here Darwin has contributed much to widen the world for us. He has shown us forces and tendencies in nature which make absolute systems impossible, at the same time that they give us new objects and problems. There is still a place for what Lessing called 'the unceasing striving after truth,' while 'absolute truth' (in the sense of a closed system) is unattainable so long as life and experience are going on."

Chapter 2

Altruism, Benevolence, and Self-Love in Eighteenth Century British Moral Philosophy

INTRODUCTION

A central theme in British moral philosophy from Hobbes to Darwin is the attempt to construct a coherent picture of human motivation in terms of a proper balance between self-regarding and other-regarding desires or motives.[1]

Within this framework, two central problems emerge. The first, encapsulated in the query "Why be moral?" is concerned with the source of moral motivation. This question, in turn, can be understood in two ways. First, we may ask why human beings are, in fact, moral. Second, we may ask why human beings should be moral.[2] That people ought to be moral was presupposed by the British moralists of the eighteenth century. In addition, there was not too much disagreement among them about what kinds of behavior were moral. Their problem was fundamentally one of showing how, given an understanding of the nature of human beings, moral action was possible.

The second central problem addressed by the eighteenth century heirs of Hobbes concerned the reconciliation of self-interest or self-love with benevolence. Sidgwick, in the nineteenth century, characterized the problem of the relation of rational self-love to rational benevolence as "the profoundest problem of Ethics" (Sidgwick, 1981, p. 386 n. 4). Given that human beings have powerful motivations to act in their own self-interest, how can we account for the fact that people sometimes act benevolently? There are three broad possibilities. The first is to deny that people, in fact, ever do act benevolently. What looks like benevolence in action is really

15

just disguised self-interest. This was the view attributed to Hobbes. Few, with the exception of cynics like Mandeville, thought that this view was in accordance with the facts of human nature. The second tack was to argue that benevolent motivations and other-regarding passions, that is, motives that defer to the interests of others, in general, were in fact more powerful than people assumed they were. As such, they could under appropriate conditions overcome the tendency to act in self-interested ways. This view was held by Hutcheson. The third alternative was to admit that the self-regarding passions were, as they appeared to be, much more powerful than the other-regarding passions but that, nonetheless, their ends often or for the most part coincided. In short, human beings are moral because it is in their self-interest to be so. Some version of this view was held by both Butler and Hume, among others.

The difference between the first and the third approaches lies in the difference between the assumption that there is only one basic motivating factor in human behavior, self-interest, and the assumption that there is more than one basic motivating factor, self-interest plus benevolence, reason, etc. The advantage of the first approach is that the coincidence between self-interest and benevolence is established in virtue of the fact that the two are, at base, the same. The case against this approach is that it is at odds with the phenomenology of everyday moral behavior. The advantage of the third approach is that it is consonant with the phenomenology in that it takes self-interest to be paramount. The disadvantage is that the coincidence between self-interest and benevolence appears to be just that—a coincidence. The eighteenth century moralists were hard pressed to account for this without appealing to providential design. Darwin, although no philosopher, was aware of the tradition, and as his notebooks make clear, his awareness of the tradition shaped his views on the nature of the problem of morality as it was to be addressed by evolutionary theory.[3]

The focus of this chapter is to situate Darwin's moral theory in the context of the British tradition from which it arose. The following section presents a historical survey of the development of the problem of altruism and self-love from Hobbes to Mackintosh. Darwin's solution is presented in the first part of the next chapter.

BENEVOLENCE AND SELF-LOVE FROM HOBBES TO MACKINTOSH

The objects of human desires, for Hobbes, are self-regarding pleasures. All apparently benevolent and altruistic impulses have to be understood in terms of disguised self-interest.[4] Hobbes argues that societies and morality that apparently are based on other-regarding interests actually arise out of self-interest. Morality arises because self-interested individuals come to see that institutions that result in thwarting some of their immediate self-interested desires are in their long-term self-interest. In effect, morality is the result of a contract between self-interested parties to forego some of their immediate desires in deference to their long-term mutual benefit.

Mandeville takes the argument one step further and argues that public benefits, or the public weal, arise out of the pursuit of self-interest, an anticipation of Adam Smith's view in *The Wealth of Nations* that public prosperity emerges under the force of an "invisible hand" that guides the self-interested behavior of citizens to the promotion of the public good. Benevolence and altruism for Mandeville, as for Hobbes, have no independent basis in human nature.

The Hobbes-Mandeville answer to the question "Why be moral?" is simple expediency. Acting morally promotes the common welfare, which in turn redounds to the benefit of the individuals that make up the society. The coincidence between the ends of morality and the ends of self-interest, such as it exists, is the result of the fact that morality is just the expression of self-interest.

This is not a completely satisfactory account for several reasons. First, there is the question of what exactly is in one's self-interest. Is one's self-interest determined by what one takes to be one's self-interest or do we need to distinguish between apparent and real self-interest? If so, how are we to do so? Second, the fact that the public good is promoted by morality, that is, that the general good is increased by the constraints individuals are willing to place on their behavior, says nothing about how this increased good is to be distributed. To the extent that agents who behave in a restrained manner to promote the common good do not reap a proportionate amount of the benefits that thereby accrue, they are faced with the problem of a conflict between their self-interest and morality. What is their motivation then to do the right thing? In Mandeville's somewhat cynical view of human institutions, the traditional moral stories are designed to fool people into thinking that by acting morally they are promoting their own interests when, in fact, they are not.

In opposition to this general view, Shaftesbury (1671–1713), Hutcheson (1694–1747), Butler (1692–1752), Hume (1711–1776) and Smith (1723–1790) all argued that human beings were motivated by genuine other-regarding passions. One of the basic concerns of post-Hobbesian moralists in the eighteenth century was the problem of integrating benevolent, other-regarding, motives and self-interest into a moral theory that would do justice to both our psychological experience and what were taken to be our moral sensibilities.

Anthony Ashley Cooper: Third Earl of Shaftesbury

Shaftesbury's *An Inquiry Concerning Virtue or Merit* was first published in an unauthorized form in 1699. Authorized versions appeared in 1711 and 1714. The *Inquiry* represents an attack on the Hobbesian and Mandevilleian conception of human beings as completely motivated by self-interest. In arguing for an autonomous role for benevolence in human action, Shaftesbury sought to develop an ethical position that was, to his mind, more consonant with the facts of human experience.

Shaftesbury argued that ethical theory ought to be based on an empirical understanding of human nature. He accepted, as a given, that organisms were designed to serve certain purposes. To determine the good for some kind of being, one need only determine what those purposes are. The purposes served by creatures are obscure but, Shaftesbury held, they can be empirically determined.

Shaftesbury's moral views are predicated on two assumptions and a model of the relationship of individuals to the wholes of which they are parts. First, each creature "has a private good and interest of his own" which he pursues. Second, "[t]here is in reality a right and wrong state of every creature" (Schneewind, 1990, p. 488). In effect, Shaftesbury assumes that human nature is everywhere the same, despite the surface differences that arise among individuals (Schneewind, 1990, p. 487).

The model of the universe that Shaftesbury employed has its roots in Stoicism. For Shaftesbury, the universe is an interconnected cosmos with interdependent parts. Sexual creatures, in particular, are "parts" of a larger harmonious whole. They obey their natures in "cooperating towards their [mutual] conservation and support." There is a well-ordered "economy of nature" with each part fitting into a whole.

Shaftesbury argues that there is an analogy between an organism's pain and the health of its body, on the one hand, and predation and the health of the "ecosystem," on the other (Schneewind, 1990, p. 489). Individual organisms are, in effect, "parts" of a larger organismic whole, and their "function" is defined in terms of their relation to the whole. Creatures are good or ill accordingly as their affections are natural (i.e., tend to promote the community good of which the individual is a member) or unnatural (fleeting, ephemeral passions whose fulfillment would not promote the common good). Shaftesbury's holistic view of individuals in society is fundamentally at odds with Hobbes's atomistic approach with regards to the relationship between individuals and their social milieu.

Shaftesbury starts off by assuming that Hobbes was mistaken and that human beings are motivated by more than self-interest. In his account, we are social creatures by nature and not, as for Hobbes, merely by convenience. He rejects the Hobbesian reduction of all passions to self-affections and all motivations to self-interest. For Shaftesbury, three types of affections constitute human nature. First are the natural affections, which he characterizes as other-regarding affections.[5] Second are the self-regarding affections relating to self-love and self-preservation. Last are the so-called unnatural affections among which Shaftesbury includes the spontaneous and violent passions. Virtue is produced by balancing our natural and self-regarding interests. The failure to balance our competing affections leads to moral ruin. This balance is determined by a moral sense. The moral sense or conscience, in his view, is akin to an aesthetic appreciation of the harmony of nature. Moral judgments are not the result of ratiocination. They are independent of the will. Shaftesbury held that musical and aesthetic harmony are natural not conventional. Similarly, for morality, the "characters and affections of mankind" give rise to a fixed standard of virtue.[6]

Even though moral judgments are arational, Shaftesbury argues that the power to reflect is a precondition of being virtuous or vicious (Schneewind, 1990, p. 490). Creatures deemed either worthy or vicious must have the concept of "a public interest" (Schneewind, 1990, p. 491). Agents are good or evil according to their motives not their deeds. Shaftesbury argues for a doctrine of "natural virtue." Society and the species are interconnected wholes whose well-being depends on the well-working of the parts. The individual-as-citizen stands to the social structure as the individual-as-organism stands to the species. The society and species to which creatures belong have a "natural" end of preservation. That which is destructive of their well-being is vicious; that which upholds and supports those structures is virtuous (Schneewind, 1990, p. 492).

The harmonization of our natural and self-affections produces virtue and goodness. There is an unresolved problem for Shaftesbury's position with respect to this. If the strengths of these affections are disproportionate to one another, *how* are they brought into harmony? The moral sense tells us *when* they are brought into harmony, but *how* is this harmony effected? For the Hobbesian, the self-regarding affections will always swamp the other-regarding affections. What is our motivation to harmonize our two sorts of affections? The desire for happiness? But, whose? *One's* own? If so, are we not back to Hobbes?

The question "Why be moral?" looms large. Why should we allow our unnatural passions to be overcome by other passions? To be happy? But, for Shaftesbury, the motivation to be happy can be only another desire. We must assume that the desire for happiness is a stronger desire than the short-term unnatural passions. Shaftesbury's "competing strength" model leaves no room for the normative component of morality.

We want to be in a position to say that some passions ought to be curbed or bridled because it is good or right that this be done. But Shaftesbury's model suggests that our passions are curbed or bridled when they are overwhelmed by the strength of competing passions. There is no guarantee that morality will prevail nor, indeed, any guarantee that any kind of coherent life will result. Butler came to criticize Shaftesbury's account on this ground.

Nonetheless, Shaftesbury sets the stage for the eclipse of the role of reason in moral theory. An appeal to reason or a priori truths about the nature of the good would provide one source of moral guidance, but Shaftesbury, along with the other empirically minded moral sense theorists of the eighteenth century, rejected this approach as arbitrary and empirically unfounded. For the moral sense theorists and their followers, human beings are passionate, feeling animals. Butler, with his doctrine of conscience, attempts to inject some element of reason into this picture without complete success. After Hume, there is a long slide in the empiricist tradition in ethics leading to Ayer and emotivism.

With respect to the coincidence between virtue and interest, Shaftesbury offers the following argument:

1. No one wants to injure oneself or create a disharmony between one's parts.
2. In injuring others, an individual injures oneself.
3. In aiding others, one is useful to oneself. Therefore,
4. Virtue (helping others) and interest (helping oneself) coincide (Schneewind, 1990, p. 488).

Nonetheless, the experiential facts indicate that human beings are constantly confronted by conflicts of interest and desire, both with respect to our own desires and interests and the desires and interests of others. How are we to reconcile the conflict between immediate, intense, short-term desires and long-term desires? Butler claims that Shaftesbury has no viable solution to this problem. Either the day-to-day desires will overwhelm the long-term desires, in which case Butler thinks the patterns of our lives would be incoherent, or the longer term desires win out—but how? Not by strength, as Shaftesbury would have it, because the day-to-day desires are so intense. So, how, Butler asks, do we account for the coherent stability of our lives in Shaftesbury's view?

Shaftesbury argues against the contractarians that their model of individuals and societies is flawed. They construe individuals and societies as two poles. But, this is a mistake according to Shaftesbury. There are not two poles but one—individuals-in-society. But, how do individuals-in-society interact with each other when their desires are in conflict? For

Butler, this becomes the question of how to produce a harmonious social order. Shaftesbury's answer to Hobbes, that human beings have irreducible benevolent motivations and other-regarding desires, does not answer the question of how we are to live with one another.

Finally, although Shaftesbury uses the notion of a moral sense, he does not say much about what the moral sense is or how it operates. For that, we must turn to Francis Hutcheson.

Francis Hutcheson

Francis Hutcheson's moral theory found its primary expression in two works published during his lifetime, *Inquiry into the Original of Our Ideas of Beauty and Virtue* (1725) and *An Essay on the Nature and Conduct of the Passions, with Illustrations on the Moral Sense* (1728), as well as the posthumous *System of Moral Philosophy* (1755).

The principal business of the moral philosopher, according to Hutcheson, is "to show, from solid reasons, that universal benevolence tends to the happiness of the benevolent." That is, the job of the moral philosopher is to show that acting for the public good produces private benefits and that there is an agreement between self-interest and benevolence. "It is true indeed, that the actions we approve in others, are generally imagin'd to tend to the *natural good of Mankind*, or that of some *Parts* of it. But whence this *secret chain* between *each person* and *mankind*? How is my *interest* connected with the most distant *parts* of it?" (Hutcheson, 1969, p. 111).

Hutcheson, following Shaftesbury, accepted the tripartite division of desires into self-regarding passions, other-regarding passions, and unnatural passions.[7] For Shaftesbury, the self-regarding passions are not in themselves bad, although they can lead to evil. A person becomes virtuous by achieving a harmonious balance between these diverse passions. For Hutcheson, on the other hand, moral action is action motivated by other-regarding or benevolent motives. Benevolence is the heart of morality for Hutcheson.

Hutcheson distinguishes the goodness or badness of the agent from the goodness or badness of an act or action. The goodness or badness of an agent is determined by the agent's motivation. Agents who are motivated by benevolence are good. Those motivated by self-interest or an unnatural passion are not. The rightness or wrongness of an act, on the other hand, is a function of whether it facilitates the common good or promotes public virtue. Hutcheson was among the first to enunciate the principle of Utilitarianism. "[T]hat action is best," says Hutcheson, "which produces the greatest good for the greatest numbers" (Schneewind, 1990, p. 515)[8].

For Hutcheson, (1) human beings have genuinely benevolent motives; (2) human beings have a moral sense; (3) the moral sense detects the approval or not of a certain kind of benevolent motivation; and (4) virtue consists in acting from benevolent motives. With respect to (1), (2), and (3), Hutcheson follows Shaftesbury, with modification. However, (4) represents a significant departure from Shaftesbury's view of virtue as harmonious action.

Given that right actions are determined by a calculation of consequences and given that we must use our reason and reflective powers to perform the calculations, do we need a moral sense? Could we not come to the same results with respect to right and wrong through the use of reason? Hutcheson thinks not. Reason is too slow and too cumbersome to serve us. We need, often, to act quickly and we do, too quickly for reason to have had time to do the requisite calculations (Schneewind, 1990, p. 521).[9] The moral sense is "implanted [in us] by the author of nature" (Peach, 1971, p. 214).[10]

The moral sense, for Hutcheson, serves a number of functions.[11] Hutcheson, following Locke, takes moral approval to be an idea of internal sense (Peach, 1971, p. 38). There is, however, no special moral sense organ. The whole person is the sensor. Normal sensing conditions correspond to conditions in which we possess moral knowledge, adopt an impartial point of view, and develop consistent moral appraisals that are general (Peach, 1971, p. 40). Whereas objects plus the dispositions of objects *cause* ideas in us, actions plus ideas in us about the actions *cause* us to feel or express moral approval or disapproval.

Moral talk is both descriptive and normative for Hutcheson. The moral sense grounds the bridge between the descriptive or benevolent and the normative or virtuous aspects of moral discourse.

Our moral judgments are subject to correction, as are our epistemic judgments, when we come to realize that we misconstrued the circumstances under which we made the original judgment. The correction of the moral sense does not mean the overriding of the moral sense by reason or conscience, as if reason now leads us to see we were mistaken in approving actions of certain types. What reason may lead us to reconsider is whether a particular act-token is of the type we originally thought (Peach, 1971, pp. 47ff.). But, can we be sure the sense is not deceitful or wrong, understood here to mean a sense that "shall make that pleasant for the present which shall have pernicious consequences"? Hutcheson cites the work of Cumberland and Pufendorf as establishing the congruence between private interest or individual happiness and benevolence (Peach, 1971, p. 214).[12]

Two principles are at the heart of Hutcheson's moral theory. The first, a strictly normative principle, is that benevolence is the root of all virtue. The second, a psychological premise, is that the moral sense approves benevolence (Peach, 1971, p. 64). Peach summarizes Hutcheson's view as follows: "Given that some act is motivated by benevolence, then if a person considers it from the moral point of view, he will, barring interference, approve it, and this approval will, again barring interference, justify the claim that the act is virtuous, which claim, again barring interference, he will make" (Peach, 1971, p. 71).

Of course, the problem is how to ensure that people will act on their benevolent motivations. With respect to the foundation of the "more important rights of mankind," Hutcheson writes:

> Probably nine tenths, at least, of the things which are useful to mankind, are owing to their labor and industry; and consequently [when men are so numerous, that the natural product of the earth is not sufficient for their support, or ease, or innocent pleasure—added in 1726] all men are oblig'd to observe such a tenour of action as shall most effectually promote industry; and to abstain from all actions which would have the contrary effect. It is well known, that general benevolence alone is not a motive strong enough to industry, to bear labour and toil, and many other difficulties which we are averse to from self-love: For the strengthening therefore our motives to industry, we have the strongest attractions of blood, of friendship, of gratitude, and the additional motives of honour, and even external interest. Self love is really as necessary to the good of the whole as benevolence; as that attraction which causes the cohesion of the parts, is as necessary to the regular state of the whole, as gravitation: without these additional motives, self-love would generally oppose the motions of benevolence, and concur with malice, or influence us to the same actions which malice would. (Hutcheson, 1969, pp. 262f.)

The import seems to be this. Benevolence, in general, is too weak a motive to get us to perform and cooperate in social endeavors that are to the benefit of both ourselves and others. Other motivating forces are at work that strengthen the push of benevolence, such as "attractions of blood, friendship, and gratitude." Without these extra forces, we would be overcome by considerations of self-interest and driven to actions that are malicious and detrimental to the well-being of others. This passage suggests that blood ties are an independent source of motivation from benevolence and that perhaps parental care should be construed as deriving from the blood ties and not from considerations of benevolence. This leaves the field open for the Darwinian: whence comes the evolution of blood ties?

We love our children, the Sophist says, because they are "part of us." But, "in what way are they part of us?" asks Hutcheson? They are formed from our parts. But, says Hutcheson, so are maggots and flies. No, says

Hutcheson, the Sophists have it backwards. Our children are part of us because we love them; it is our natural affection that binds us together (Hutcheson, 1969, pp. 143f.).

The importance of the moral sense to the happiness of humankind lies in the fact that "[i]n . . . the sentiments which men universally form of the state of others, when they are no way immediately concern'd; . . . [we find] . . . human nature is calm and undisturb'd, and shews its true face" (Hutcheson, 1969, p. 222). Hutcheson goes on to argue that when we reflect we realize that our lives would be impoverished without the long term "moral pleasures of friendship, love and beneficence" (Hutcheson, 1969, p. 223).

Our "public affections" excite in us the desire to promote the happiness of many. "Without such affections this truth, 'that an hundred felicities is a greater sum than one felicity,' will no more excite to study the happiness of the one hundred than this truth, 'an hundred stones are greater than one,' will excite a man, who has no desire of heaps, to cast them together" (Peach, 1971, p. 126).

For Utilitarians if some is good, more is better. But why? What makes the greatest happiness a goal worthy of pursuit? Hutcheson's answer is twofold: it is part of our nature to pursue such a goal *and* we have a moral sense that approves of such pursuits. The moral sense, for Hutcheson, both detects and endorses. In this way it bridges the gap between "is" and "ought."[13] But what is the source or warrant for that endorsement? Hutcheson does not say. Butler will invoke a principle of reflection or conscience to provide the warrant. Hume suggests that any views that attempt to glibly infer from how we behave to what we ought to do need to be scrutinized very closely indeed.

Joseph Butler

Joseph Butler (1692–1752) was a Presbyterian convert to Anglicanism. As a preacher at Rolls Chapel at the Inns of Court he preached about sixty sermons of which fifteen were printed in 1726. Among other things, these sermons present a model of human nature in terms of which Butler sought to ground an ethical theory.

There are two ways to study morals according to Butler. The first proceeds from first principles or self-evident truths; the second, from the investigations into the "particular nature of man." Both paths lead to the same conclusions with respect to our "obligations to the practice of virtue" (Butler, 1983, p. 13). In the *Sermons*, Butler follows the second path and seeks to answer three questions: (1) What is the nature of man? (2) What does it mean to say that virtue follows the nature of man and vice deviates from it? (3) To what extent is it true that virtue follows the nature of man and vice deviates from it? (Butler, 1983, p. 13).

What is a system with a nature? For Butler, a system with a nature is a collection of parts or components that are organized or interrelated in some way. The system is the totality of the parts plus their interrelationship. He suggests as two such systems a watch and a man. The nature of man stands to virtue, he suggests, as the nature of a watch stands to telling time. The normal working of both requires a harmony between the parts. The former is an artificial system, the latter is a natural one. The difference between the former and the latter is that a watch is merely a machine whereas a human being is an agent—"Our constitution is put in our own power. We are charged with it; and therefore are accountable for any disorder or violation of it" (Butler, 1983, p. 14). The problem with this approach is that, whereas we know what the virtue of a watch is because we have designed it to perform a certain task, we do not know (do we?) what the virtue of a man is other than that it consists in the harmonious balance of the components of human nature. We must discern what those parts are through empirical investigation.

Butler begins by arguing that we can determine the nature of man from an empirical investigation into what we have called the *phenomenology of moral experience*. The principal tools are an adaptational and functional argument. Butler cites the case of the eye and how it is manifest that it was "intended for us to see with." The contrast with Darwin is striking and must give us pause as we try to unpack the implicit assumptions that underlie the world-view Butler is articulating. Even so, Butler urges, we must exercise the greatest caution in using this line of reasoning with respect to morals that we not be misled by the idiosyncratic aspects of our own behaviors, which may be due to "particular customs." Nevertheless, we may appeal to our inner sense of right and wrong to the same extent and with the same degree of confidence that we appeal to our outward senses and perceptions. "Now obligations of virtue shown and motives to the practice of it enforced, from a review of the nature of man, are to be considered as an appeal to each particular person's heart and natural conscience, as the external senses are appealed to for the proof of things cognizable by them. Since then our inward feelings, and the perceptions we receive from our external senses, are equally real; to argue from the former to life and conduct is as little liable to exception as to argue from the latter to absolute speculative truth" (Butler, 1983, p. 34).

This empirical investigation is guided by a theory or, more precisely, a model of human nature and the place of human beings in the scheme of things. This model gets elaborated in the first three sermons on human nature. Butler summarizes his views on human nature at the end of Sermon III.

The Nature of man is adapted to some course of action or other. [This is a theoretical normative postulate of Butler's model] Upon comparing some actions with this nature, they appear suitable and correspondent to it; from comparison of other actions with the same nature, there arises to our view some unsuitableness or disproportion. [This is an implication of the model and its content. It forms the theoretical analysis of the rightness and wrongness of given actions] . . . the correspondence arises from the action being conformable to higher principle, and the unsuitableness from its being contrary to it. Reasonable self-love and conscience are the chief or superior principles in the nature of man, because an action may be suitable to this nature, although all other principles be violated; but becomes unsuitable, if either of those are. Conscience and self-love, if we understand our true happiness, always lead us the same way. Duty and interest are perfectly coincident, for the most part in this world, but entirely and in every instance if we take in the future and the whole, this being implied in the notion of a good and perfect administration of things. (Butler, 1983, p. 45)

Every human being is an integrated system and individuals-in-society form a system as well. The parts of a human being stand to the whole as individuals do to the society to which they belong. There is a nearly perfect coincidence between "the nature of man as respecting self and tending to private good, his own preservation and happiness, and the nature of man as having respect to society and tending to promote public good, the happiness of that society" (Butler, 1983, p. 26). Butler continues on to argue that human beings are naturally constituted by social ties. The bonds of kinship, real and presumed, play a role in eliciting the aid and affection of our fellow humans. This lays out a conception of human nature and social nature at odds with that of Hobbes. The organic metaphor holds together the interests of the individual and the social realm. He concludes: "And therefore to have no restraint from, no regard to, others in our behavior is the speculative absurdity of considering ourselves as single and independent, as having nothing in our nature which has respect to our fellow creatures, reduced to action and practice. And this is the same absurdity as to suppose a hand or any part to have no natural respect to any other or to the whole body" (Butler, 1983, p. 31).

Human beings have "natural principles" of benevolence and self-love. The principle of benevolence stands to society, to its general happiness, as the principle of self-love stands to the happiness of the individual. In a long footnote with reference to Hobbes's view, Butler argues that the testimony of mankind and experience proves, as strongly as possible in these regards, that "there is some degree of benevolence among men" (Butler, 1983, p. 26). In addition, it is ludicrous to construe this degree of benevolence as disguised self-interest. It is a *sui generis* component of human nature. I take this to be the force of Butler's famous dictum: "Everything is what it is, and not another thing" (Butler, 1983, p. 20).

In addition, "though benevolence and self-love are different, though the former tends more directly to public good, and the latter to private, yet they are so perfectly coincident that the greatest satisfactions to ourselves depend upon our having benevolence in a due degree, and that self-love is one chief security of our right behavior toward society" (Butler, 1983, p. 27).

In the preceding account, when Butler goes on to claim that "it is as manifest that we were made for society and to promote the happiness of it, as that we were intended to take care of our own life and health and private good," he is tacitly appealing to the model of human nature that he has just sketched in terms of the principles of motivation and the principle of reflection. What is manifest, if anything, is that we behave in ways that promote the common good. What is not manifest is why we do so. The debate between Butler and Hobbes cannot be resolved by appeal to what is manifest at the phenomenological level. The a priori ethicists, the Cambridge Platonists such as Cudworth and More and the rationalists such as Clarke and Wollaston, might believe in the manifest truth of a model of human ethics but that tack seems hardly appropriate for Butler who was at pains to distance his naturalistic approach from theirs. It is true that, in his account, both lead to the same conclusions but those conclusions have to be understood as the same only insofar as the same precepts of morality, love thy neighbor, for example, are forthcoming from both (Butler, 1983, p. 30).

In Sermon III, Butler elaborates further on the organic analogy that drives his model of human nature. The civil constitution, he suggests, stands to the individual's constitution as the sovereign does to our individual conscience. For Butler, there appear to be only two options with respect to the moral constitution of human beings. One is the individualism of Hobbes, where human beings, like brutes, act in accordance with their strongest immediate passions. This leads to random, whimsical, unreflective behavior.[14] But, reason and experience both indicate that human beings are reflective, so the Hobbesian model must be wrong. The other option is that man has been so created and designed by his Maker to be "a law to himself" wherein conscience dictates our notions of right and wrong (Butler, 1983, p. 41).

Darwin's theory presents a third option. The moral nature of human characters, judgments, and actions is due to the shaping effects of natural selection. An argument for the superiority of the principle of reflection can be constructed along these lines to the extent that superiority is due to the selective advantages conferred upon men and women of conscience. Conscience in the phenomenological sense does not disappear but what grounds it has been reinterpreted.

When we look into the nature of our being, according to Butler, we see that we have these principles of self-love, benevolence, and the power to reflect. But we also find passions and appetites opposed to them, and sometimes overcoming them.[15] These impulses are no less natural than the guiding principles. "Thus, as in some cases we follow our nature in doing the works contained in the law, so in other cases we follow nature in doing contrary" (Butler, 1983, pp. 36f.).[16] The fact of the matter is that all our actions are the resultant of the composition of various principles and affections in us and that, in general, it is impossible to decompose these motivating principles in a way that allows us to determine the extent to which they are the result of self-love or some particular passion (Butler, 1983, p. 19).

Butler, following St. Paul, holds that "every man is naturally a law unto himself." But, he asks, what does *natural* mean here? There are two senses of *natural* that are no help. In the first, whatever is a part of us is natural. In the second, howsoever we are impelled by the strongest impulse of the moment is what is natural. In neither of these cases are we a law unto ourselves (Butler, 1983, pp. 37f.).

But, in addition to the principles and the passions, we have a conscience. This is, for Butler, "a superior principle of reflection or conscience in every man which distinguishes between the internal principles of his heart as well as his external actions, which passes judgment upon himself and them, pronounces determinately some actions to be in themselves just, right, good; others to be in themselves evil, wrong, unjust. . . . It is by this faculty, natural to man, that he is a law to himself" (Butler, 1983, p. 37).[17]

Acting against one's immediate inclinations does not constitute going against one's nature but "to go against cool self-love [which dictates that we should preserve the harmonious balance of our being] for the sake of [some immediate] gratification is an 'unnatural action'." Following the dictates of our conscience or cool self-love is to follow a "superior" part of our nature. The argument for the superiority of cool self-love over passion is that contradicting the latter does not violate the harmony of our nature, whereas contradicting cool self-love does violate the harmony of our nature (Butler, 1983, p. 39). For Butler, then, to act against our nature is to act in such a way to disturb the equilibrium of our being (Butler, 1983, p. 38).

This argument hinges on the assumed natural superiority of the principle of reflection or conscience. That we have some such principle and that it works much as Butler thought may be admitted but the superiority of it rests either on an implicit theological point of view or on a model of the good for our nature that puts harmonious balance as the good for human individuals. This rests then on a theoretical model not on a manifest fact of our moral phenomenology.[18]

Which is to be obeyed, our appetites or reflection? Butler argues that the appetites stand to reflection as strength stands to authority. Just as in society, mere power may coerce us to do things but would not make them right whereas authority compels what is right, so too with the management of our private selves. We may give in to our strong inclinations against our better judgment but our better judgment, which has our true self-interest as its standard, is the guide to what is good or right (Butler, 1983, p. 39).

Butler concludes the sermon by considering what the consequences would be if human beings did not have a conscience. They would be as he imagined the brutes, acting on the strongest impulse of the moment. Without the existence of such an authority the parricide and filial pietist would be on a moral par. They are not, at least for us. Therefore, something in us must mark the difference. Mere strength of passion, as we have seen, is not enough. The "something else" is what Butler calls *conscience* or the *principle of reflection* (Butler, 1983, p. 40).

But this latter conclusion is not a mere restatement of the problematic data namely, that as a matter of fact we do reflect on what we do and make appeals to what we call our *conscience*. That conscience is, as it were, the phenomenological conscience of our moral experience. The conscience that Butler argues is the ground for our activity is the theoretical construct of Butler's model.

The essentialistic nature of Butler's model is illustrated in his remarks on deviant personalities. We have within us ungoverned passions that if unchecked would lead to self-destruction as well as social evil (Butler, 1983, p. 31). But for Butler, there is no principle of self-hatred, no love of injustice. When we act against our own cool self-interest or in ways that tend to social evil, we do so out of ignorance about where our true interests lie.[19]

Butler acknowledges the existence of a few individuals without these normal affections toward themselves or their fellow man, but he dismisses them as aberrations (Butler, 1983, p. 32). Man's nature is not to be determined with respect to these outliers but by the bulk of mankind. This bears the stamp of the essentialist. Outliers are deviant.

For Butler, the essence of vice and injustice is disharmony; the essence of virtue is harmony. Particular affections or inclinations are neither so vicious nor so virtuous as the imbalance or balance of the whole (Butler, 1983, p. 15). The moral goodness or badness of an action is a function of whether that action contributes to or detracts from the harmonious equilibrium that constitutes our virtue and *not* a matter of whether the action is interested or disinterested (Butler, 1983, p. 21).

Butler summarizes his argument for the authority of conscience as follows:

1. Both human beings and brutes have various instincts and principles, some of which are directed to the good of the community and some of which are directed toward the good of the agent.
2. In addition, human beings are capable of reflection and have a conscience. They can thereby reflect upon what they do and approve or disapprove accordingly.
3. Brutes behave "mechanically." They act in accordance with the sum of the principles and instincts they feel at the moment and in accordance with their natures, the "constitution of their bodies."
4. Most human beings, as well, act in accordance with the sum of the principles and instincts they feel at the moment and in accordance with their natures.
5. But, this is not the whole story. Human beings have a conscience and the ability to reflect on what they should or should not do. Our conscience has an authority over the rest of our principles and instincts and can (and does) overrule our momentary inclinations.
6. Human beings cannot be said to be acting in accordance with their natures unless they concede to their consciences the "absolute authority which is due to it" (Butler, 1983, p. 17).

But why should we obey our conscience? For Butler, "[y]our obligation to obey . . . [your conscience] . . . is its being the law of your nature. That your conscience approves of and attests to such a course of action is itself alone an obligation" (Butler, 1983, p. 43). Prefigurations of Hume indeed. We see here an instance of the easy passage from what is, that we do obey our consciences, to an ought, that we should obey our consciences.

Butler rejects the view that we can reasonably not be concerned, in general, with the well being of others. Such a view supposes, falsely according to Butler, that our virtues and even our vices are not dependent upon our regard for others. Without such regard we would be indifferent to the garden variety of vices, infamy, covetousness, ambition, the disgrace of poverty, etc. "[T]here can be no doubt concerning ambition and covetousness, virtue and a good mind . . . which temper and which course is attended with most peace and tranquil of mind, which with most perplexity, vexation, and inconvenience" (Butler, 1983, p. 44). Butler here appeals to the facts of human life. At first, he thinks, the demands of virtue may seem like a constraining force. When acting virtuously becomes second nature to us, we choose the good with delight. "It is manifest that, in the common course of life, there is seldom any inconsistency between our duty and what is *called* interest; it is much seldomer that there is any inconsistency between duty and what is really in our present interest— meaning by 'interest' happiness and satisfaction. Self-love then, though confined to the interest of the present world, does in general perfectly coincide with virtue, and leads us to one and the same course of life."

The key to Butler's moral theory is the role of conscience. Conscience ("the voice of God within us"—III. 2) is a two-dimensional concept. It is a reflective faculty that has an emotive, moving power.[20]

Guilt and shame are motivating forces for all human beings except the amoralists. How these are exercised, which actions or situations give rise to feelings of shame or guilt, may vary from culture to culture. Nonetheless, the measure of the strength of the dictates of our conscience is the length to which we go when we act in ways which violate our inner voice.

Reason provides "cool" reflection, a detached level-headed analysis minus the pressures which push in one direction or another. Had conscience the strength it has in authority, it would rule the world. Conscience can overrule benevolence, self-love, and individual fleeting powerful passions. Conscience should overrule, but does not always do so. Sometimes our passions get the best of us.

How does conscience know what action to pick to condone or condemn? An act is wrong if it produces disequilibrium. Conscience, benevolence, and self-love control the straining passions. Immediate passions, such as the desire for heroin, if satisfied, may lead to disaster. Immoderate benevolence, if unchecked, leads to unrestrained altruism (St. Francis run amok), and this in turn leads to disaster.

Neither consequences nor egoistic considerations are relevant to morality. What is relevant? For Butler, as for Shaftesbury and Aristotle, accordance with human nature. Reason reflects on the nature of the act.

There are two fundamental underlying assumptions of Butler's view: (1) rationality is the same for everyone; and (2) there is a universal agreement about the facticity of particular tokens of murder, theft, etc. For Butler, morality is grounded in human nature and comprises both elements of the passions and reason. Hume will focus on the passions; Kant, on the elements of reason. A richer Butlerian position emerges in Adam Smith's view of conscience as the impartial spectator.

David Hume

David Hume's moral views appear, in their most extended development, in part III of *A Treatise of Human Nature*, which appeared in 1739–40 and in a revised version in 1751 as *An Enquiry Concerning the Principles of Morals (Second Enquiry)*.

Before Hume, a long intellectual and moral tradition, dating back to the ancient Greeks, maintained that from indubitable premises, self-evident moral truths, one could by deduction derive truths about morality. This was the position of the Church Fathers and the Cambridge Platonists, for example. Hume challenges this tradition and the view that there are objective moral truths. Hume's attack on the notion of moral knowledge parallels in many respects his arguments against the certainty of empirical knowledge.

At the beginning of the *Second Enquiry*, Hume considers three questions concerning the general foundation of morals: (1) Are morals "derived from *reason* or from *sentiment*"? (2) Do we come to our knowledge of morals "by a chain of argument and induction or by an immediate feeling and finer internal sense"? (3) Are morals "the same to every rational, intelligent being, or . . . [are they] . . . like the perception of beauty and deformity, . . . founded entirely on the particular fabric and constitution of the human species"? (Hume, 1946, p. 2).

Hume's view, in a nutshell, is that morals are derived from sentiments by an immediate feeling and finer internal sense and founded on the particular fabric and constitution of the human species.[21]

Hume's approach is empirical. Recall that the subtitle of the *Treatise* is *An Attempt to Introduce the Experimental Method of Reasoning into Moral Subjects*. In the *Abstract* to the *Treatise* , Hume approvingly lumps together "Mr. Locke, my Lord Shaftesbury, Dr. Mandeville, Mr. Hutchison [sic], [and] Dr. Butler," presumably on the grounds that, despite their differences, they agree in (1) banishing "hypotheses" from moral philosophy and (2) founding their conclusions about human nature on "experience" (Hume, 1978, p. 646).

What are the respective roles of reason and sentiment in morals for Hume? Reason plays a role in helping us to calculate the utilities (Hume, 1946, p. 126). Reason provides calculations of potential consequences and the sentiment of humanity tilts in favor of the useful and the beneficial. Hume then undertakes to defend "this partition" by arguing that no theory that supposes reason to be the "sole source of morals" will be successful.

The bottom line is the claim that reason giving must come to an end. Hume says: "It is impossible there can be a progress *ad infinitum*; and that one thing can always be a reason why another is desired. Something must be desirable on its own account, and because of its immediate accord or agreement with human sentiment and affection."[22]

The point of moral speculation, for Hume, is to provide us with theoretical knowledge of our duty, and inculcate us with virtuous habits.[23]

In the *Second Enquiry*, Hume seems to assume that the theory of human nature he puts forth is universally true. For all time and all places, human beings are much the same.[24] They have the same general concerns and motivations although the specific codes and rules that they formulate and live by are historically constrained.[25] What is surprising about this is that he is apparently not exercised by those worries about the warrant for universal claims that so bedeviled him in the *First Enquiry*.

All the eighteenth century British moralists seem to have assumed the uniformity of human nature. But Hume, unlike the others, has an epistemological stance that makes this assumption dubious. He does not allow his epistemological opponents this kind of assumption. What warrant does he have for making it himself?[26]

How, despite the alleged universality of our moral reactions, can we explain the fact that people make different moral judgments? Hume's point is that we are all feeling creatures; he does not maintain that we all judge things in the same way. Why don't we? (1) Either those who judge differently from us do not understand the case in the same way that we do; or (2) one or the other of us has not had his or her moral sense properly cultivated.

In an essay, "Of the Standard of Taste," Hume explores the question of whether there can be a universal standard of taste. He focuses on beauty and style, but the argument is couched in such a way that it appears to apply to any judgment that arises from sentiments.

Hume begins by noting that there is a great variety of opinions and sentiments throughout the world. With respect to the variety in taste, it is greater upon examination than it appears to be at first sight. All agree that the beautiful is to be admired and the ugly condemned, but they disagree about what particulars fall under those classes. With respect to the difference in opinions, there is a great deal of consensus with respect to the particulars, but people differ with respect to their general or theoretical accounts of these matters.

Those, like Hume, who found morality on sentiment are apt to "maintain, that, in all questions which regard conduct and manners, the difference among men is really greater than at first sight it appears" (Hume, 1825, p. 222). What unanimity exists can be traced to the linguistic fact that all praise virtue and condemn vice. What actions or people fall under these labels is a function of circumstances.

Some hold that no standard of taste or sentiment is possible because, as the proverb has it, there is no disputing about tastes (Hume, 1825, p. 224). The reason is "no sentiment represents what is really in the object. It only marks a certain conformity or relation between the object and the organs or faculties of the mind; and if that conformity did not really exist, the sentiment could never possibly have being. Beauty [moral value?] is no quality in things themselves: It exists merely in the mind which contemplates them; and each mind perceives a different beauty [moral value]" (Hume, 1825, p. 225). A corollary of this view is that if no sentient evaluators exist then the world is devoid of beauty or value.

Nevertheless, another commonsensical point of view suggests that it is absurd to think that there is no difference between great writers and lesser hacks. Hume suggests over the next few pages that there are "general principles of approbation or blame" that rest on the common sentiments and "whose influence a careful eye may trace in all operations of the mind" (Hume, 1825, p. 228). Not all will adhere to them, and they are subject to distortion if the external circumstances are amiss—if we are not calm, cool, collected, and if we do not have a sufficiently delicate and educated palate (cf. p. 237: "Though the principles of taste be universal, and nearly, if not entirely, the same in all men; yet few are qualified to give judgment on any work of art, or establish their own sentiment as the standard of beauty"). Yet, "[s]ome particular forms or qualities, from the original structure of the internal fabric [of the human mind], are calculated to please, and others to displease; and if they fail of their effect in any particular instance, it is from some apparent defect or imperfection in the organ" (Hume, 1825, p. 229). Hume goes on to remark that "[t]hough it be certain, that beauty and deformity, more than sweet and bitter, are not qualities in objects, but belong entirely to the sentiment, internal or external; it must be allowed, that there are certain qualities in objects, which are fitted by nature [both our nature and the nature of the objects] to produce those particular feelings" (Hume, 1825, p. 230).

So, there are universal principles of taste, but individual evaluators must be properly educated and free from any number of biases to use them aright. All things considered, however, "there still remain two sources of variation, which are not sufficient indeed to confound all the boundaries of beauty and deformity, but will often serve to produce a difference in the degrees of our approbation or blame" (Hume, 1825, p. 240). These two sources are "the different humors of particular men" and "the particular manners and opinions of our age and country" (Hume, 1825, p. 240).

"The general principles of taste are uniform in human nature: Where men vary in their judgments, some defect or perversion in the faculties may commonly be remarked; proceeding either from prejudice, from want of practice, or want of delicacy: and there is just reason for approving one taste, and condemning another. But where there is such a diversity in the internal frame or external situation as is entirely blameless on both sides, and leaves no room to give one the preference above the other; in that case a certain degree of diversity in judgment is unavoidable, and we seek in vain for a standard, by which we can reconcile the contrary sentiments" (Hume, 1825, pp. 240f.).[27]

Hobbes was construed by the eighteenth century writers including Hume as holding that human beings are egoistic by nature—and that they could not be changed. Hume rejects the view that the social virtues are derived from considerations of self-love: " . . . the voice of nature and experience seems plainly to oppose the selfish theory" (Hume, 1946, pp. 49f.).[28] The assumption that disinterested benevolence is distinct from self-love is the *simpler* hypothesis and "more conformable to the analogy of nature." Nor is self-love a primary desire. Consider bodily appetites and mental passions. In each case there is a primary object whose gratification leads to pleasure. This pleasure may, in turn, give rise to a secondary desire. Hunger has eating as its end. Our primary pleasure comes from satisfying our hunger. In the process the very activity of eating becomes desirable. Primary mental passions include the desire for fame, power, and vengeance. Self-love, Hume suggests, is activated only by the presence of these primary desires, since if we had none of them, the "propensity [to self-love] could scarcely ever exert itself" (Hume, 1946, pp. 143f.).

Hume then suggests that the propensity for benevolence might be part of the "original frame of our temper" that, when exercised, gives rise to feelings of pleasure in us and that we thereafter pursue both from motives of "benevolence and self enjoyments." The alternative is to embrace a "malignant philosophy . . . more like a satyr than a true delineation or description of human nature." All human beings are affected by the happiness and misery of others to some degree or other. This fundamental sympathy forms the basis of morality. "The human countenance, says Horace, borrows smiles and tears from the human countenance" (Hume, 1946, pp. 54f.).

Hume takes it as a virtue of his account that it is indifferent to considerations of the varying degrees to which benevolence or self-love prevail in human nature. This dispute, Hume allows, "is never likely to have any issue, both because men, who have taken part, are not easily convinced, and because the phenomena, which can be produced on either side, are so dispersed, so uncertain, and subject to so many interpretations, that it is scarcely possible accurately to compare them, or draw from them any determinate inference or conclusion." It suffices for us that some small modicum of the "dove" be instilled in our nature that suffices, when everything is equal, to a tilting toward the common good. "A *moral distinction*, therefore, immediately arises; a general sentiment of blame and approbation; a tendency, however faint, to the objects of the one, and a proportionable aversion to those of the other" (Hume, 1946, p. 109).

Despite concluding that the "question concerning the universal or partial selfishness of man be not so material as is usually imagined to morality and practice," Hume allows that a few remarks on it may not be out of place. First, the selfish hypothesis is "contrary to common feeling" and requires a reconceptualization of phenomena that on the surface appear quite different. The same may be said for Freud and the sociobiologists. Second, in a footnote, Hume distinguishes between general benevolence and particular benevolence. The former, he identifies with a general sense of humanity, fellow feeling, or sympathy. Of it he says, "I assume it as real, from general experience, without any other proof." The latter, he identifies with friendship that is prompted by the recognition of virtue in others. Thus, your mere humanity arouses in me feelings of general benevolence. When I learn of your virtues, I am moved to feelings of particular benevolence (Hume, 1946, p. 140). Third, in physics, appearances are often deceiving and what appears to be one way subsequently turns out another. But, in investigations into the origins of our passions and the internal operations of the human mind, the presumption is against reductionism. Hume recognizes that people often disguise their true feelings from themselves, as when a man who loses his patron deceives himself into thinking that his grief is all due to "generous sentiments" and not at all to self-interested motives. This, he thinks, is a far cry from some "metaphysical" reduction of all motives to motives of self-interest. In an unfortunate analogy, Hume concludes, "We may as well imagine that minute wheels and springs, like those of a watch, give motion to a loaded wagon, as account for the origin of passion from such abstruse reflections" (Hume, 1946, p. 141). Fourth, animals are capable of evincing kindness. Are we to attribute their behavior to disguised self-interest?[29] (Hume, 1946, p. 142). Finally, a mother loses her child and grieves unto her death. What is self-interested about that, Hume asks.[30] A "thousand" such cases could be cited[31] (Hume, 1946, p. 143).

The social virtues of benevolence and humanity are part of our original nature. Each act is beneficial (Hume, 1946, p. 146).[32] The utility of the social virtues of justice and fidelity, which are indispensable for our well-being, does not arise from each act but results from the general scheme of things (Hume, 1946, p. 147). Hume rejects the view that the social virtues are all acquired by education or conditioning in the light of their utility. If human beings did not have a natural bent to practice them, no urging by politicians or clergy could induce them to do so (Hume, 1946, p. 48).

That the whole merit of benevolence is *not* utility is evidenced by the facts that expressions of benevolence evoke warm feelings of satisfaction independent of considerations of utility, and we often remark on the fact that someone can be "too good." How could this be? In such cases, persons exceed the bounds of decency—hence, utility must be produced within the proper bounds (Hume, 1946, p. 94).

Hume distinguishes between artificial and natural virtues. The paradigm example of an artificial virtue for Hume is justice. At the beginning of the *Second Inquiry*, Hume states that "[t]hose who have denied the reality of moral distinctions, may be ranked among the disingenuous disputants . . . [who really do not believe the opinions they defend]; nor is it conceivable, that any human creature could ever seriously believe, that all characters and actions were alike entitled to the affection and regard of everyone" (Hume, 1946, p. 1). The very idea of "artificial" virtues, as Hume explores them, undermines a long moral tradition. For Hume, the Sermon on the Mount and the Ten Commandments, two of the pillars of the traditional morality, are, at best, useful pieces of advice for unreflective persons.

What is the distinction between the artificial and the natural virtues for Hume? The artificial virtues are virtues that exist solely in virtue of the existence of rules. Justice derives its rationale from considerations related to the equitable distribution of property. But human beings do not possess a natural sentiment about property rights. Property rights are codified in rules that vary from culture to culture and time to time. Hume illustrates this by focusing on the arbitrariness and superstitious nature (in the Skinnerian sense that pigeons can be conditioned to exhibit superstitious behavior) of property laws. The wide variety of property laws that human beings have formulated attests to the impossibility of tracing them to "original instincts" (Hume, 1946, p. 35). As justice is not derived from a natural sentiment, it must be an artificial virtue.

Justice is not based on conventions if by *convention* is meant a "promise." Keeping promises is itself a part of justice. If by convention one means because of common interests, then justice is based on conventions (Hume, 1946, p. 149). Is justice then natural? Natural may be opposed to unusual, miraculous, or artificial. Justice is natural as opposed to unusual and miraculous; not so with respect to artificial (Hume, 1946, p. 150).

How does Hume's theory of justice relate to the theory of the passions? If people were genuinely altruistic, there would be no need for justice. In a world populated by individuals who had no strong self-regarding affections but for whom everyone's needs and desires counted as one's own, there would be no room for justice (Hume, 1946, p. 17).

There is no question that justice is useful for society. What is not so obvious is that the origin of justice and the basis of its merit are public utility. In a world where there is no want or scarcity, considerations of justice do not arise (Hume, 1946, p. 15). "The common situation of society" gives rise to the concepts of property and justice. That justice involves merit and incurs moral obligation rests solely on its "usefulness to the public" (Hume, 1946, p. 22). "Human nature cannot by any means subsist, without the association of individuals; and that association never could have place, were no regard paid to the laws of equity and justice." Unlike individuals, nations can exist without commerce and hence the sense of

moral obligation that exits between states is nowhere as strong as that
which exits between individuals (Hume, 1946, p. 40).

An examination of the particular laws and regulations that direct and
promote justice reveals that their only object is to promote the good of
humankind (Hume, 1946, p. 25).

Writers on social and political issues, whatever their ideological starting point, converge on a single reason for the rules that they propose;
namely, "the convenience and necessities of mankind." No other reason is
possible, thinks Hume, for deciding what is mine and what is yours. But,
Hume glosses over the fact that the public welfare may be promoted to
the same degree in many ways and that the micro-distribution of goods
and benefits need not be the same in all those systems.

Sometimes, considerations of "analogy" allow one to discriminate
between situations that equally promote the global welfare in favor of one
form of local distribution over another. Such principles are subordinate to
the considerations of the "safety of the people" (Hume, 1946, pp. 28f.).
When these fail as well, we resort to civil codes which are dictated by considerations of public utility.

"In general . . . all questions of property are subordinate to the
authority of civil laws, which extend, restrain, modify, and alter the rules
of natural justice, according to the particular *convenience* of each community" (Hume, 1946, p. 30).[33]

"The necessity of justice to the support of society is the sole foundation of that virtue; and since no moral excellence is more highly esteemed,
we may conclude that this circumstance of usefulness has, in general, the
strongest energy, and most entire command over our sentiments."

The sole foundation of justice is its social necessity—its utility is its
imprimatur. Using a Newtonian maxim, Hume argues that what is the
case in this one instance, vis à vis justice, is so in the case of similar
instances, other virtues as well—utility is the sole basis of their validity
(Hume, 1957, p. 34).

"Usefulness is agreeable, and engages our approbation. This is a matter of fact, confirmed by daily observation." But useful for what or whom?
Not just ourselves, says Hume, but "the interest of those who are served
by the character or actions approved of; and these we may conclude, however remote, are not completely indifferent to us" (Hume, 1946, p. 52).
The distinction between what is useful and what is pernicious "is the same
in all its parts, with the *moral distinction*, whose foundation has been so
often, and so much in vain, enquired after." Hume here again invokes
Newton's rule that similar effects are presumed to be due to similar causes
in order to conclude that the "same endowments of the mind, in every circumstance, are agreeable to the sentiment of morals and to that of humanity" (Hume, 1946, pp. 70f.).

Hume argues that just as our ordinary sensory images are corrected for perspective effects, so are our moral judgments. The same object seen up close looks larger than it would seen from a distance. We correct for the distortion and "see" the object as having the same size in both cases. In moral matters, we correct for the accidental consequences that might result from our actions and consider only the intended consequences as morally relevant. Thus, "the tendencies of actions and characters, not their real accidental consequences, are alone regarded in our moral determinations or general judgments. . . . Why is this peach-tree said to be better than that other; but because it produces more or better fruit? And would not the same praise be given it, though snails or vermin had destroyed the peaches, before they came to full maturity? In morals too, is not *the tree known by the fruit*? And cannot we easily distinguish between nature and accident, in the one case as well as in the other?" (Hume, 1946, p. 63 n. 1).

In this same passage, Hume indicates that we correct our true sentiments to account for the "distance" between us and those whose actions and characters we judge. This is an adumbration or reflection of Smith's doctrine of the disinterested observer, which is itself a reflection of a "God's-eye" perspective in morals analogous to the "God's-eye" point of view in perception. We want to see things as they are, free from distorting influence. This gives us the truth both in morals and in science (Hume, 1946, p. 63; cf. p. 65).[34]

Why are and should we be moral? With the threat of eternal damnation no longer viable, what is there to make us moral? What is the source of moral obligation?

Ethics, for Hume, turns out to be no different from cookery. Just as cookery consists of recipes for producing tasty dishes, so morality consists of recipes for producing good in situations. Morality is analogous to aesthetics.

How then is morality acquired? Consider a child learning how to ride a bike. The child undergoes a series of trials and falls and eventually gets the hang of how to do it. But for the child to learn how to ride a bike, the child must have antecedently had the ability to learn how to ride the bike. The learning how is acquired but the antecedent ability seems to be innate—a mysterious je ne sais quoi.

Part II of Section 9 of the *Second Enquiry* raises the question: What is an "interested obligation" to duty; what is our motivation to do our duty? Hume answers: It is in our interest to do so. We must show that *all* our duties are in our own interest.

The close coincidence between the public interest and the private interest of each individual is an observable fact. This provides the ground for thinking that a unity in principle underlies both (Hume, 1946, p. 53).

It was this coincidence that Darwin sought to explain on the basis of his evolutionary theory.

Hume notes that, even though the coincidence is not exact, the moral sentiment continues. In addition, where the coincidence is more exact the sentiment is stronger. This leads us to conclude that two principles are at work.

We assume therefore that there is a "public affection" and that social utility is not a matter of indifference to us, independent of effects that may redound to ourselves. This principle accounts "in great part, for the origin of morality" (Hume, 1946, p. 53).[35]

In a footnote, Hume argues that, having determined that we are motivated by a principle of public affection, we need not pursue our investigations any further to determine the source of this principle. "It is sufficient, that this is experienced to be a principle in human nature. We must stop somewhere in our examination of causes; and there are, in every science, some general principles, beyond which we cannot hope to find any principle more general" (Hume, 1946, p. 54).[36]

The question now remaining is to determine the nature and extent of our obligation to perform in accordance with the moral injunctions here described (Hume, 1946, p. 118): "What theory of morals can ever serve any useful purpose, unless it can show, by a particular detail, that all the duties which it recommends, are also the true interest of each individual?" Of those virtues that are immediately useful or agreeable to the agent there is no dispute and no need for further argument. The same goes for the companionable virtues that are immediately agreeable to others (Hume, 1946, p. 119). The only case in which vice might have an advantage over virtue, as Hume sees it, is with respect to justice, where one might see oneself coming out on the short end by maintaining one's integrity. Such a person would endorse the general maxim "Honesty is the best policy" unless it be advantageous to do otherwise. Free rider problems come into play here. Hume appeals to one's sense of character that one would sacrifice "for the acquisition of worthless toys and gewgaws." In Hume's view no sensible person would so succumb (Hume, 1946, pp. 122f.).

Two central tensions emerge in Hume's ethical theory. On the one hand, Hume argues that reason is the slave of the passions. On the other, Hume condemns the "selfish view" of Hobbes and Mandeville, but reduces our duty to what is in our interest.

With respect to the first tension, if reason cannot motivate, then passions can be thwarted only by countervailing passions. If we have them, fine; if not, then we must develop them. But, to what extent can passions be developed or nurtured? Without countervailing passions, we act on the strength of our original passions.

The seventeenth and eighteenth century British moralists from Hobbes to Mandeville, Shaftesbury, Hutcheson, Butler, Hume, and Smith express a single theme with different variations. It culminates with Hume's idea that reason is the slave of the passions. Reason, which for the Cambridge Platonists motivates us to virtue, is increasingly relegated to an instrumental role. Butler argued, and Hume followed, that reason cannot motivate us to virtue. Hutcheson, as well, says much the same in his discussion of the force of the greatest good principle. From this point of view, to know what is right or wrong is one thing; to be motivated to act accordingly is another.

Adam Smith

The Theory of Moral Sentiments by Adam Smith was published in 1759, one hundred years before the appearance of *The Origin of Species*. Smith's theory was grounded in the empirical and naturalistic spirit of the age and is similar in many respects to Hume's view. Edmund Burke wrote to Smith commending his approach on the ground that "[a] theory like yours founded on the Nature of man, which is always the same, will last, when those that are founded on his opinions, which are always changing, will and must be forgotten" (Smith, 1982, p. 20). Both Smith and Hume relied on the centrality of the notion of "sympathy," although Smith's usage differed from Hume's. Smith also rejected what he saw to be Hume's grounding of morality in utility.

In section VII of *The Theory of Moral Sentiments*, Smith argues that two questions are central to a theory of moral sentiments. The first concerns the nature of virtue or morality. The second concerns our inclination to be moral: why do we prefer virtue? (Smith, 1982, pp. 265f.). Smith holds that the first question is more important than the second, as it has a practical import. The second question is, he says, merely academic.

Smith's analysis of virtue owes much to the Stoic tradition. He characterizes Stoicism as holding that virtue consists of assuming a measured indifference to the events of human life (Smith, 1982, p. 277). For the Stoics, the "sublime contemplation" of the workings of the universe under its "superintendant" is the "great business and occupation of our lives" (Smith, 1982, p. 292). However, Smith takes some exception to this. Nature, in his view, directs us to be concerned with ourselves, our interests, and the interests of those who are closest to us. Nature has, it is true, "provided a proper remedy and correction [for any imbalance of self-concern]. The real or even the imaginary presence of the impartial spectator, the authority of the man within the breast, is always at hand to overawe them into the proper tone and temper of moderation" (Smith, 1982, p. 292). Although Stoicism enjoins us to be indifferent and apathetic and unconcerned about all things, Nature prescribes otherwise and the "reasonings of philosophy" are not up to putting asunder the relations between the causes of our concerns and the concerns we feel as effects (Smith, 1982, pp. 292f.). "The judgments of the man within the breast, however, might be a good deal affected by those reasonings, and that great inmate might be taught by them to attempt to overawe all our private, partial, and selfish affections into a more or less perfect tranquility. *To direct the judgments of this inmate is the great purpose of all systems of morality*" (Smith, 1982, p. 293; added emphasis).[37]

Smith also takes Epicurus to task for his reductionist approach in seeking the root of all virtues in the pursuit of pleasure and the avoidance of pain (Smith, 1982, p. 299). He criticizes the benevolence theorists on the grounds that there are clearly other virtues than benevolence, and these accounts do not sufficiently explain the source of approbation for these "inferior" virtues (Smith, 1982, p. 304). We are, Smith notes, often motivated by considerations of self-interest to various degrees. "The condition of human nature were [=would be] particularly hard, if those affections, which, by the very nature of our being, ought frequently to influence our conduct, could upon no occasion appear virtuous, or deserve esteem and commendation from any body" (Smith, 1982, p. 305). To act always and only from considerations of benevolence, Smith notes, is worthy of a deity but not the imperfect creatures that we are.[38]

On the relation between his own view and the utility view that he associates with Hume, Smith says that "[t]he only difference between it and that which I have been endeavoring to establish, is, that it makes utility, and not sympathy, or the correspondent affection of the spectator, the natural and original measure of . . . [the] . . . proper degree . . . [of the affections which constitute virtue]" (Smith, 1982, p. 306).

The mark of all the previously considered systems of virtue is that they make a "real and essential" difference between right and wrong, good and evil, virtue and vice. Although they may be biased in what they consider to be the best, they all agree in encouraging the best (Smith, 1982, pp. 306f.). Mandeville, in earlier editions La Rochefoucauld as well, on the other hand, is an exception insofar as he reduces virtue to vanity or a "love of praise and commendation" (Smith, 1982, p. 308). Smith objects that what we qualify as virtuous cannot, with propriety, be termed vanity (Smith, 1982, p. 309). Yet Smith argues Mandeville's view must "border on the truth" because if it did not, his view would have been unmasked in an instant.[39] The point, I take it, is not that Mandeville's doctrine contains a kernel of truth, that after all we are only creatures of vanity, but rather that the pursuit of esteem, for example, can be the result of both noble and ignoble motives. But that some are unjustly honored for some virtue that in fact they do not possess does not mean that all are unjustly honored.

For Smith, three virtues are the cornerstones of human happiness: prudence, which is a regard for our own happiness, and justice and beneficence, which have regard for the happiness of others. Justice is concerned with not hurting that happiness; beneficence with its promotion (Smith, 1982, pp. 262f.).

Four alternatives account for our preference for and approval of virtue, according to Smith: (1) Approval is dictated by self-love (Hobbes); (2) Approval is dictated by reason (Wollaston); (3) Approval is dictated by sentiment (Hutcheson and Hume); and (4) Approval is dictated by a "modification of sympathy." This last is Smith's view. In Smith's view, moral approval derives from four sources, which together account for all the moral sentiment that exists as far as he can see. The moral sense is welcome to what remains, if anything. First, we may sympathize with the motives of the agent. Second, we may sympathize with the gratitude of those who benefit from the actions of the agent. Third, we note whether the conduct of the agent is in accord with general rules "[b]y which those two sympathies [with the motives of the agent and the gratitude of the benefactor of the agent's action] generally act" (Smith, 1982, p. 326). Fourth, "when we consider such actions as making a part of a system of behavior which tends to promote the happiness either of the individual or of the society, they appear to derive a beauty from this utility, not unlike that which we ascribe to any well-contrived machine" (Smith, 1982, p. 326).

When A confers a bounty on B, we say that B deserved it if (1) we directly approve of A's motive; (2) we indirectly sympathize with B's gratitude. The case is similar for demerit (Smith, 1982, pp. 74f.). The sympathy must, however, be appropriate.

In a letter to Gilbert Elliot upon publication of the first edition wherein Smith sought to make clear the standard of evaluation, Smith says: "Man is considered as a moral, because he is regarded as an accountable being. But an Accountable being, as the word expresses, is a being that must give an account of its actions to some other, and that, consequently, must regulate them according to the good liking of this other" (Mossner and Ross, 1987, p. 52). The other, to whom we are all accountable, is ourself as we reflect the views of an "average" neighbor. That is, we must discount any bias we might bring to an analysis of any situation and judge by the standards of the average spectator who might be viewing our actions. For Smith, the beginning of morality is our desire to be well thought of by our compatriots and to think well of ourselves. Society is a "mirror" that serves as a reflection of what we deem it proper to do. But, as Elliot and others objected, individual conscience is often at odds with the social norms. The correction that Smith worked into subsequent editions is Smith's major contribution to moral theory—the "impartial spectator" or the "man within the breast."

The "impartial spectator" is, in effect, Smith's version of Butler's conscience. It is the "voice of God" or the "Voice of Nature" within us. The impartial spectator is, in effect, ourselves viewing our situation from a disinterested point of view. Smith sees the judgments of the impartial spectator as standing to our untutored appraisals as "corrections" in much the same way that Hume thought our judgments about physical objects were "corrections" to the untutored judgments of our senses. Partiality in moral matters is playing the same role as perspectival distortions do with respect to sensory phenomena (Mossner and Ross, 1987, pp. 55f.).[40] The solution is to find a perspective in terms of which the deplorable but natural misfortunes that befall others can be weighed with the intense pain we endure when similar misfortunes befall us. In this way the minor but intense pains we suffer can be justly weighed with the great, but unfelt by us, pains of others. "It is from this station only that we can see the propriety of generosity and the deformity of injustice; the propriety of resigning the greatest interests of our own for the yet more important interests of others, and the deformity of doing the smallest injury to another in order to obtain the greatest benefit to ourselves. The real littleness of ourselves and of whatever relates to ourselves can be seen from this Station only; and it is here only that we can learn the great lesson of Stoical magnanimity and firmness, to be no more affected by what befalls ourselves than by what befalls our neighbor, or, what comes to the same thing, than our neighbor is capable of being affected by what befalls us" (Mossner and Ross, 1987, p. 56).

The introduction of the notion of an "impartial spectator" into moral theory is a major development and represents an attempt on Smith's part to give a naturalistic account of the nature and role of conscience. Smith's "impartial spectator" is akin to but not to be identified with the "ideal observers" that subsequently came to prominence in moral theory. The impartial spectator, although impartial, is far from ideal; that is, it is not a perfectly rational being with full information who decides issues solely through reason alone. To attempt to ground morality in such a notion would have seemed wrongheaded to Smith and not consonant with what he took to be the nature of human beings.

True to his Stoical inclinations, Smith often represents nature and society as efficient machines that work by the smooth interaction of their component parts. Human beings are individuals who, in the pursuit of their own goals, promote what Smith calls the two "great ends" for which Nature fashioned animals—self-preservation and the propagation of the species. In an anticipation of a theme running through *The Wealth of Nations*, Smith writes

Though man, therefore, be naturally endowed with a desire of the welfare and preservation of society, yet the Author of nature has not entrusted it to his reason to find out that a certain application of punishments is the proper means of attaining this end; but has endowed him with an immediate and instinctive approbation of that very application which is most proper to attain it. The economy of nature is in this respect exactly of a piece with what it is upon many other occasions. With regard to all those ends which, upon account of their peculiar importance, may be regarded, if such an expression is allowable, as the favorite ends of nature, she has constantly in this manner not only endowed mankind with an appetite for the end which she proposes, but likewise with an appetite for the means by which alone this end can be brought about, for their own sakes, and independent of their tendency to produce it. Thus self-preservation, and the propagation of the species are the great ends which Nature seems to have proposed in the formation of all animals. . . . But though . . . [humans] . . . are . . . endowed with a very strong desire of these ends, it has not been intrusted to the slow and uncertain determinations of our reason, to find out the proper means of bringing them about. Nature has directed us to the greater part of these by original and immediate instincts. Hunger, thirst, the passion which unites the two sexes, the love of pleasure, and the dread of pain, prompt us to apply those means for their own sakes, and without any consideration of their tendency to those beneficent ends which the great Director of nature intended to produce by them. (Smith, 1982, pp. 77f.)

Adam Smith, the author of *The Theory of Moral Sentiments*, which holds that the foundation of morality is sympathy, is also the author of *The Wealth of Nations*, which argues that society is best served by individuals pursuing their own self-interest. Several commentators in the nineteenth century were struck by the apparent contradiction and gave birth to an academic industry known as the *Adam Smith problem*. However, a careful reading of *The Theory of Moral Sentiments* dispels the appearance of contradiction. There would be a problem only if one construes sympathy as akin to benevolence and then takes the youthful Smith to be arguing for a theory of human nature based upon the centrality of benevolence in human nature and the older Smith as arguing for a more Hobbesian view of human nature with selfishness at the core. But this interpretation is not borne out by the text. Smith is at great pains in *The Theory of Moral Sentiments* to point out that human beings are motivated by a variety of considerations. Self-interest or concern for oneself is one of the fundamental endowments of nature. Recall that Smith rejected the Stoical view of morality as based on too austere a view of the nature of human beings.

Indeed, sympathy and self-interest, far from being incompatible or even at odds with one another, fit together in an essential way in the theory of moral sentiments. The key to the role of sympathy for Smith, recall, is that the judgment of the "impartial spectator" is based on a sense of propriety or what is appropriate for a situation. Some situations require and demand that an agent be motivated by self-interest. If someone does another an injustice and by so doing threatens not only one's well-being but one's life as well, it is proper that the person being victimized should respond in a self-interested way. If one does not, then the impartial spectator, the man within my breast, condemns the person on the grounds that one's reaction is not appropriate to the indignities one is subjected to. An agent who does not look out for oneself, where it is appropriate that one should, is the subject of our disapprobation not our approval. Had Hutcheson written *The Wealth of Nations*, then we should either see a contradiction or conclude that, for Hutcheson, no economic agent, as such, could be moral. But, not so for Smith.

Darwin, in *The Descent of Man* (Darwin, 1981, p. 81), complains of Smith's view "that the basis of sympathy lies in our strong retentiveness of former states of pain or pleasure" does not account for why we are more sympathetic to those close to us. Darwin is here using *sympathy* in the sense in which it is associated with benevolence, as his reference to Bain makes clear. This is not the primary sense of *sympathy* for Smith, although he does use the word to connote "beneficence." (See especially Smith, 1982, pp. 219–222.) Smith claims that "natural affection" is "more the effect of the moral than of the supposed physical connection between the parent and the child" (Smith, 1982, p. 223). From a Darwinian point of view, no doubt, this does seem the wrong way around. The example Smith cites to make his point is that men who suspect their wives of infidelity often regard the offspring of their wives' infidelity "with hatred and aversion." This is presumably a result of the failure of the "moral bond" between husband and wife. But, of course, there is a presumed biological explanation of why this should be so. Smith construes "physical" here as amounting to proximity and nurturing—the illegitimate offspring "having been educated in his own house." In general, Smith's account hinges on proximal nurturance and the effects of custom. Darwin allows in his discussion that these factors may have been the origin of sympathy but that, in the course of evolution, it has become an "instinct."

The question vexing Darwin in his argument with Smith and Bain is whether sympathy and its features are innate or learned. Smith's view appears to be that, whereas we have a natural disposition to be beneficent, it is a manifestation of what we would today label *reciprocal altruism*. Smith has it that "Of all the persons, however, whom nature points out for our peculiar beneficence, there are none to whom it seems more properly directed than to those whose beneficence we have ourselves already experienced. Nature, which formed men for that mutal [sic!] kindness, so necessary for their happiness, renders every man the peculiar object of kindness, to the persons to whom he himself has been kind" (Smith, 1982, p. 225).

THE EIGHTEENTH CENTURY LEGACY

Two problems form the core of the eighteenth century discussions on moral motivation. The first "Why be moral?" is really two questions, "Why are we moral?" and "Should we be moral, and if so, why?" The first descriptive question is one of moral motivation. In this chapter, we have explored some of the variations that emerged in the literature as an aftermath of Hobbes's challenge. That we should be moral and that being moral involved acting to promote the common good were presupposed by these writers. As to why we should be moral, although the eighteenth century British moralists rejected a radical Hobbesian position, more often than not they wound up defending a version of the view that we should be moral because it is in our self-interest to do so.

The second problem was how to reconcile self-interest and benevolence, which in the nineteenth century became the problem of reconciling self-interest with altruism. This problem was bequeathed to the eighteenth century by a Hobbesian view of humankind that forced moralists to deny that real benevolence existed or to show how (1) benevolence could overcome self-interest and (2) why the two often if not usually coincided. Two options emerged as alternatives to Hobbes's view that benevolence is an illusion. One option was to argue that benevolence is stronger than often supposed and overwhelms self-interest. This is basically Hutcheson's view. The other was to argue that the self-regarding passions often, if not nearly always, coincided with duty and benevolence. This is basically the Butler-Hume view.

All had read Newton and Locke and were influenced by the new physics. All appealed, more or less explicitly, to a "force" model of moral motivation. The underlying model, which draws heavily on the Newtonian paradigm, involves a composition of forces, where the components are "self-interest," "benevolence," and motivations for specific ends. The basic idea is that the agent is under the influence of competing and cooperating motivational forces that determine the course of his or her action. In terms of such a vector-sum model, the problem of accounting for benevolently motivated actions is immediately clear. Even if one did not agree with the Hobbesian view that, in effect, benevolent motives were disguised self-interested ones or decomposable into self-interested ones, the problem of the relative strength of the different motives posed a major problem. All, with the possible exception of Hutcheson, agreed that self-interested motives were much more powerful than benevolent motives, so how was it that agents ever acted benevolently? Shaftesbury avoided this problem by characterizing moral behavior in terms of a balance of motives but, for those who saw the heart of morality to lie in benevolence, this was a real problem. The resolution, more often than not, took the form of an argument for the coincidence of self-interest and benevolence, so that both "vectors" as it were, more often than not pointed in more or less the same direction.

The two building blocks in the eighteenth century response to Hobbes by the British moral theorists were the perceived independent reality of benevolent or other-regarding motives and the recognition that the strength of such motives was, in general, much less than the strength of self-regarding or self-interested motives. Both were consequences of the naturalistic attitude that sought the springs of human action through empirical studies of human behavior and human nature. The relative strengths of self-regarding as opposed to other-regarding motives may not seem to pose much of a problem, but how could the eighteenth century critics be so sure that Hobbes's reductionist position was flawed? How could they be so sure that benevolent motives were an independent factor in human motivation? The answer, I suggest, lies in their implicit acceptance of what might be called the *Transparency Assumption*, that individuals have an unbiased access to their interests and motives. One need only look into one's own motivations and reflect upon the common experience of humankind—open and clear to all—to see that Hobbes and the reductionist position were mistaken. They assumed to a man, Mandeville excepted, that human motives and especially one's own motives were easily accessible to a disinterested observer. They assumed, in effect, that human motives were transparently obvious to any observer who took the least precautions to guard against self-deception. A simple examination of the motivational structure of human beings revealed to these investigators not only the relative strengths of alternative motives but the fact that benevolent motives were sui generis. Even the skeptical Hume, who recognized the tendency of human beings to practice self-deception and who took pride in the fact that his analysis of morality was not so tied as that of his predecessors to evaluating the relative strengths of various motivational forces, rejected the "selfish view" as being clearly contrary to the facts. The investigations of Freud and contemporary sociobiologists, which suggest that self-deception is at the center of human behavior and human nature, reveal the innocence of the age. Nevertheless, this is the legacy left to the nineteenth century theorists and to Darwin, who can be construed as attempting to provide an evolutionary resolution of the problem of reconciling self-interest and benevolence.

James Mackintosh

James Mackintosh provides a direct link between the eighteenth century British moral tradition and Charles Darwin. Darwin's uncle by marriage, Mackintosh wrote a well-known treatise on moral philosophy that Darwin knew well (Mackintosh, 1834). Mackintosh argued against the reductionist thesis that all passions or interests could be reduced to self-love. Virtue is not disguised vice. Using the chemistry and physics of the day, Mackintosh argued for the reality of complex phenomena that may, in fact, be constituted by simpler parts. Water, for example, was known to be a compound of hydrogen and oxygen. The liquidity of water, however, was not something that could be reduced to or explained by the then known properties of hydrogen and oxygen. Such compounds are real and irreducible. In a similar vein, acts of benevolence are not reducible to acts of self-love.

Human morality, for Mackintosh, was characterized by the striving for universality, necessity, and immutability in moral judgments. With Butler, Mackintosh postulated conscience as a supreme moral principle. Conscience is a universal, independent principle that guides our voluntary actions (Mackintosh, 1834, pp. 380f.). At the same time, Mackintosh argued for the contingent malleability of conscience. Our conscience morally approves as virtuous those actions that promote the general good, although the general good is rarely if ever our deliberate aim. Our moral sentiments "coincide" with the dictates of conscience. But, Mackintosh asks " . . . 'whence arises the coincidence between [conscience] and the moral sentiments?' It may seem at first sight, that such a theory rests the foundation of morals upon a coincidence altogether mysterious, and apparently capricious and fantastic" (Mackintosh, 1834, p. 382).

Mackintosh was as hard pressed as Butler to account for the "social dimension" of morality. Darwin, who expressed admiration for Mackintosh's mental powers, was unhappy at Mackintosh's attempt to explain the coincidence between the universal judgments of conscience and socially useful behaviors by an appeal to "mental contiguity." Mackintosh's solution, to which Darwin objected, is that "It may truly be said, that if observation and experience did not clearly ascertain that *beneficial tendency* is the constant attendant and mark of *all virtuous dispositions and actions*, the same great truth would be revealed to us by the *voice of conscience*. The coincidence, instead of being arbitrary, arises necessarily from the *laws of human nature*, and the *circumstances in which mankind are placed*" [emphasis added] (Mackintosh, 1834, p. 383).

In his notebooks, Darwin posed the fundamental problem of morality as the attempt to reconcile and explain the "coincidence of morality with individual interest." Darwin mused that conscience, *a la* Mackintosh, is supreme only insofar as it is part of our inherited habitual natures (Gruber, 1974, pp. 398f.).[41] Darwin's objection hinges on his evolutionary perspective, which denies the universality or immutability of human nature. The changing circumstances in which humans find themselves modify both human beings and their natures. For Darwin, Mackintosh's "solution" merely reposes the problem of coincidence.

NOTES

1. The pre-Darwinian literature is couched in terms of considerations of benevolence rather than altruism. The latter term was coined by Auguste Comte in the 1830s. The approaches are either reductionistic or pluralistic. They are embedded within implicit or explicit models of human nature. They are, of course, concerned with proximate rather than evolutionary analyses.

2. These questions presuppose that some sense of what it is to be moral is antecedently understood or accepted. One of the functions of the embedding theory of human nature is to provide a sense of what it means to be a moral agent and to be moral.

3. Darwin was related by marriage to the Scottish philosopher James Mackintosh, who wrote an influential summary of moral philosophy with which Darwin was acquainted. See Manier (1978) for a discussion of Mackintosh's influence on Darwin.

4. See, e.g., Dawkins (1976) and Ghiselin (1974) for a contemporary sociobiological variation on this theme.

5. See Grean (1967) for a discussion of six different senses of the term *natural* in Shaftesbury.

6. By appealing to concepts of harmony derived from the Stoics, Shaftesbury attempted both to establish the aesthetic dimension of moral action and to develop a Deistic ethical position that did not rely for its warrant on the Christian religion.

7. The "unnatural" passions, for Hutcheson, are a result of the Fall. Whereas Shaftesbury was a Deist, Hutcheson was a Theist.

8. Hutcheson goes on to claim that the calculation of consequences requires us to consider what might occur versus what might not (Schneewind, 1990, p. 516). This is the adumbration of rule utilitarianism. Hutcheson argues that we often frame laws against kinds of actions where particular instances would do good if the general tendency of acting on such would be the promotion of evil. One can well see how one could use such a principle to argue against state welfare systems on the grounds that, whereas particular acts of public welfare may alleviate the conditions of the unfortunate, a general reliance on such schemes would or might lead to a dissolution of the moral fibre of the community. Spencer, for one, was prone to such arguments and tended to favor laissez-faire systems of social welfare.

9. Darwin, in response to Mill on the status of the Greatest Happiness Principle, makes a similar point (Darwin, 1981, pp. 97f.). Mill's response is to distinguish between motives and criteria. In Mill's view, the Greatest Happiness Principle is a criterion for right or wrong but agents do not appeal to it as a source of psychological motivation. (See later, pp. 62f.)

10. Darwin attempts to give an evolutionary account of its origin (Darwin, 1981, ch. 3). Compare in this respect Butler's view of conscience as the "voice of God within us." Midgley (1979a) argues that evolution takes over the role that God plays in Butler's theory of human nature.

11. The following discussion of the moral sense in Hutcheson is heavily indebted to Peach (1971).

12. This congruity, asserted by Mackintosh, is queried by Darwin, who tries to give an evolutionary account (Manier, 1978, p. 163). The evolutionary account lays the groundwork for accounting for "mistakes" insofar as organisms may evolve capacities and behavioral repertoires that misfire or that the organism displays in inappropriate circumstances. Just as, say, the moth's attraction to light enhances its fitness but becomes dysfunctional when the moth is attracted to flames, so one might try to account for the cases where benevolence and self-interest dictate opposing courses of action.

13. Compare, in this regard, the argument by Richards (1987) that a selectionist account can provide both empirical and moral justifications of ethical principles. Richards's argument is discussed later in Chapter 5.

14. But, the brutes do not behave randomly. Ethnological studies reveal that there are patterns to their behaviors as well, although perhaps not patterns that indicate reflection. (See Tinbergen (1989), or any number of comparative studies of animal behavior.)

15. In footnote 6 to Sermon I, Butler argues that self-love is to be distinguished from the particular passions. But, in addition to benevolence, here construed as a general passion, and self-love, individuals have particular passions whose immediate end is their satisfaction by some reward. These passions can be either private or public. As an instance of the former, Butler cites hunger, which is satisfied by food. As an instance of the latter, Butler cites the desire for esteem, which is satisfied by esteem. In that same note, Butler observes that although the particular passions are desires for particular ends, their gratification contributes to the more general ends of self-love and benevolence. Thus, "the . . . [public passions] . . . can no more be gratified without contributing to the good [note: not the preservation!] of society, than the . . . [private appetites] . . . can be gratified without contributing to the preservation [note: not the good!] of the individual." But, the parallel seems somewhat forced. First, are we to assume that the good of the individual is preservation and the preservation of the society is good? Radicals may challenge the latter and sociobiologists may challenge the former. Second, the means-ends relationships in the two cases do not appear to be the same. In the case of gratifying my hunger, my eating food contributes to my preservation, all things considered. In the case of gratifying my desire for esteem, are we to infer that my being held in high esteem contributes to the good of the society? Surely, it is that I am held in esteem to the extent that by word, deed, or example I contribute to the good of society (by being magnanimous, helpful, a role model, etc.). In the former case, gratifying my private appetite contributes to my preservation. In the latter case, my contributing to the public good leads to the gratification of my public passion.

16. Cf. Huxley's remark to the effect that the murderer and the thief follow nature as much as the saint (Huxley, 1989, p. 138).

17. Butler here alludes to the possibility that the dictates of conscience may be checked by appeal to a "higher" power, but the further consideration of this goes beyond his present purpose.

18. In §8 of Sermon I, Butler argues that the principle of reflection (or conscience) "tends to restrain men from doing mischief to each other, and leads them to do good, is too manifest to need being insisted upon" (Butler, 1983, p. 30). Butler goes on to assert that "It cannot possibly be denied that there is this principle of reflection or conscience in human nature."

Here, I suggest, Butler slides between the phenomenological and the theoretical levels of analysis, which were distinguished in Chapter 1. That we behave in such and such a way is a fact about human behavior. That we act in such a way because we have a principle of reflection or conscience is a model construct. The slide is obscured because the term *conscience* is serving a double function. It is a term with phenomenological application and also a term of art. It may be useful to compare the situation here with that of geometry. The term *straight line*, for example, has both a phenomenological and a theoretical application. In the former case, it is something that is produced using a straight edge, a ruler, or by stretching a taut string between two points on a flat surface. In the latter case, it is a concept whose meaning is fixed by its embedding within an axiomatic system. When only one geometry is available the ambiguity is no problem. The existence of non-Euclidean geometries creates a difficulty. The axiomatic geometry of Euclid is one theoretical system among many, competing as the best account of the phenomenological facts of our geometrical experiences. So, too, can one construe Butler's moral system. It is one of a number of competing theoretical accounts that attempt to make sense of and do justice to our moral experience.

19. Modern psychology and its emphasis on unconscious motivation puts the lie to, or at the very least, a new twist upon, this.

20. Cf. Butler's remarks in the "Dissertation" (Butler, 1983, p. 69).

21. There are elements of reason and sentiment in all our moral judgments but "The final sentence, it is probable, which pronounces characters and actions amiable or odious, praise-worthy or blameable . . . depends on some internal sense or feeling, which nature has made universal in the whole species" (Hume, 1946, p. 5).

22. This claim is a manifestation of Hume's foundational approach to ethics. Human beings certainly do act, but the conclusion that there must therefore have been an initial or original motivating cause rests on a model of human action (involving among other things, the distinction between reason and sentiment) that we are not compelled to accept (Hume, 1946, p. 134). Hume's foundationalism and essentialism is apparent in the final paragraph of Appendix 1. He again claims a sharp distinction between reason and taste. "The former conveys the knowledge of truth and falsehood: the latter gives the sentiment of beauty and deformity, vice and virtue."

23. "The end of all moral speculations is to teach us our duty; and, by proper representations of the deformity of vice and beauty of virtue, beget corresponding habits, and engage us to avoid the one, and embrace the other" (Hume, 1946, p. 4).

24. "The notion of morals implies some sentiment common to all mankind."

When we say of something that we disapprove of it we are, Hume says, speaking the language of self-love. When we say of something that it is wrong, we say more—not merely that we disapprove but that it is something of which all right-minded individuals, free from prejudice, would disapprove of as well (Hume, 1946, p. 110). These common sentiments also extend to all human beings—the range of those who fall within the moral realm extends to all humankind (Hume, 1946, p. 111).

25. "Particular customs and manners alter the usefulness of qualities: they also alter their merit." Private virtues are more arbitrary and variable than public ones because what counts as virtuous is a function of the differing circumstances in which we find ourselves (Hume, 1946, p. 77).

There are, it is to be admitted, qualities that are useful to individuals but not the public at large, and these are praised as selfish virtues. We account for them not by deriving them from self-love but on the grounds that the approval and disapproval of others is not a matter of indifference to us. When we are, for example, impatient rather than patient, the resulting misery that we induce in others is a matter of concern to us (Hume, 1946, p. 79).

26. For Hume, the assumption of the uniformity of human nature is a very peculiar assumption. Hume is in somewhat of a quandary. He denies that human beings are empirically warranted in believing in the uniformity of nature but his ethics assumes that human nature is uniform. The question is: How can one be an arch skeptic in epistemology and have any positive moral philosophy at all?

27. In the *Second Inquiry*, Hume claims that the standard of truth and false-hood "being founded on the nature of things, is eternal and inflexible, even by the will of the Supreme Being: the standard . . . [of matters of taste] . . . arising from the eternal frame and constitution of animals [!], is ultimately derived from the Supreme Will, which bestowed on each being its peculiar nature, and arranged the several classes and orders of existence" (Hume, 1946, p. 135).

28. Hume argues that the principle of self-love is so powerful and pervasive in human beings that it is understandable why some philosophers have felt that "all our concern for the public might be resolved into a concern for our own happiness and preservation" (Hume, 1946, p. 53).

29. The sociobiologists will say: *yes*

30. The sociobiologist replies—this is parental affection gone awry. Humans are shaped by natural selection just as watches are designed by master artisans. Watches sometimes fail to keep the proper time, nonetheless, so human beings do not always act in ways that are conducive to their own survival and self interest.

31. The sociobiologists will have a general answer for these as well. Hume might object: what is the test or proof of this? Is there nothing more than post hoc reconstructions? If so, then we must admit that the matter does not admit of test. But, tests, in principle, are forthcoming. We should be able to make statistical predictions about the distributions of behaviors in cases like that of the bereaved mother. That we cannot perform the tests is a measure of technical and ethical considerations not theoretical ones. This hypothesis is "metaphysical" only to that extent and unlike other metaphysical hypotheses that invoke untestable, in principle, spirits, pixies, or fairies.

32. On benevolence, Hume holds that "nothing can bestow more merit on any human creature than the sentiment of benevolence in an eminent degree; and that a part, at least, of its merit arises from its tendency to promote the interests of our species, and bestow happiness on human society" (Hume, 1946, p. 14).

33. Note the focus on each community; there are no universal laws of justice here. Hume, in a footnote here on Montesquieu, argues against founding principles of justice on reason. The "sole foundation of property and justice" is the "interest of society." Indeed, "our obligation itself to obey the magistrate and his laws is founded on nothing but the interests of society" (Hume, 1946, p. 30).

34. "It is wisely ordained by nature, that private connexions should commonly prevail over universal views and considerations; otherwise our affections and actions would be dissipated and lost, for want of a proper limited object. Thus a small benefit done to ourselves, or our near friends, excites more lively sentiments of love and approbation than a great benefit done to a distant commonwealth: But still we know here, as in all the senses, to correct these inequalities by reflection, and retain a general standard of vice and virtue, founded chiefly on general usefulness" (Hume, 1946, p. 65).

35. In terms of our framework, this is a proximate principle, which stands in stark contrast to the quite different proximate starting point of Hobbes. Hume's principle needs to be supplemented by an evolutionary account in place of the static human nature account or divine law model that might be forthcoming from the Hobbes-Smith crowd.

36. Two points are of interest here. First, the move to the evolutionary model opens up a new dimension of the problem. Second, the point about unexplained explainers is well taken, but can be taken in either of two ways. There can be an absolute or relative interpretation. In the first, some principles serve as the first principles no matter what. In the second, for every investigation, there are first principles, because every particular investigation must come to an end. The first claim is an existentially quantified universal claim. The second is a universally quantified existential claim. The first entails the second but not vice versa.

37. This discussion brings to mind Huxley's analysis of Stoicism and its failings in Huxley (1989). Huxley criticizes the Stoic view insofar as it promotes indifference where what is needed, in Huxley's view, is struggle against the forces of the cosmos.

38. Compare, in this regard, the austere morality of Kant.

39. It is otherwise with speculations about physical nature because there the most extravagant systems may appear very plausible to many for a long time and yet turn out in the end to have no foundation whatsoever. Smith cites as an example the vortex hypothesis of Descartes (Smith, 1982, p. 309). The hypothesis, which was held in high esteem for close to a century, had, at the time of Smith's writing, been replaced by the theories of Newton. The idea that an incorrect analysis of moral phenomena could enjoy such a reign was unthinkable to Smith. This marks an important difference between the natural and the moral sciences in Smith's view, according to Raphael and Skinner in their General Introduction to Smith's *Essays* (Smith, 1980, p. 12). The point has merit, however, only on the assumption that moral phenomena wear their analysis on their face, so to speak. It

is one thing, though, to reject the view that vanity, as experienced, is experientially the same as, say, benevolence and quite another to say that the "hidden springs" of both are or are not the same. In that sense, the moral sciences or, in particular, moral psychology, is no different from the natural sciences. After all, from our point of view, psychology is a natural science.

40. In that same letter to Gilbert Elliot, Smith rehearses the "perceptual correction" thesis endorsed by Hume: "As to the eye of the body objects appear great or small, not so much according to their real dimensions, as according to the nearness or distance of their situation; so do they likewise to, what may be called, the natural eye of the mind: and we remedy the defects of both these organs pretty much in the same manner" (Mossner and Ross, 1987, pp. 55f.).

41. See Manier (1978) for a discussion of the influence of Mackintosh on Darwin.

Chapter 3

The Moral Realm of Nature: Nineteenth Century Views on Ethics and Evolution

I cannot forbear adding to these reasonings an observation, which may, perhaps, be found of some importance. In every system of morality, which I have hitherto met with, I have always remark'd, that the author proceeds for some time in the ordinary way of reasoning, and establishes the being of a God, or makes observations concerning human affairs; when of a sudden I am surpriz'd to find, that instead of the usual copulations of propositions, *is*, and *is not*, I meet with no proposition that is not connected with an *ought*, or an *ought not*. This change is imperceptible; but is, however, of the last consequence. For as this *ought*, or *ought not*, expresses some new relation or affirmation, 'tis necessary that it shou'd be observ'd and explain'd; and at the same time that a reason should be given, for what seems altogether inconceivable, how this new relation can be a deduction from others, which are entirely different from it. (Hume, 1978, p. 469)

INTRODUCTION

Hume's caution sets the stage for subsequent attempts to force a wedge between facts and values. In particular, it sets the stage for a distinction between science, which deals with the "facts" of nature, and ethics, which deals with one aspect of the values that one finds expressed by certain organisms as they attempt to cope with those facts. In the nineteenth century the difference was not so sharp as it appears to be today. Ethics was construed to be a subject matter that could be put on a scientific basis just as much as geometry or physics.

As sentient and sapient creatures, we find ourselves immersed in a value-laden *Lebenswelt*. Many of the nineteenth century writers, including the evolutionists Darwin, Huxley, Spencer, and Kropotkin, were not loathe to draw moral implications from the facts and theory of evolution although they differed among themselves on the extent and the nature of such implications. In the twentieth century, such speculations were quieted by philosophical considerations, such as Moore's charge that ethical positions inspired by evolutionary considerations committed the naturalistic fallacy, and by political considerations such as the fact that a broad spectrum of social and political positions claimed to draw comfort from evolutionary theory. The recent emergence of sociobiological theory has rekindled interest in drawing moral conclusions from evolutionary considerations and rekindled charges that such inferences commit an egregious fallacy.

In the first section of this chapter I present a representative sample of nineteenth and twentieth century views on the relevance of evolutionary facts for moral values. The second section explores the role of culture in the determination of value.

NATURAL FACTS AND NATURAL VALUES

Charles Darwin

"A moral being is one who is capable of comparing his past and future actions and motives,—of approving of some and disapproving of others; and the fact that man is the one being who with certainty can be thus designated makes the greatest of all distinctions between him and the lower animals" (Darwin, 1981, part ii, p. 392). Darwin is quick to point out, however, that he believes this great difference is still only a difference in degree and not in kind.

Darwin summarizes his view of the evolution of the moral sense in the last chapter of part ii of *Descent* (1981, part ii, pp. 389ff.). He reminds us of the main conclusion of the book. Human beings are descended from some "less organized form." Mental faculties as well as physical characteristics are variable. These variations are inherited. He conjectures that the increase in relative brain size, which is a feature of human beings, is partly a result of the development of language and the subsequent interaction of mental faculties with the physical brain. The "culture of the mind" contributes, in both the race and the individual, to the development of the higher intellectual powers in humankind.

The foundations of morality lie in the social instincts. For human beings, Darwin notes, these include family ties, love, and sympathy. These foundations are shared by other social animals although, given their intellectual limitations, they do not have morality in any true sense of the word. These instincts "have in all probability been acquired through natural selection" (Darwin, 1981, ii, p. 391).[1]

The moral sense in human beings evolved through the interaction of the social instincts and the higher mental powers. The crucial intellectual capacities for the development of morality in Darwin's view are memory, anticipation, and the power of reflection. We remember deeds done or not done in the past, and upon reflection these memories give rise to feelings of satisfaction or dissatisfaction. The feelings of dissatisfaction in turn give rise to feelings of regret, and we resolve to act differently in the future. Such is the origin of conscience. Our sense of obligation arises from the presence of permanent, stronger, and more enduring instincts. These turn out, for Darwin, to be the social instincts.

We share with other social animals certain social instincts that manifest themselves in a general desire to aid members of our community. In the lower animals, these desires manifest themselves in "hard-wired" actions or responses. Human beings, on the other hand, are "soft wired." They have a general desire to aid members of their community but no built-in responses or specific patterns of behavior. The implementation and satisfaction of these general desires is enhanced by the human capacity for language. Through language, human beings can make their desires and needs clearer to others who might be in a position to satisfy them. Praise and blame become possible and once instituted become selective shapers of behavioral repertoires. In addition, the formulation of moral rules and codes becomes possible and this in turn contributes to the spread of moral practices and the development of "higher" moralities; that is, moralities that embrace wider and wider human communities.[2]

Four propositions lie at the heart of Darwin's ethical theory:

1. The foundation of morality lies in the social instincts.
2. The evolution of mentality-intelligence leads to the evolution of the social instincts.
3. The development of language leads to the development of common opinions and the development of public approval and disapproval based upon considerations of mutual sympathy.
4. The evolution of morality is aided and abetted by the formation of habits (cf. Kropotkin, 1947, pp. 33–34).

The evolution of intelligence leads to the evolution of conscience or a moral sense. Feelings of regret, shame, remorse, repentance, and guilt are part of our moral conscience, and they evolve as part of a mechanism to ensure automatic acceptance of certain rules of conduct that are necessary for group survival. These sentiments arise from a conflict between instincts. All organisms with a sufficiently developed social nature are subject to these conflicts. Instincts are often in conflict and have different strengths. The migratory instinct in birds sometimes overcomes the maternal instinct when, for example, a mother bird will abandon her late-hatched and underdeveloped chicks to fly south (Darwin, 1981, part i, p. 82). Of two instincts, Natural Selection generally will make that which promotes the good of the species more "potent" because individuals with instincts that promote the good of the species would tend to survive in greater numbers, but, as Darwin notes, the migratory-maternal conflict in birds is an exception to this rule. Human beings, unlike other animals, have the ability to reflect upon and judge their intentions and actions. This ability for second order reflection results in *conscience*. But, how are we to account for it? Darwin distinguishes between social instincts and self-directed instincts. When we act against the inclinations of our social instincts we experience regret. If we attempt to explain action in the presence of conflicting instincts by appealing to the strength of instincts and if we assume that the social instincts are "higher" because of their greater strength, we are unable to explain why humans often act counter to their social inclinations. In this simple model, our other-directed motives ought to outweigh our self-directed motives every time.

Butler, in the eighteenth century, faced a similar problem in trying to account for the nature and effectiveness of conscience. Butler distinguished between the *strength* and the *authority* of an instinct and argued that, in effect, our social instincts have a higher authority. Butler argued that the principles and propensities that motivate us can be hierarchically organized. The hierarchical ordering is based upon two criteria: strength and authority. The idea then seems to be this: We have a postulated hierarchical *model* of motivation that consists of two factors—benevolence and self-love in some mixture—with an appropriate strength and authority. Every individual action is presumed to be the product of a "mixed" motivation of the same factor. We can, in principle, compare the "motivational profile" of a given real-world action against the standard model—"the correspondence of actions to the nature of the agent renders them natural: their disproportion to it, unnatural" (Butler, p. 31, also see pp. 32f., 39f.). But Darwin could not accept such an answer, as his notebooks reveal.

Rachels argues that Darwin's solution is to appeal to a modified model based on strength considerations alone. The strength of our instincts or motives varies from time to time and circumstance to circumstance. When we act against our social instincts we do so because, *at that moment,* our self-directed instincts are stronger. We act and the moment passes. As it does, the strength of our self-directed instincts wanes with respect to the strength of our other-directed instincts. We reflect again and experience remorse, guilt, and so forth. The "authority" of the social instincts rests, in Darwin's view, solely on their longevity and permanence (Rachels, 1990, pp. 7f.). But why have the social instincts evolved to be more permanent and lasting than the self-directed motives or instincts? Darwin's answer is that these instincts emerge as more "potent" because natural selection singles them out in virute of their conduciveness to group survival.

Darwin accepted a version of the inheritance of acquired characteristics in the form of the "use and disuse" principle.[3] Virtue practiced becomes virtue habituated. Habits turn into instincts and are inherited. The moral fiber of humankind becomes stronger and more advanced. "The moral nature of man has reached the highest standard as yet attained, partly through the advancement of the reasoning powers and consequently of a just public opinion, but especially through the sympathies being rendered more tender and widely diffused through the effects of habit, example, instruction, and reflection. *It is not improbable that virtuous tendencies may through long practice be inherited*" (Darwin, 1981, part ii, p. 394; my emphasis).[4]

What does this higher morality look like? Darwin is careful not to suggest that any specific moral codes can be derived from evolutionary considerations. Indeed, although the instincts upon which morality rests may have evolved through natural selection, the development and practice of specific virtues owes much to education, enculturation, and social contingencies.[5] Nonetheless, "[a]s all men desire their own happiness, praise or blame is bestowed on actions and motives, according as they lead to this end; and as happiness is an essential part of the general good, the greatest-happiness principle *indirectly* serves as a nearly safe standard of right and wrong" (Darwin, 1981, part ii, p. 393).

Was Darwin a utilitarian? More important, did he hold that the theory of natural selection served as an explanation or justification for the greatest happiness principle? Many nineteenth century commentators interpreted him this way, including J. G. Schurman (1888). Schurman takes the struggle for life and survival of the fittest as the two fundamental components of Darwin's theory (Schurman, 1888, p. 116). The first component he took to derive from Malthus and hence from political economy; the second he took to derive from Utilitarianism. "No one uninfluenced by the ethics of the school of Hume and Bentham would have ventured to interpret the evolution of life as a continuous realization of utilities" (Schurman, 1888, p. 117). Schurman argues that "[n]atural selection rests upon a biological utilitarianism, which may be egoistic [corresponding to individual selection] or communistic [corresponding to group selection], but never universalistic" (Schurman, 1888, p. 118). This is then turned by Schurman into a critique of both natural selection as an explanation of morality and of Utilitarianism. Human evolution by natural selection has produced bodily changes, along with the evolution of mental powers that render human beings "independent of nature." The ethical systems that men have developed are not completely explicable as the results of the working of natural selection.

"We began by remarking that the biological theory borrowed the notion of utility from empirical morals; but we must now confess the loan has been so successfully invested that there is some ground for believing the proceeds suffice, not only to wipe out the obligation, but even to make the ethics debtor to biology" (Schurman, 1888, p. 122).

Schurman argues that some form of Utilitarianism is a necessary implication of Darwinism. But, there is more to morality than can be accounted for by Utilitarianism, hence, there is more to morality than can be accounted for by an appeal to natural selection. Biology, he concludes, does not afford a "complete scientific explanation of the phenomena of morals" (Schurman, 1888, p. 127).

There is other evidence in the *Descent* that Darwin construed his theory as quite distinct from Utilitarianism and neither entailing it nor being entailed by it. At best he saw Utilitarianism as a useful guide to determining right and wrong. To see where Darwin saw his view as different from Utilitarianism, we have to examine the argument for the development of the social instincts in somewhat more detail.

The heart of Darwin's argument is contained in Chapters 3 and 5 of part i of the *Descent*. For Darwin, the foundation of morality lies in sympathy. But what is the origin of sympathy? Sympathy is distinct from love. How is it acquired? In the view of Smith and Bain, sympathy is induced by the recollection of past suffering plus association with the misfortune of others. But, says Darwin, this does not explain why we feel a stronger sympathy for those more closely related to us (Darwin,1981, part i, p. 81). Darwin's answer is that human survival depends on cooperation. Rudimentary forms of cooperation exist in lower animals and are selectively advantageous. These form the basis of the social instincts.

Darwin's argument in the *Descent of Man* is that we have three options in explaining the evolution of social instincts that, when conjoined with the power to reason and reinforced by habit, form the basis of the moral sense or conscience:

1. By trying to understand their evolution as a result of selfishness. Darwin rejects this as the basis of an appropriate analysis on the grounds that animals exhibit phenotypic other-regarding behavior that cannot be understood as self-regarding or selfish.
2. In terms of the Greatest Happiness Principle. This Darwin rejects on the ground that natural selection is not concerned, primarily, with the pleasure and pain of organisms but rather with

producing structures and traits conducive to the promotion of reproductive success. The social instincts, as he sees it here, have evolved because of their contribution to the common good. That good is not the sum of pleasures or happiness in the community, but rather is the development of a social life that enhances the reproductive success of its members. Pleasure and happiness are, at best, derivative ends. For Darwin, X promotes pleasure because it is good and has been selected because it promotes reproductive success. For the Utilitarians, from whom Darwin is here trying to distance himself, X is good because it promotes pleasure or the greatest happiness. The Utilitarians have the argument backwards.

3. For Darwin, the evolution of the social instincts is driven by selection for the common good or the common welfare. This is to be understood as just sketched. Natural selection does not "see" the happiness of organisms or the total happiness of the communities they form. Selection "sees" the potentialities for differential reproductive success and rewards them. Those instincts emerge and survive that tend to promote reproductive success. The engendered behaviors may result in pleasure or happiness for the organisms that pursue them but the evolutionary ("ultimate") rationale for performing them is not that they are pleasure inducing but that they promote reproductive success. The organism's immediate ("proximate") rationale may indeed be the anticipated pleasure that will be enjoyed *but* the evolutionist is unhappy with leaving the explanation there. Why are *these* activities pleasure inducing and *those* not? The answer must be that the former are fitness enhancing and the latter not. The evolutionary argument is committed to denying that there can be systematic pressure for the evolution of characteristics that, however pleasure inducing, are not contributing to enhanced reproductive success or are not in some way implicated in the enhancement of reproductive success. Of course, in some mosaic interpretation of behavioral repertoires, it may be difficult in practice to isolate just which behaviors are enhancing what and to what extent. The point here is both empirical and conceptual. The conceptual point is that enhanced reproductive success drives the evolution of the social instincts *not* the correlated enhanced pleasure or happiness, which may or may not accompany their exercise.

Darwin's model is an improvement, from a naturalistic point of view, over Butler's. It provides a naturalistic account of the emergence of conscience and attempts to account for the "authority" of considerations of conscience and the interests of others over the considerations of self. But it falls somewhat short of being completely successful. Explanations of abilities of any sort in terms of natural selection are quite limited. First, they do not explain the emergence of *particular* traits. Even if we were to accept the idea that having the capacity to be moral was selectively advantageous, that in itself does not explain why *morality* as such evolved and not some equally enhancing alternative mechanism. Second, when Darwin distinguishes between 'higher' and 'lower' moral values, he classifies the social (other-regarding) values as higher and the individual (self-regarding) values as lower (Darwin, 1981, part i, p. 100). But why identify "moral" with "social"? And why give the social values higher priority than the individual values? (cf. Murphy, 1978). Virtue based moralities include self-regarding virtues as well as social virtues in the realm of the moral. Darwin, as the inheritor of the eighteenth century moral debate, is in accord with one of the central conclusions of the post-Hobbesian tradition in British moral philosophy in locating social values as "higher" than self-regarding values. But does it follow from any evolutionary argument that social values *are* "higher," more moral, than self-regarding values? Even if it could be shown that evolution leads to a strengthening of the social values vis à vis self-regarding values, the question of the moral authority of such values remains.

The gap between evolved *strength* and *moral* authority is the chasm between the natural and the moral. For those to whom this gap is unbridgeable, such as Michael Ruse and E. O. Wilson, the conclusion to be drawn from the evolutionary argument is the rejection of ultimate justifications in questions of morality. For those naturalists to whom the gap is bridgeable, such as Robert Richards, the task remains to show how the evolutionary argument can be molded to provide a justification of moral principles.

T. H. Huxley

Thomas Henry Huxley was a staunch defender of the Darwinian approach to biological questions. He was less sanguine about attempts to draw moral conclusions from Darwinian theory or from the Darwinian picture of nature. In the first Romanes lecture on ethics and evolution and in a paper on the population question, he was concerned to combat what he thought were wrongheaded attempts by thinkers such as Spencer to draw unwarranted moral conclusions from the biological circumstances of human existence.

The essence of Huxley's position on ethics and evolution can be summarized in four propositions. He defends the Hobbesian vision of the state of nature as a war of all against all. He rejects attempts to find a sanction for ethics in nature. He distinguishes what he calls the *ethical process*, which involves the struggle between good and evil, from the *cosmic process*, which involves the struggle for existence. He rejects attempts to read progressivism into the history of biological evolution and by extension into the evolution of morality.

Huxley endorsed the Hobbesian view for both nature and primitive society. He held that the life of primitive man is correctly characterized as a war of all against all. On nature in general he says, "[f]rom the point of view of the moralist the animal world is on about the same level as a gladiator's show" (Huxley, 1888, p. 330).

With respect to the possibility of finding moral sanctions in the natural world, Huxley responded with a vehement No! "Nature is not evil but morally indifferent" (Huxley, 1989, p. 117). We live in neither the best nor the worst of possible worlds. It is not the best, for those who point out contrivances to produce pleasure and infer that principles of benevolence are at work in nature are loath to point out contrivances that conduce to the production of pain and infer the workings of principles of malevolence (Huxley, 1888, p. 329).[6] It is not the worst of all possible worlds either. "Men with any manhood in them find life quite worth living under worse conditions than these" (Huxley, 1888, p. 331).

In the Romanes lecture, Huxley argues that those who profess to draw moral consequences from evolutionary history are prone to commit two fallacies, one of which involves the attempt to find a moral sanction in nature. But, Huxley argues, both the thief and the murderer follow nature as much as the saint. The facts of evolution cannot provide a *reason* for preferring what we call *good* to what we call *evil*—both are evolutionary products (Huxley, 1989, pp. 138f.).

The opposition between the cosmic process and the ethical process is illustrated in the Romanes lecture by the metaphor of a cultivated garden that stands in stark contrast to the wild and untamed jungle from which it has been carved. The garden is the representation of human attempts to tame nature through artifice and the development of civilization. No matter how well-cultivated the garden is, however, the threat of nature to overwhelm the garden remains. Our outposts of civilization are just that—outposts—surrounded by wild and uncompromising nature (Huxley, 1989, pp. 67–74). The struggle for existence is driven by Malthusian considerations, by conditions of scarcity that engender competition and violence (Huxley, 1888). Visionaries may foresee the end to the struggle for existence but we will not arrive there as long as the "natural man increases and multiplies without restraint" (Huxley, 1888, p. 333).

Are human beings part of the cosmic process or not? If so, how does Huxley account for the conflict between what he calls the *cosmic process* and the *ethical process*? Huxley's stand in the Romanes lecture was criticized by fellow Darwinians as a breach of faith. It seemed to them that Huxley was, on the one hand, saying that man was a part of nature and, on the other, saying he was not. When it came time to publish the lecture, Huxley sought to redress the issue by clarifying his position. Yes, he said, human beings were a part of nature but once a degree of civilized society is reached, social institutions, internally at least, are not driven by the "struggle for existence." The ethical process is, for Huxley, the attempt to control the circumstances under which the struggle is possible to mini-mize its effects on human beings. In this sense, the two processes are opposed to one another. In footnote 20 to the original lecture Huxley had suggested that the relation of the ethical process to the cosmic process was analogous to the relation between the governor of a steam engine and the steam engine itself. The cosmic process encompasses all aspects of change in the universe but some aspects of the process can be in conflict with other aspects.

In his 1888 paper, Huxley had argued that society is, of course, a part of nature but differs from those parts of nature not under the direct con-trol of human intervention "in having a definite moral object; whence it comes about that the course shaped by the ethical man—the member of society or citizen—necessarily runs counter to that which the non-ethical man—the primitive savage, or man as mere member of the animal king-dom—tends to adopt. The latter fights out the struggle for existence to the bitter end" (Huxley, 1888, p. 331).

Kropotkin objected to this characterization of primitive man on the grounds that no human society is devoid of an ethical sensibility. Kropotkin also argued that this is a distortion of Darwin's view. But just as Kropotkin exaggerated the importance of mutual aid as a corrective to what he saw as Huxley's overindividualistic interpretation of Darwin, so Huxley might be excused for exaggerating the violent aspect of natural selection as a corrective to those who he perceived were illegitimately see-ing benevolence at work in natural phenomena. In either case, such exag-gerations complicate our attempts to sort out what ethical conclusions are warranted on the basis of a study of nature.

One of the points of Huxley's population paper was to argue for and justify the need for educational reform. True to his colors he does not infer, as have Herbert Spencer, Julian Huxley, Richard Alexander, and E. O. Wilson among others, an individualistic social ethic from what he takes to be the individualistic bias of natural selection as it operates in the wild. Huxley was dismayed by the state of technical education in Britain in the 1880s. The breakdown of the medieval system of apprenticeship had left much to be desired with respect to teaching technical crafts (Huxley, 1888, p. 338). Reform was desperately needed. The question was, Should these reforms come at the hands of a state or through the actions of individuals? Although professing himself to be an individualist at heart, Huxley argued that intervention by the state is often necessary and justified however inefficient and wrongheaded it may often or always prove to be. "To abolish State action, because its direction is never more than approximately correct, appears to me to be much the same thing as abolishing the man at the wheel altogether, because, do what he will, the ship yaws more or less" (Huxley, 1888, p. 339).

Again, in keeping with his separation of nature and morality, he argued that human beings do not come into this world with unalienable and natural rights. What they become is in no small respect due to the nurturance of the society into which they have been fortunate enough to be born. Should that society now request that they contribute to its upkeep by, for example, paying for the paving of roads upon which they may never trod, it would, he thought, be churlish to refuse (Huxley, 1888, p. 340).

Finally, Huxley was at pains to reject any hint of progressivism in either the workings of natural selection or in the natural evolution of ethics. It is, he holds, " an error to imagine that evolution signifies a constant tendency to increased perfection" (Huxley, 1888, p. 330). The second fallacy of evolutionary ethics condemned by Huxley in the Romanes lecture concerns this point. What is fit is a function of circumstances, which are liable to fluctuate and change. What was progressive with respect to some environment will no longer prove to be progressive should the environment change. The ethical process aims towards survival of the *best* not the *fittest* (Huxley, 1989, p. 173, n. 20). The cosmic process has no relation to moral ends.

Ethical progress, such as it exists, results from combating the cosmic process. Progress in ethics involves rejecting the Buddhist-Stoic flight from evil that Huxley interprets as the passive acceptance of the world as one finds it. On the contrary, Huxley avers, we must constantly strive to combat the cosmic process and modify the conditions that make it possible. We cannot hope to completely alleviate the struggle for, as Huxley suggests in the *Prolegomena*, no matter how carefully and zealously we cultivate our gardens, the cosmic process (evolution) maintains a presence that constantly threatens to overwhelm us and throw us back into a state of natural struggle as soon as we become too complacent and let down our guard.[7] Those who seek to base moral principles on the struggle for existence are completely misguided. The "imitation of ... [the cosmic process] ... by man is inconsistent with the first principles of ethics" (Huxley, 1888, p. 330). For Huxley, these first principles are restraints on the assertion of self-interest which is the "essence" of the cosmic process.

What then from Huxley's view is the business of the moral and political philosopher? The business of the moral and political philosopher is the scientific determination of the best means for "facilitating the free expansion of the innate faculties of the citizen, so far as it is consistent with the general good" (Huxley, 1989, p. 101). This will not put an end to external struggle. Given human frailty, there is no hope for an evolutionary amelioration of the human condition—a "perfect" society.

Dewey sees Huxley's essay as marking a watershed in the history of the discussion of the relation between evolution and ethics (Dewey, 1972, pp. 34ff.). In the 1860s, the focus was on ethics as a distinguishing mark between the human and the nonhuman. In the 1890s, the focus was on evolutionary forces versus ethical "forces." Huxley's essay changed the tone of the discussion. Dewey sees what Huxley calls the struggle between the cosmic and the ethical processes as a manifestation of the fact that practices and so forth that were selected for in earlier times and have been maintained have yet to confront changing circumstances. Practices that originally helped the organism "fit" in with its environment, under changed social conditions, create tensions (Dewey, 1972, p. 46).

Herbert Spencer

Herbert Spencer was one of the leading intellectual lights of the nineteenth century. His systematic writings range far afield, and he was widely read and admired by his contemporaries. He was already embarked on the development of systematic philosophy along general evolutionary lines well before Darwin wrote the *Origin*. He became a supporter of Darwin's views when they were published, although he felt that he had anticipated most of the theory himself. The term *survival of the fittest*, which Darwin introduced into later editions of the *Origin*, was originally used by Spencer.

His reputation has not survived him, and he is not widely read today. The reasons for this are partly matters of substance and partly matters of style. His philosophical evolutionism was more theory driven than Darwin's data-driven approach. For Spencer, biological evolution was merely one example of a general process of cosmic evolution. That organisms should evolve was a corollary of his view that everything in the universe was evolving. The fine details of biological evolution in particular did not matter to him as they did to Darwin. On the other hand, the synthetic approach, which is characteristic of his work, has gone out of style. In addition, the contemporary verdict on his work is that, however grandiose it is, it is not of the first rank. Nonetheless, Richards (1987) contains a recent sympathetic reassessment of Spencer's work on evolution and ethics.[8]

Spencer's Theory of Population

In 1852 Spencer wrote an essay entitled "A Theory of Population, Deduced from the General Law of Animal Fertility." In it he criticizes the implications drawn by Malthus and his supporters from the struggle for existence and the competition for scarce resources. There is in nature, he thinks, a series of checks and balances that will prevail against any apparent local tendency to a worsening of the human condition. We observe, in the organic and inorganic worlds alike, a general tendency toward the good, the harmonious (witness the solar system), and the stable. Any theory, such as the Malthusian theory of population, that then proposes that there is an irremediable defect in nature is immediately suspect.

To understand the mechanism whereby life is maintained, we need to first say what life is. Spencer is inclined to a definition that does not restrict life to the organic alone—therefore, he defines life as "the coordination of actions" (Spencer, 1852, p. 472).

The difference between inorganic and organic or between higher and lower forms hinges on the degree of complexity involved in each. The organic and higher forms are more complex than the inorganic and lower. Among the organic forms, races are maintained by a balance between destructive forces such as, for example, death, and preservative forces such as swiftness, sagacity, and strength, which tend toward an equilibrium. Preservative forces include self-maintenance and reproductive prowess which vary inversely with one another. The more energy one invests in maintenance, the lower one's fertility and vice versa (Spencer, 1852, p. 476).[9]

Surveying the human condition as it was in the middle of the nineteenth century, Spencer concluded that, with respect to human beings, there has been an increase in fertility, which will tend to equilibrate with the maintenance of life. As that occurs, we should expect the quality of maintained lives to increase as the fertility of the race declines. Increase in quality, for Spencer, implies an increase in coordination, but of what kind? More likely, Spencer thinks, in mechanical skill than in bodily prowess of some kind, in intelligence and even more so in morality (Spencer, 1852, p. 497). However it occurs, a decrease in fertility is to be expected. According to Spencer's view, the more intelligent and the more moral beings ought to reproduce at lower rates than the less intelligent and the less moral.

The more fertile a people are the more intelligent they must become to cope with feeding and tending their population. This in turn leads to the enlargement of their nervous systems and a consequent decline in their fertility (Spencer, 1852, p. 499). Those who are least capable of contending with the circumstances created by increased fertility tend to die young and leave in their wake individuals who are better at self-preservation: more coordinated and intelligent (Spencer, 1852, p. 500).

What is the limit of this "progress"? The general increase in "complexity" and attendant increase in coordination, intelligence, and morality will continue until the forces balance each other out so that the rate of multiplication equals the rate of mortality. At this point, Spencer concludes, "the obtainment of subsistence will require just that kind and that amount of action needful to perfect health and happiness" (Spencer, 1852, p. 501).

For Spencer, the pressure of population leads to an increased development of intellectual and moral capacities. Population pressure is the proximate cause of civilization and its subsequent progress. In the limit, a state of equilibrium is reached when no further evolution is possible. At that point the whole world will be part of a global human economy and population pressure will be counterbalanced by other forces (Spencer, 1852, p. 501).

Spencer's answer to Malthus is that population pressure, far from creating ravages and leading to the decline of civilization, in fact promotes civilization to the state of perfection at which point such pressures cease to be a problem.

Spencer's Ethical Theory

This general sketch was developed and incorporated into Spencer's general evolutionary philosophy in the *Data of Ethics*, published in 1879. Here the problem is recast in terms of Spencer's holistic vision. Chapter 1, on "Conduct in General" argues that parts and wholes are interconnected and neither can be properly understood without consideration of its correlative aspect. Ethical conduct is a part of conduct as a whole and "the whole must be understood before the part can be understood" (Spencer, 1966, p. 5). Conduct itself is a part of action: conduct involves "acts adjusted to ends, or else—the adjustment of acts to ends." Most conduct is morally indifferent and the slide from the one to the other is a matter of degree.

Human conduct is itself a part of animate conduct in general, and "to fully understand human conduct as a whole, we must study it as a part of that larger whole constituted by the conduct of animate beings in general" (Spencer, 1966, p. 7). "Nor," he continues, "is even this whole conceived with the needful fulness, so long as we think only of the conduct at present displayed around us. We have to include in our conception the less-developed conduct out of which this has arisen in course of time. We have to regard the conduct now shown us by creatures of all orders, as an outcome of the conduct which has brought life of every kind to its present height.

And this is tantamount to saying that our preparatory step must be to study the evolution of conduct" (Spencer, 1966, p. 7).

In Chapter 2, on "The Evolution of Conduct," Spencer distinguishes between the evolution of structures, the evolution of functions, and the evolution of conduct.[10]

What, Spencer asks, "constitutes advance in the evolution of conduct, as we trace it up from the lowest types of living creatures to the highest?" (Spencer, 1966, p. 10). He answers: The emergence of acts adjusted to ends, purposeful action. The distinction between purposeful and purposeless action arises through the course of evolution by degrees (Spencer, 1966, p. 10).[11]

As one progresses up the scale of being, the conduct of organisms becomes better adjusted in terms of their ability to adjust means to ends. Their actions become more complex and more integrated. In humans, "we not only find that the adjustments of acts to ends are both more numerous and better than among lower animals; but we find the same thing on comparing the doings of higher races of men with those of lower races. If we take any one of the major ends achieved [e.g., nutrition, warmth, dwellings], we see greater completeness of achievement by civilized than by savage; and we also see an achievement of relatively numerous minor ends subserving major ends" (Spencer, 1966, p. 13).

Spencer distinguishes between conduct that is conducive to the life of the individual from conduct conducive to the preservation of the race or species. These two coevolve. As for humans, "[c]ompared with brutes, the savage, higher in his self-maintaining conduct, is higher too in his race-maintaining conduct. A larger number of the wants of offspring are provided for; and parental care, enduring longer, extends to the disciplining of offspring in arts and habits which fit them for their conditions of existence. Conduct of this order, equally with conduct of the first order, we see becoming evolved in a still greater degree as we ascend from savage to civilized. The adjustments of acts to ends in the rearing of children become far more elaborate, alike in number of ends met, variety of means used, and efficiency of their adaptations; and the aid and oversight are continued throughout a much greater part of early life" (Spencer, 1966, p. 16). "In tracing up the evolution of conduct, so that we may frame a true conception of conduct in general, we have thus to recognize these two kinds as mutually dependent. Speaking generally, neither can evolve without evolution of the other; and the highest evolutions of the two must be reached simultaneously" (Spencer, 1966, pp. 16f.).

The evolution toward perfection by each kind of organism is tempered by the "struggle for existence" of individual versus individual and species versus species. The result is "imperfectly evolved conduct." The highest form of conduct involves "adjustments that each creature may make . . . without preventing them from being made by other creatures" (Spencer, 1966, p. 18). "That the highest form of conduct must be so distinguished, is an inevitable implication; for while the form of conduct is such that adjustments of acts to ends by some necessitate non-adjustments by others, there remains room for modifications which bring conduct into a form avoiding this, and so making the totality of life greater" (Spencer, 1966, p. 18).

The formation of social groups and the elimination of internecine strife and the decrease of wars is a necessary condition for the approach of individual conduct to well-adjusted completeness. "There remains a further advance. . . . For beyond so behaving that each achieves his ends without preventing others from achieving their ends, the members of a society may give mutual help in the achievement of ends. And if, either indirectly by industrial co-operation, or directly by volunteered aid, fellow citizens can make easier for one another the adjustment of acts to ends, then their conduct assumes a still higher phase of evolution; since whatever facilitates the making of adjustments by each, increases the totality of the adjustments made, and serves to render the lives of all more complete" (Spencer, 1966, p. 19).

The argument thus far has led us to

> see that Ethics has for its subject-matter, that form which universal conduct assumes during the last stages of its evolution. [No argument however has been given for assuming that human beings represent the "last" stages of evolution unless the remark is intended to be comparative.] We have also concluded that these last stages in the evolution of conduct are those displayed by the highest types of being, when he is forced, by increase of numbers, to live more and more in the presence of his fellows. And there has followed the corollary that conduct gains ethical sanction in proportion as the activities, becoming less and less militant and more and more industrial, are such as do not necessitate mutual injury or hindrance, but consist with, and are furthered by, co-operation and mutual aid. (Spencer, 1966, p. 20)

It now remains to show the harmony between "[t]hese implications of the Evolution-Hypothesis . . . [and] . . . the leading moral ideas men have otherwise reached" (Spencer, 1966, p. 20).

In Chapter 3, "Good and Bad Conduct," Spencer holds that objects, situations, and so on are good or bad in relation to how well they serve or fail to serve human wants (Spencer, 1966, p. 21). "The entanglement of social relations is such, that men's actions often simultaneously affect the welfares of self, of offspring, and of fellow-citizens . . . when we disentangle the three orders of ends, and consider each separately, it becomes clear that the conduct which achieves each kind of end is regarded as relatively good; and is regarded as relatively bad if it fails to achieve it" (Spencer, 1966, p. 22).

With respect to self-welfare, "other things equal, conduct is right or wrong according as its special acts, well or ill-adjusted to special ends, do or do not further the general end of self-preservation" (Spencer, 1966, p. 23). The ethical judgments we make with respect to "self-regarding" acts are often passed over because ordinarily "self-regarding desires . . . do not need moral reinforcement, and partly because the promptings of the other-regarding desires, less strong, and often over-ridden, do need moral enforcement" (Spencer, 1966, p. 23).[12]

With respect to that conduct which conduces to the raising of offspring, it is good or bad insofar as it efficiently or inefficiently leads to that end or is supportive or not of that end.

With respect to social ends,

the words good and bad have come to be specially associated with acts which further the complete living of others and acts which obstruct their complete living. Goodness, standing by itself, suggests, above all other things, the conduct of one who aids the sick in re-acquiring normal vitality, assists the unfortunate to recover the means of maintaining themselves, defends those who are threatened with harm in person, property, or reputation, and aids whatever promises to improve the living of all his fellows. Contrariwise, badness brings to mind, as its leading correlative, the conduct of one who, in carrying on his own life, damages the lives of others by injuring their bodies, destroying their possessions, defrauding them, calumniating them. (Spencer, 1966, p. 25)

[J]ust as . . . evolution becomes the highest possible when the conduct simultaneously achieves the greatest totality of life in self, in off-spring, and in fellow men; so here we see that the conduct called good rises to the conduct conceived as best, when it fulfills all three classes of ends at the same time. (Spencer, 1966, p. 26)

The foregoing arguments assume that life is worth living and therefore that what promotes a long and prosperous life is good as well. But this optimistic view is not the only one possible. Pessimists deny these points, and their view of what is good and bad would vary accordingly. There is a postulate that both pessimists and optimists hold in common though. Both positions "assume it to be self-evident that life is good or bad, according as it does, or does not, bring a surplus of agreeable feeling" (Spencer, 1966, p. 27). The difference between the optimist and the pessimist, according to Spencer, comes down to different factual assumptions about the distributions of pleasures and pains involved in living: "there is no escape from the admission that in calling good the conduct which subserves life, and bad the conduct which hinders or destroys it, and in so implying that life is a blessing and not a curse, we are inevitably asserting that conduct is good or bad according as its total effects are pleasurable or painful" (Spencer, 1966, p. 28). The only alternative, he thinks, is to assume that "men were created with the intention that they should be sources of misery to themselves; and that are bound to continue living that their creator may have the satisfaction of contemplating their misery" (Spencer, 1966, p. 28). We are led to conclude that "the good is universally the pleasurable" (Spencer, 1966, p. 30).[13]

Spencer criticizes what he calls the *intuitional* theory of morals, which alleges that human beings have an innate divinely inspired sense of right and wrong or good and bad. In any case, the confidence of the intuitionist in his "verdicts of conscience" rests, Spencer contends, on their agreement with the ultimate test of whether the acts in question do or do not tend to promote the happiness and well-being of others. It all boils down to the "fundamental assumption that acts are good or bad according as their aggregate effects increase men's happiness or increase their misery" (Spencer, 1966, p. 40).

Spencer concludes that "no school can avoid taking for the ultimate moral aim a desirable state of feeling called by whatever name—gratification, enjoyment, happiness. Pleasure somewhere, at some time, to some being or beings, is an inexpungible element of the conception. It is as much a necessary form of moral intuition as space is a necessary form of intellectual intuition" (Spencer, 1966, p. 46).[14]

Several points emerge from this discussion. First, it is clear that Spencer was a progressionist both with respect to evolution in general and the evolution of morality in particular: "[W]e must interpret the more developed by the less developed" (Spencer, 1966, p. 7). Second, his view is holistic and hierarchical. Third, his ethical position is clearly interwoven with his views on biological evolution to the extent that one might well suspect that his ethical conclusions will stand or fall with the biological theories, such as the inheritance of acquired characteristics, that they rely on. Finally, and most significant from the point of view of the contemporary discussion of evolution and ethics, he seems to commit the naturalistic fallacy with a vengeance.

This last point was made most forcefully by G. E. Moore. As Moore sees it, Spencer commits the naturalistic fallacy insofar as he identifies "the gaining of ethical sanction with the being more evolved" (Moore,

1962, p. 49). Moore allows that he is not sure this is really Spencer's view because Spencer elsewhere denies the implication that Moore attributes to him. Even so, Spencer takes *more evolved* to be an indicator of "better", because being more evolved leads to a more pleasant life overall. But then, Moore asserts, Spencer is guilty of identifying *good* with *pleasant*. [15]

What is, for Spencer, "the relation of Pleasure and Evolution in ethical theory?" (Moore, 1962, p. 51). Moore argues that Spencer vacillates between two views, that the more evolved is better because it is more evolved and that the more evolved is better because it produces more pleasure, and the more pleasant is better than the less pleasant because it is more pleasant (Moore, 1962, p. 52).

Remarking on Spencer's claim that "life is good or bad, according as it does, or does not, bring a surplus of agreeable feeling," Moore suspects that Spencer thinks this is true because he commits the naturalistic fallacy of identifying the meaning of *good* with "productive of pleasure" (Moore, 1962, p. 53).

At best, the appeal to evolutionary theory can provide us only with a criterion of *good*. That which is more evolved is better than that which is less evolved. But, what we want is a "clear discussion of the fundamental principles of Ethics, and a statement of the ultimate reasons why one way of acting should be considered better than another" (Moore, 1962, p. 54)

There is no doubt that Moore's critique was instrumental in undermining support for Spencer's views on ethics. However, these are different times. Moore's critique of naturalism appears to be riddled with unwarranted assumptions. The question of whether the naturalistic "fallacy" is indeed a fallacy and whether Spencer's argument commits it has been reopened by Richards (1987) among others. What is clear is that, for Spencer, inferences from the physical and biological conditions of the world to moral conclusions were warranted. The warrant derives, in large part, from Spencer's holistic point of view. To the extent that we no longer share Spencer's vision we may well charge him with some fast and loose reasoning, if not a fallacy.

Petr Kropotkin

Petr Kropotkin (1842–1921) was a Russian prince and a naturalist who today is best known for his anarchistic views. He wrote two books that relate to the implications of evolution for ethics. The first, and best known, is *Mutual Aid: A Factor of Evolution*, which first appeared in 1902. The second, lesser known work, which he left incomplete at his death, is *Ethics: Origin and Development*, which first appeared in 1924.

Mutual Aid was compiled from a series of articles written for the periodical, *The Nineteenth Century*, to which Kropotkin added a concluding section and some updating appendices. His rationale for writing the book was to provide a corrective to that brand of Darwinism that sees evolution and natural selection purely in terms of "competition" and the "struggle for existence." Kropotkin singles out Huxley's essay as an especially glib and facile insinuation of the "law of the jungle" interpretation of Darwin.[16] He sets out instead to detail and expound upon the role of cooperation and mutual aid in evolution. His aim was not to replace competition with cooperation but to locate the proper role of the latter. Individual survival is, Kropotkin argues, often enhanced more by cooperation than by competition, strictly understood. "I should certainly be the last to underrate the part which the self-assertion of the individual has played in the evolution of mankind" (Kropotkin, 1955, p. xvi).

Nevertheless, the "law" of mutual aid is paramount. Communal nesting, migration, the predominance of social mammals over solitary mammals, beaver dam building, lion pack hunting, the behavioral patterns of organisms such as marmots, wild horses, reindeer, and elephants, among others, are cited as evidence of the working of a law of mutual aid: "those mammals, which stand at the very top of the animal world and most approach man by their structure and intelligence, are eminently sociable" (Kropotkin, 1955, p. 50).

"Association is found in the animal world at all degrees of evolution ... [and] colonies are at the very origin of evolution in the animal kingdom" (Kropotkin, 1955, p. 53). Sociality, Kropotkin urges, is conducive to protection from predation, longevity, population maintenance, and migration (Kropotkin, 1955, p. 57). "The fittest are ... the most sociable animals, and sociability appears as the chief factor of evolution, both directly, by securing the well-being of the species while diminishing the waste of energy, and indirectly, by favoring the growth of intelligence" (Kropotkin, 1955, p. 58).

As Kropotkin points out, none of this is inconsistent with the Darwin-Wallace "theory of the struggle for life." Darwin, we are reminded, talks of "struggle" in two senses, literal and metaphorical. Darwin "often speaks of regions being stocked with animal life to their full capacity, and from that overstocking he infers the necessity of competition" (Kropotkin, 1955, p. 61). But, according to Kropotkin, the evidence for *literal* competition is sparse. What we see are species succumbing because they could not adjust to changing circumstances—what Darwin called the *metaphorical* struggle. *Inter*group "competition" is not so much a fact as a requirement of the logic of the situation and only in the extended metaphorical sense does Kropotkin see evidence it exists. The situation is similar for *intra*group "competition." Darwin talks of the "extermination of transitional varieties"; however, Kropotkin points out, this is not a *literal* extermination but again a metaphorical extermination, where the problem is often ill-adaptedness to deal with changing environments and not literal conflict between conspecifics (Kropotkin, 1955, p. 67).

> . . . if the evolution of the animal world were based exclusively, or even chiefly, upon the survival of the fittest during periods of calamities; if natural selection were limited in its action to periods of exceptional drought, or sudden changes of temperature, or inundations, retrogression would be the rule in the animal world. . . . All that natural selection can do in times of calamities is to spare the individuals endowed with the greatest endurance for privations of all kinds. (Kropotkin, 1955, p. 73)[17]

> "Don't compete—competition is always injurious to the species, and you have plenty of resources to avoid it!" That is the *tendency* of nature, not always realized in full, but always present. That is the watchword which comes to us from the bush, the forest, the river, the ocean. "Therefore combine—practise mutual aid! That is the surest means for giving to each and to all the greatest safety, the best guarantee of existence and progress, bodily, intellectual, and moral." That is what Nature teaches us; and that is what all those animals which have attained the highest position in their respective classes [!] have done. That is also what man—the most primitive man—has been doing; and that is why man has reached the position upon which we stand now, as we shall see . . . [when we consider the workings of] . . . mutual aid in human societies. (Kropotkin, 1955, p. 75)

Having established to his satisfaction that mutual aid is a predominant factor in the evolutionary history of nonhuman animals, Kropotkin proceeds to devote the bulk of *Mutual Aid* (six chapters) to the role of mutual aid in the evolution of human civilization. First, he argues that so-called savages are not the bloodthirsty individualists they are often popularly portrayed to be. They form bands and communities from which the family structure as we know it has evolved. They are not individualistic but clannish and communal. In a nutshell, they practice mutual aid (Kropotkin, 1955, ch. 3).[18]

Next, Kropotkin considers "Mutual Aid Among the Barbarians." So-called barbarians also exhibit legal frameworks that promote cooperation. Wars are unavoidable when cultures clash through migration and other causes, but Kropotkin cites a number of "barbarian" institutions that ritualize warfare and that indicate, in his view, attempts to restrain and circumscribe the devastation and mayhem of conflict. In addition, for intra-group acts of personal aggression and murder there are ritualized codes of compensation in many cultures—blood revenge and vendettas in a few, but many where payment or adoption is prescribed rather than further bloodshed (Kropotkin, 1955, Ch. 4).

Kropotkin argues that the scenario that depicts the evolution of civilization as progressing from individual to family to clan is mistaken. Instead, he thinks, the clan structure comes first. The family and the idea of an individual he takes to be a rather late development.[19]

In his discussion of the rise of the medieval city, Kropotkin posits that they evolved from walled village communities and the rise of guilds, both temporary and permanent, as loci of brotherhood. Guilds formed to further common aims or common functions. Each was self-policing and served as a judicial district. The rise of the modern state involves, in part, a usurping of the functions of these guilds and their eradication.

The medieval city was a federation of village communities plus guilds as can be seen from the old city charters. The cities originally served as communal merchants buying and selling for the community as a whole. Individual merchants were originally commissioners. Trade prices were set by neither the buyer nor the seller but by some third party (Kropotkin, 1955, Ch. 5). The medieval cities, rich or poor, independent of location, had a common structure.[20]

The market served as a neutral zone where violence and feuding were strictly proscribed. The cities rose in power as burghers confronted the power of the lords that served originally to protect them. The burghers compromised by failing to include the supporting peasantry of the countryside as part of their pacts with the lords and thereby started the rifts between city and country that Kropotkin saw still evidenced in the nineteenth century and which have persisted to our own time albeit tempered somewhat by the all pervasive global cable television. The cities served as centers of learning, culture, and trade.

The rise of kings was correlated with the decline in power of the local lords and the shift of church support from emperors to local kings. The peasants were supporters of the kings against the lords and the burghers and the invasions by the Turks and Mongols served to accentuate the need for centralized power.

In Kropotkin's view, the cities made a number of mistakes that in time led to their decline, the chief of which was that they circumscribed the use of the principle of mutual aid. Inside the cities, the burghers faced off against the newcomers. Outside, the city united against the peasants of the country. Their biggest mistake, according to Kropotkin, was in basing their economies on commerce and industry and not on agriculture (Kropotkin, 1955, Ch. 5).

Kropotkin contrasts the social institutions that arise "from the masses," and are based upon cooperation and mutual aid, with the coercive authoritarian state. "New economical and social institutions, in so far as they were a creation of the masses, new ethical systems, and new religions, all have originated from the same source, and the ethical progress of our race, viewed in its broad lines, appears as a gradual extension of the mutual-aid principles from the tribe to always larger and larger agglomerations, so as to finally embrace one day the whole of mankind, without respect to its divers creeds, languages, and races" (Kropotkin, 1955, p. 224).

The peasant revolts were motivated in part by the desire to establish "free, brotherly communities." "The absorption of all social functions by the State necessarily favoured the development of an unbridled, narrow-minded individualism. In proportion as the obligations towards the State grew in numbers the citizens were evidently relieved from their obligations toward each other." These mutual support obligations had been codified in the rules of the guilds (Kropotkin, 1955, p. 227).

"[T]he theory which maintains that men can, and must, seek their own happiness in a disregard of other people's wants is now triumphant all around—in law, in science, in religion. . . . Science loudly proclaims that the struggle of each against all is the leading principle of nature, and of human societies as well. To that struggle Biology ascribes the progressive evolution of the animal world" (Kropotkin, 1955, p. 228). Given all this, we might expect to find no vestiges of mutual aid left in modern times but, in fact, Kropotkin urges, cooperative efforts will not die out.[21]

Why did the village communities die out? The received wisdom is that they could not compete successfully against more modern forms of social organization. But,

> to speak of the natural death of the village communities in virtue of economic laws is as grim a joke as to speak of the natural death of soldiers slaughtered on a battlefield. The fact was simply this: The village communities had lived for over a thousand years; and where and when the peasants were not ruined by wars and exactions they steadily improved their methods of culture. But as the value of land was increasing, in consequence of the growth of industries, and the nobility had acquired, under the State organization, a power which it never had had under the feudal system, it took possession of the best parts of the communal lands, and did its best to destroy the communal institutions. (Kropotkin, 1955, p. 236)

Still peasant communes and cooperative activities persist. They are not of great economic importance in modern times "but from the ethical point of view . . . their importance cannot be overrated. They prove that even under the system of reckless individualism which now prevails the agricultural masses piously maintain their mutual-support inheritance; and as soon as the States relax the iron laws by means of which they have broken all bonds between men, these bonds are at once reconstituted, notwithstanding the difficulties, political, economical, and social, which are many, and in such force as best answer to the modern requirements of production. They indicate in which direction and in which form further progress must be expected" (Kropotkin, 1955, pp. 249–250).

To support this, Kropotkin sketches the suppression of the medieval guilds and modern trade unions. He cites the survival of mutual aid among the poor and of neighborhood solidarity among children.

> In short, neither the crushing powers of the centralized State nor the teachings of mutual hatred and pitiless struggle which came, adorned with the attributes of science, from obliging philosophers and sociologists, could weed out the feeling of human solidarity, deeply lodged in men's understanding and heart, because it has been nurtured by all our preceding evolution. What was the outcome of evolution since its earliest stages cannot be overpowered by one of the aspects of the same evolution.[22] And the need of mutual aid and support which had lately taken refuge in the narrow circle of the family, or the slum neighbors, in the village, or the secret union of workers, re-asserts itself again, even in our modern society, and claims its rights to be, as it always has been, the chief leader towards further progress. Such are the conclusions which we are necessarily brought to when we carefully ponder over each of the two groups of facts briefly enumerated in the last two chapters. (Kropotkin, 1955, p. 292)

In his book on ethics, Kropotkin concludes that "not only does Nature fail to give us a lesson of a-moralism, i.e., of the indifferent attitude to morality which needs to be combated by some extra-natural influence, but we are bound to recognize that the *very ideas of bad and good*, and man's abstractions concerning 'the supreme good' have been borrowed from Nature" (Kropotkin, 1947, p. 16). When he claims that Nature is the "first ethical teacher for man," Kropotkin intends this in two senses. First, he means that mutual aid is the principal factor in evolution (Kropotkin, 1947, p. 45). Second, he speaks of primitives, and presumably our ancestors, as living with the animals and deriving inspiration from their ways and from human interpretations of their ways (Kropotkin, 1947, pp. 55f.).

Kropotkin's analyses share some common features with the other nineteenth century analyses we have considered. There is no clear distinction between "earlier" in the phylogenetic sense and "less developed" in the sense that extant taxonomic categories are assumed to exhibit a hierarchical structure and "primitive" societies are assumed to be "lower" or less developed than more "advanced" modern societies. This in turn is reflective of the general "progressionist" bias of the age. Although both Darwin and Huxley warn against this point Darwin, at least, implicitly betrays his "progressionist" perspective in his comments which are more reflections of his Victorian upbringing than they are of biological or sociological "fact."

NATURE, CULTURE, AND CONFLICT

Two competing metaphors, "struggle" and "cooperation" or "mutual aid," shaped the evolutionary accounts of social change in the nineteenth century. Malthus was read as arguing for the view that competitive struggle was the primary engine of social change. He drew pessimistic conclusions about the future of humankind from this fact. Charles Darwin's Malthusian revelation led him to characterize natural selection among natural populations in terms of the struggle for existence. Darwin was somewhat more optimistic about social progress. He saw the development of modern civilizations as reducing the effect of natural selection as a factor in social change.

Spencer, who embraced Darwin's view when it appeared, assimilated it to his own view of cosmic evolution. Spencer starts from the Malthusian assumption that the motor of evolutionary change is competition. But, unlike Malthus, Spencer drew optimistic conclusions from this fact. For Spencer, cosmic evolution, left to its own devices, leads to physical, moral, and social progress. Insofar as the evolutionary process is unhampered, evolution will "naturally" tend toward the good. The result will be a stateless society where there is an equilibrium between population growth and resource consumption. For Spencer, states interfere with evolutionary progress.

Huxley accepts Spencer's Malthusian assumption with respect to physical evolution but rejects Spencer's linking of physical and cultural or ethical evolution. The emergence of civilization means the decoupling of physical and social or moral evolution. For Huxley, evolution does not entail progress but merely change. Once decoupled, human nature evolves more slowly than the environment. Cultural evolution swamps physical evolution and is in conflict with it. Unlike Spencer, Huxley is a statist because he sees culture and morality as acting as a brake on the competitive struggle that characterizes physical or biological evolution. The state serves as an institutional guarantor for moral and social norms. States aid in the protection of civilizations that serve as the bulwark against the encroachment of natural selection in the wild against civilized order.

Kropotkin stands in contrast to both Spencer and Huxley in his rejection of the Malthusian assumption that the primary motor of evolutionary change is competitive struggle. For Kropotkin, the primary motor is mutual aid and cooperation. Kropotkin stands with Spencer and against Huxley in his rejection of states as detrimental to the evolutionary process. Both Kropotkin and Spencer are much more progressionist than Huxley. Both argue that evolution left to its own devices will lead to the development of good social environments. In Kropotkin's romantic vision, this state was realized in the guild structure of the Middle Ages. With the decline in guilds, which for Kropotkin are the epitome of cooperative ventures, states have taken over many of the social roles of the guilds. Unfortunately, they do badly what the guilds did well. When states are abolished, the mutual cooperative drives that, in Kropotkin's view, led to the guild structure in the first place will reassert themselves. The result will be the development of communal, stateless societies where free associations maximize the potentialities of all individuals.

As we have seen, the nineteenth century evolutionary ethicists did not, in general, make a clear distinction between biological and cultural evolution. In addition, as Quillian points out, the nineteenth century evolutionary ethicists tended to accept the doctrine of a moral sense. This doctrine, in proposing that human beings have an innate and natural sense of right and wrong, ignored the cultural and contextual component of moral considerations (Quillian, 1945, esp. p. 77).

The moral sense theorists tended to blur the distinction between two different doctrines. One was that the moral sense was analogous to an organ of sensibility like the eye or the ear. In this sense, the moral sense of humans would have been, for the evolutionary ethicists, an evolved organ to be used in the determination of right and wrong, good and evil, in much the same way that the eye functions as an organ that aids in the detection of color. The existence of such an organ would not in itself dictate what was right and wrong, just that organisms so equipped have the capacity to make such judgments. In another sense, however, possession of a moral sense was tantamount to having an innate sense of right and wrong. The very principles of ethics were held to be inborn and subject to evolution. The first kind of moral sense theory is a version of moral descriptivism. The second kind of moral sense theory is a kind of moral prescriptivism.

Once the distinction between nature and culture is clearly articulated, the two versions can be sharply distinguished in terms of their relative plausibility. The idea that human beings or ethical organisms have evolved physical mechanisms that enable them to make moral judgments retains a certain degree of plausibility. That there might exist an "ethical organ" akin to the eye is not currently plausible. So the capacity exists but how to spell out the physiological basis for it remains very much a mystery. That moral principles have a physiological basis is much less plausible despite the claims by some sociobiologists to that effect. The moral principles that human beings adopt seem tailored, at some level, to their particular circumstances. They appear to be more the product of culture than of nature.[23]

NOTES

1. It is well to note that the reason Darwin gives for holding that the social instincts have "probably been acquired by natural selection" is that "they are highly beneficial to the species."

2. "As the reasoning powers advance and experience is gained, the more remote effects of certain lines of conduct on the character of the individual, and on the general good, are perceived; and then the self-regarding virtues, from coming within the scope of public opinion, receive praise, and their opposites receive blame. But with the less civilized nations reason often errs, and many bad customs and base superstitions come within the same scope, and consequently are esteemed as high virtues, and their breach as heavy crimes" (Darwin, 1981, part ii, p. 393).

3. Darwin writes: "It is well known that use strengthens the muscles in the individual, and complete disuse, or the destruction of the proper nerve, weakens them. When the eye is destroyed the optic nerve often becomes atrophied. When an artery is tied, the lateral channels increase not only in diameter, but in the thickness and strength of their coats. . . . [etc.] . . . Whether the several foregoing modifications would become hereditary, if the same habits of life were followed during many generations, is not known, but is probable" (Darwin, 1981, part i, pp. 116f.).

4. Darwin, of course, had no means of distinguishing between genetic-based inheritance and cultural inheritance of habits, customs, and lifestyles. See the editor's introduction to Darwin (1981).

5. Murphy (1982, pp. 82f.) argues on the basis of this that Darwin recognized as Freud did not that there are elements to morality that may lie beyond the scope of his theory. That is, the theory of natural selection is not the be-all and end-all of moral phenomena.

6. Compare, on this point, Darwin's remark in Chapter 3 of *Descent* to the effect that the tendency of animals to expel the wounded from their packs ranked as "the blackest fact in natural history" (Darwin, 1981, pp. 76f.).

7. The periodic rise of natural plagues such as the AIDS epidemic and the recent resurgence of tuberculosis as a serious health problem serve as reminders of this as it applies to purely natural processes. William Golding's *Lord of the Flies* is a fictional representation of what might happen in the moral realm.

8. For a discussion of Richards's thesis see Chapter 5.

9. One can detect an echo of this doctrine in the current biological literature on life history strategies. See Stearns (1992).

10. The distinction between mere acts and conduct rests on the adjustment of acts to ends. The distinction is not sharp.

11. Spencer does not clearly distinguish between phylogenetic development and the extant hierarchical structure suggested by systematics. Various extant cate-

gorical structures are thought of as superior or inferior as well as subdivisions within them. For example, the Molluscs are a "superior sub-kingdom" with "high" and "low" molluscs within (Spencer, 1879, p. 11).

12. Do we not need an evolutionary account of why this should be so, if in fact it is so? That it is so is taken to be self-evident. For what kinds of creatures might it not be so? Clones? Is it a testable assumption? Is it something that can be measured without significant bias?

13. Mill criticized Spencer for being an "anti-utilitarian." In a letter to Mill, reprinted in Bain (1884, vol. 2), Spencer defends his Utilitarian credentials and argues that his view provides a theoretical superstructure for Utilitarianism and stands to it as modern theoretical astronomy stands to the empirical generalizations from ancient astronomy about the orbits of the planets (Bain, 1884, vol. 2, p. 722).

14. See the similar point in the letter to Mill (Bain, 1884, vol. 2, p. 722). Spencer accepted the inheritance of acquired characters. Moral intuitions, honed as they are by the advance of civilization, are inherited. Compare, in this regard, the analogous position developed by Lorenz with respect to cognitive categories (Lorenz, 1982). To the extent that Mill and the Utilitarians opposed the view that moral "intuitions" were innate, this puts them at odds with Spencer.

15. Moore does not call this "naturalistic" identification a fallacy but it would seem to be so, because it identifies a nonnatural property, *good*, with a natural property, *pleasant*.

16. The phrase *the law of the jungle* was first used by Kipling in *Jungle Tales* to designate not a Hobbesian state of war of all against all but rather a state of cooperation between different species of animals (see the paper by J. L. Mackie of that title [Mackie, 1978]) although it is now construed in the opposite or Hobbesian sense.

17. Kropotkin here evinces his progressionist inclinations. If natural selection, on the whole, *is* progressive and if natural selection *as competitive* is retrogressive, then there must be another factor in natural selection to balance the account. In such a way, room is made for the principle of mutual aid. But, suppose we reject the progressionist assumption? This weakens the case for endorsing the principle of mutual aid.

18. In his *Ethics*, Kropotkin cites the fact that primitive peoples have legends about isolates and hermits but none about life in societies. This suggests to Kropotkin that social life is the ingrained norm (Kropotkin, 1947, p. 60).

19. Kropotkin corrects this view somewhat in Appendix 8 of 1955.

20. It is not clear from Kropotkin's account whether he takes this to be due to the fact that they were allegedly prompted by a common motive, mutual aid, or because they were serving a common function.

21. Cf. Darwin's remarks about the emergence of social norms first and then the emergence of individualism. From this one might perhaps construct an argument about the motivating power of other-regarding behavior as more primitive than the self-serving motives of egoism.

22. This perspective should be contrasted with Huxley's view of the ethical process as arising out of and yet acting in a direction contrary to what he calls the

cosmic process. That argument illustrates the incorrectness of Kropotkin's point of view. Even if we discount Huxley's perspective, evolution is not of a piece but represents the results of a compromise between tendencies and forces that can very well act contrary to one another.

23. This distinction is somewhat artificial because every phenotypic characteristic of biological organisms is a reflection of an interaction between the genotypes of such organisms and their environments. For human beings, part of the relevant environment is social and cultural. Some disputes among sociobiologists and between sociobiologists and others hinge on how widely or narrowly the term *biological* is construed. In a broad interpretation, as appealed to at points by Richard Alexander, there is a "biological" basis to morality because the contribution of the environment is counted as part of the "biological" input. Thus, even in cases where environmental effects swamp narrowly construed "biological" effects, or genetic effects, the traits in question still have a strong biological basis. In general, however, to say of a characteristic that it has a biological basis is to allege that the narrowly construed biological factors tend to swamp the environmental factors.

Chapter 4

Human Nature

INTRODUCTION

That organisms have natures is an integral part of both common sense and our intellectual tradition. "That's human nature for you," is a quick and dirty way to justify or explain a wide range of human actions or activities, usually nefarious. The philosophical and religious traditions are filled with books and tracts on the subject from Plato to E. O. Wilson and beyond. There is an especially deep connection between the concept of human nature and the problems of ethics. What kind of creatures we are is reasonably thought to be relevant to what we can be expected to do or refrain from doing. Although I shall not argue for it in detail here, a close examination of any moral system that has been put forth either explicitly or implicitly rests on assumptions that may be properly called *assumptions about human nature*. These underlying assumptions form a framework within which ethical principles take shape and upon which they are grounded. To the extent that we are biological creatures, it is not unreasonable to suppose that whatever generic nature we may be said to possess is in part to be understood in terms of our biological endowments, both developmental and evolutionary.

The focus of this chapter is to see what content can be given to the above suppositions. The following section takes up the question of what we are to understand by the concept of human nature. In the next section, the connection between human nature and moral theory is established. The section on "Human Nature and Ideology" explores the sense in which concepts of human nature function not merely descriptively but also ideologically. The section entitled "Does Darwinism Undermine the Concept of Human Nature?" addresses the question of the implications of Darwinism for the concept of human nature. Some take concepts of human nature to be products of essentialistic modes of thinking which are

87

effectively undermined by Darwinian considerations. To the extent that this is so, it undercuts appeals to Darwinistic theories to provide crucial clues as to what our nature is, because we do not have any. Such attacks, if successful, would constitute significant objections to drawing moral implications from Darwinism, especially if there is a tight connection between assumptions about human nature and moral theories or moral systems. The idea is that such attacks would constitute an uncovering of the basically ideological nature of the concept of human nature and of the irrelevance of biological considerations for moral theory.

THE CONCEPT OF HUMAN NATURE

The concept of human nature is one of those chameleon concepts that can mean many things to different people at different times. In this section, we shall look at a number of different readings that are relevant to the themes of this book.

A prior meta-conceptual question relates to the force of the concept itself. Are we to understand attributions of human nature to be *descriptive* of some value-neutral sense of the way human beings, as a matter of scientific fact, are constituted? Or are we to understand attributions of human nature to be *prescriptive* in the sense that they are reflective of certain ideological assumptions about what it means to be human? A review of the literature reveals that authors often use them, consciously or not, in both senses. The prescriptive sense is obviously value laden in a way in which the descriptive sense is not. Recognizing that authors tend to slip between the two senses may go a long way to understanding the seductive inclination to infer values from facts. This issue is discussed in detail in the following section but it is well to get it out front at the beginning so that the reader can constantly bear in mind that each putatively descriptive reading has a prescriptive shadow dogging its tracks.

Charles Cooley (1956) distinguishes several senses of the term *human nature*. In one sense, it can be taken to mean the strict genetic endowment of individuals (Cooley, 1956, p. 31). E. O. Wilson uses the term in this sense in his book *On Human Nature*. The glossary defines *human nature* as "[in] the broader sense, the full set of innate [= genetic] behavioral dispositions that characterize the human species; and in the narrower sense, those predispositions that affect social behavior" (Wilson, 1979, p. 226). In a second sense, human nature is sometimes understood to be the social nature that results from the basic interactive relationships characteristic of most humans; that is, "certain primary social sentiments and attitudes" (Cooley, 1956, p. 32). Cooley takes this to be the ordinary usage of *human nature*. Finally, the term is sometimes used to designate more specific traits such as "pecuniary selfishness, generosity, belligerency or peacefulness, efficiency or inefficiency, conservatism or radicalism, and the like" (Cooley, 1956, p. 33). These characteristics are more obviously variable and subject to alteration. Focusing on them, as opposed to the traits associated with the second sense, is more liable to lead to the conclusion that you *can* change human nature.

In an even more general sense, a cluster of traits characterize human nature, the most important of which is "teachability," or "malleability," or "plasticity" (Cooley, 1956, p. 34). From this perspective, the key that distinguishes human nature from other organismic natures is that humans need not change their "natures," as less plastically endowed organisms must, to adapt to changing circumstances. Alexander and the sociobiologists, in general, trade off between these four notions. They sometimes focus on the first and the third, especially the "selfish" features at either the genic or organismic level, and treat them as if they were one idea. They tend to ignore the more general sense even when, like E. O. Wilson and Richard Alexander, they recognize the importance and centrality of human plasticity (cf. Cooley's use of the term *plastic* on p. 31 in Cooley, 1956).

HUMAN NATURE AND MORAL THEORY

When Aristotle reasoned about the good for human beings, he did so against a set of background assumptions about human nature. Critics of Aristotelian naturalism argue that Aristotle's concept of human nature smuggled in normative considerations, which then appeared to have been derived from the facts as he saw them. When Kant says that a study of the "abiding *nature* of man" is a precondition for the application of morality to the solution of problems of human conduct, this illustrates the pervasive role of the concept of human nature in moral theory even among non-naturalists (Schilpp, 1977, p. 76). There is a crucial difference between the appeals to human nature made by the eighteenth century British moral philosophers and those made by Kant. For the former, the concept of human nature plays a central role in determining what constitutes the good or the right. For Kant, the emphasis is on the need to understand the nature of the beast to correctly apply the lessons of morality—which one presumes are truths independent of the facts of human nature. If this is correct, then Kant's position opens the possibility that human beings might be so constituted as not to be able to realize the good or consistently make progress toward it.

In this section, I want to illustrate these two interrelated themes. Moralists often present sketches of human nature from which they draw moral conclusions but often without adequate argumentation for the underlying conceptual scheme. To the extent that we are biological creatures, one of the potential contributions of biology to morality would be to supply relevant information about the nature of human beings that would serve as empirical input into the construction of moral systems. Bishop Butler presents a typical case.

Virtue, Butler says, "consists in following human nature; vice, in deviating from it" (Butler, 1983, Preface § 13). By a system or nature, Butler understands a series of component parts and the interrelations between them. The constitutive parts of human nature for Butler are appetites, passions, affections, and the principle of reflection or conscience, plus the interrelations between them. The supreme principle is reflection or conscience (Butler, 1983, Preface, § 14).

A system running smoothly is virtuous; one out of kilter, out of balance, is vicious. Thus, although both misery and injustice are vices, injustice is a disequilibration of the whole and a more serious breach of harmony than misery (Butler, 1983, Preface, § 15). It is not clear whether Butler here means injustice *internal* to an individual or injustice in relation to the community. If the former, then the difference between misery and injustice, or disequilibrium, is like the difference between a system failure due to a component failure versus a system failure due to an interactive imbalance between components.

The essence of Butler's argument is as follows. Humans and brutes act under the influence of several directing principles or instincts. Some of these principles are directed at the social good; some at the private good. Humans have more motivating principles than brutes. In particular, humans are directed by a principle of reflection or conscience. In the Preface, Butler rejects the Hobbesian reductionist position that humans are "wholly governed by self-love" (Butler, 1983, Preface, § 21). In addition, he argues, "one of these principles of action, conscience or reflection, compared with the rest as they all stand together in the nature of man, plainly bears upon it marks of authority over all the rest, and claims the absolute direction of them all" (Butler, 1983, Preface, § 24). According to Butler it is not enough merely to avoid evil, one must, to act in conformity with one's nature, actively subject one's actions to the authority of conscience, because it is part of our nature that conscience has this authority and that it should be exercised.

In Sermon I, Butler suggests that the *parts of the body* stand to the whole body as particular persons stand to society (Butler, 1983, Sermon I, § 4).[1] For Butler, it follows that just as the parts of the body work together for the benefit of the whole, so we as individuals, were intended [by God]? to do good to others. Hence, Butler, in opposing Hobbes, is starting from a metaphor and analogy that Hobbes would presumably reject. Because bodies, as such, are *inert*, Butler proposes the analogue: individuals stand to society as the internal principles of human nature stand to the whole nature of man. Butler then concludes that the comparison will be between the nature of man as respecting self and tending to private good, his own preservation and happiness, and the nature of man as having respect to society and tending to promote public good, the happiness of society. These ends, do indeed perfectly coincide (Butler, 1983, Sermon I, § 4).

What follows, according to Butler, is "that we were [just as much] made for society and to do good to our fellow creatures, as we were intended to take care of our own life and health and private good" (Butler, 1983, Sermon I, § 5). Here Butler clearly appeals to design to account for the workings of conscience. An empirical survey of the moral phenomenology of human experience reveals, according to Butler, that the principle of reflection or conscience works in such a way. Given that we have this marvelous faculty that affords us the ability to distinguish between right and wrong, who could fail to conclude that "this faculty was placed within to be our proper governor, to direct and regulate all other principles, passions and motives of action" (Butler, 1983, Sermon II, § 15)?

Butler gets a lot of milage out of the fact that humans have the capacity to reflect on what they do. But our moral sensibilities, such as they are, cannot merely reside in our ability to reflect. So wherein does the capacity to reflect rightly lie (Butler, 1983, I, § 8ff.)?

Butler assumes, according to Roberts, that there is a norm or standard for human nature. This, in turn, means that most individuals have appropriate sentiments in certain circumstances. Not to have them would be "unnatural" (Roberts, 1973, p. 32).

Butler's approach to human nature is "teleological." For Butler, human individuals are invested with a nature constituted in us by God to promote our "proper end." Once we determine what that end is, we can designate it, and what promotes it, as "natural" and other ends, or misguided means, as "unnatural." This, Roberts points out, allies Butler with the Aristotelian tradition and the Schoolmen, and would seem to distance his view from a proper "Darwinian" one. With respect to the Schoolmen, this approach clearly emerges in Aquinas and his strictures against fornication and homosexuality as being "unnatural." Teleological views of human nature clearly exemplify the dual descriptive and prescriptive roles that the concept of human nature is called on to play. The question raised by Darwinism is this: If we abandon teleological approaches to understanding human beings, and with it the idea of design, does the concept of "human nature" provide any useful ideologically neutral bearing or point of reference in terms of which one can measure what is good or evil and right or wrong?

From Cooley's (1956) sociological perspective, society and individuals form an organic unity. They are "simply collective and distributive aspects of the same thing" (Cooley, 1956, p. 37). He goes on to say that "just as there is no society or group that is not a collective view of persons, so there is no individual who may not be regarded as a particular view of social groups" (Cooley, 1956, p. 38). Thus, neither the individual nor the group is primary. But strictly speaking, from an evolutionary (phylogenetic) point of view, this must be false because organic species existed long before social groups.

For Dewey, morality is a function of the interaction between human nature and the physical and social environments within which humans live (Dewey, 1957, p. 1). What, Dewey asks, is the authority and claim upon us of ideas and standards developed through custom and habit (Dewey, 1957, p. 75)? In one sense, he says, such questions have no answer. This is the sense in which the only acceptable answer is an appeal to a first principle. But, first principles, like ultimate ends, have no currency for pragmatists. In another sense, Dewey says, the answer is the authority of life itself. It is a matter of fact that we find ourselves engaged in the processes of living subject to the constraints we find ourselves in. We can no more do away with morality and standards than we can do away with breathing and still live: "the choice is not between a moral authority outside custom and one within it. It is between adopting more or less intelligent and significant customs" (Dewey, 1957, p. 75).

The upshot of Dewey's view is that psychological individualism is untenable. Human beings are, aboriginally, social beings whose individuality proceeds from their social constitution and not psychic individuals whose sociality emerges from their original psychical natures (Dewey, 1957, p. 6). Nevertheless, Dewey sees himself as following in the footsteps of Hume. Hume held that "a knowledge of human nature provides a map or chart of all humane and social subjects" (Dewey, 1957, p. vi). For Dewey, Hume correctly emphasized habit and custom as the foundations of sociality "but he failed to see that custom is essentially a fact of associated living whose force is dominant in forming the habits of individuals" (Dewey, 1957, p. vii).

"Morality is largely concerned with controlling human nature" (Dewey, 1957, p. 1). Dewey's instrumentality leads him to the view that controlling human nature is akin to conquering or controlling physical nature. Just as the task of physics is the latter, so the task of morality is the former. The important point to note is that Dewey, although he was one of the first to point out the antiessentialist implications of Darwinism for philosophy, takes the concept of human nature seriously (cf. Dewey, 1910). This is in sharp contrast to Rorty's recent diagnosis that what is disturbing about Pragmatism is that it undermines appeal to our biological nature and undercuts the significance of "human nature" as a useful moral concept (Rorty, 1989, p. 177). Pragmatism, he argues, undermines the comfort of the sense of continuity of the cultural line, the sense that, even if we were to be annihilated tomorrow, *our* culture and *our* values would reemerge wherever sufficiently "rational" investigations of the cosmos were to appear, because *our* view of the world is taken to be a reflection of the way things are. Incidentally, this conceit is also undermined by evolutionary considerations. If we hold on to the concept of human nature despite accepting the evolution of human beings from nonhuman forms, then whatever concept of human nature survives intact must be admitted to be variable. To the extent that what *we* take to be "rational" is determined in part by that "nature," evolutionary considerations alone begin to undermine the "God's-eye" point of view that is the target of Pragmatism.[2]

The dual aspect of the concept of human nature, its prescriptive as well as descriptive force, is clearly articulated in a recent work by C. J. Berry that explores the role of the concept of human nature in political theory (Berry, 1986). According to Berry, theories of human nature serve as "relevance sieves" that act to determine what factors are or are not relevant to the adjudication of an issue (Berry, 1986, p. 20). They serve to determine salience. Different theories or concepts of human nature are likely to filter out different factors of a situation as relevant. "Human nature," as Berry understands it, is *not* a purely descriptive theoretical concept. It has a *practical* dimension as well. Such concepts exhibit what Berry calls *duality*. A concept or theory of human nature shapes how people act and what they do in ways that purely theoretical or epistemic classifications do not (Berry, 1986, p. 33). The Lockean and Marxian concepts of human nature, for example, are in competition in a way in which the alternative conceptions of physicists and geologists with respect to the nature of rocks are not. The former, Berry claims, lead to disputes over practical consequences that the latter do not. One can argue just as well, however, that the different theoretical constructs of the physicist or geologist have practical consequences as well, especially if the physicist tells us that the rock in question is radioactive or a meteor. But even in a mundane sense, the alternative theoretical conceptions of scientists regarding natural phenomena have a host of practical consequences, which range from differing programs of experimental research to infighting for scarce resources during funding cycles. That there is a distinction between the natural or nonhuman world and the human world is however well taken as far as the latter is a world of practices or, as Berry puts it, of *conduct* (Berry, 1986, p. 34).

In their prescriptive guise, concepts of human nature implicitly put forward an *ideal* (Berry, 1986, pp. 41ff.). Berry notes that the Stoics were the first to make an effective use of the universality of human nature as they and the Epicureans formulated their views in the light of the collapse of the *polis* or city-state as ideal. For the Stoics, the goal of the individual was "self-sufficiency" and not, as Plato and Aristotle argued, to be realized in the life of the *polis*. For the Stoics, living according to nature was the ideal, where *nature* has to be understood in a dual sense as both descriptive of the way things are and prescriptive of a view of the way things ought to be (Berry, 1986, p. 62).

Appeals to human nature are then faced with a dilemma. Insofar as they are ideologically constrained, they are question begging. Insofar as they are *not* ideologically constrained, they border on the vacuous as any behavior within the range of human endeavor could be said to be according to "nature." Is the concept of human nature vacuous? As used by Rawls and Hart, professedly so, although their use has been criticized as based on particular assumptions and cultural biases (Berry, 1986, pp. 87f.). Can there be an ideology-free concept of human nature? Given the critiques that suggest that particular views of human nature are hopelessly biased, we can either do away with the concept altogether (as, for example, Rorty and Hull suggest) on the grounds that it does not do any *real* work or try to produce an ideology-free concept of human nature (Berry, 1986, Ch. 8). Even if that is not possible, the concept of human nature may be one of those that we cannot seem to do without. Does it produce the same kinds of pernicious effects in moral and political theory that the relationalists like Mach argued the concepts of absolute space and time produced in physical theory? Even so, the concept of absolute space and time has reappeared in a new guise, absolute space-time, in the general theory of relativity. Perhaps there *are* concepts without which the human mind cannot think.

HUMAN NATURE AND IDEOLOGY

To label a belief as ideological is to suggest that the merits of the belief rest more on conceptual presuppositions of the believer than on a dispassionate regard for the facts. Ideology connotes bias. Can there be an ideology-free or unbiased concept of human nature? Berry suggests not but argues that the concept may prove indispensable nonetheless. What the concept of human nature does for us is help to define an ideal by singling out certain features or capacities as salient, that is, relevant to determining what is or is not the good life. "To involve human nature is to argue that one form of life is superior to another" (Berry, 1986, p. 134).

The eighteenth century histories, which were written using what Comte came to call the *comparative method*, were tainted by a theoretical assumption, that "since the powers of nature (including human nature) are uniform and unfailing, it may be taken for granted that civilizations will grow up independently and spontaneously and follow, more or less, the same general course." The acceptance of this assumption contaminated the evidence truly comparative histories might have provided by assuming that the gross morphology of all cultures and all civilizations were everywhere and anytime the same (Bryson, 1945, pp. 109ff.).

The concept of human destiny is one manifestation of the ideological aspect of the concept of human nature and design. Kant, in his *Anthropology*, claims "Man is destined by his reason to live in a society of other people, and in this society he has to cultivate himself, civilize himself, and apply himself to a moral purpose by the arts and sciences. No matter how great his animalistic inclination may be to abandon himself passively to the enticements of ease and comfort, which he calls happiness, he is still destined to make himself worthy of humanity by actively struggling with the obstacles that cling to him because of the crudity of his nature" (Kant, 1978, pp. 241f.).

Darwinism, one would think, seriously undermines the concept of human destiny but not everyone agrees. Julian Huxley, for one, argues that evolutionary biology provides a new view of human destiny. The evolutionary destiny of human beings is "to be the agent of the evolutionary process on this planet, the instrument for realizing new possibilities for its future" (Huxley, 1960, p. 262).

The central idea of Huxley's evolutionary ideology is that "our human destiny is to have the unique privilege and responsibility of leadership in the process of evolution: There is one reality, and man is its prophet and pioneer" (Huxley, 1960, p. 236).[3]

As Huxley sees it, human destiny involves the expansion and fuller realization of the potentialities of individuals (Huxley, 1960, p. 110). "[H]uman individuals . . . [are] biologically and intrinsically higher than the state" (Huxley, 1960, p. 112). The development of individual personalities is one of the open possibilities of human nature. Huxley concludes that communitarian social and political philosophies are inconsistent with human destiny. Huxley identifies communitarianism with statism whereas Kropotkin is careful to make a distinction between the two. This helps explain how some "Darwinists" come to see the principle of natural selection, at least the principle of individual selection, as incompatible with communitarianism and others do not.

Ashley Montagu notes that concepts of human nature help shape and determine the attitudes of conduct that human beings display toward each other. This is an expression of the ideological component of the concept of human nature. "Facts" themselves cannot determine attitudes. Human attitudes are "spins" on the facts, or what people take to be the facts, and no mere setting straight of the "facts" will ensure that one spin will emerge and others fall by the wayside. Consider the sort of humble case that has beleaguered moral philosophy for the past 300 years. A gentleman lays down his coat on the ground for a lady to trod upon. That is a fact. Is Sir Walter acting from benevolence or self-love? Are men basically selfish or self-serving or are they motivated by benevolent and altruistic feelings as well? Opinions divide: Hobbes, Mandeville, Dawkins, Ghiselin, and Alexander are to one side. Butler, Hutcheson, Smith, and Kropotkin are on the other. Both camps claim Darwin for their own.

In discussing Hitler's deliberate mis-use of the concept of race to further political ends, Montagu notes that "Pathological thoughts . . . can be quite as lethal as pathological germs. Hence, the importance for human beings of understanding the true facts concerning the nature of man cannot be overestimated" (Montagu, 1956, p. 11).

Here Montagu suggests that the perniciousness of false theories is correctable by getting the "true facts" of human nature. But, do such ideologically "true facts" exist for the concept of "human nature" (Montagu, 1956, p. 1)? This view should be contrasted with Darwin's claim that false theories do no damage but false facts are pernicious. Montagu's point about pathological thoughts shows the falsity of Darwin's view, but insofar as he takes such views to be correctable by pristine facts he overstates the case. "The proper attitude in the face of facts or theories is not belief or disbelief, but dispassionate inquiry" (Montagu, 1956, p. 38). With respect to questions of human nature, however, we may ask whether *dispassionate* inquiry is possible.

In addition, one must realize that these views have practical and not purely speculative consequences. "Theories spun by men desirous of rationalizing their otherwise unjustifiable conduct towards other men, and discussions of the nature of man in the learned academies, have never long remained within the bounds of private discourse, for what affects the lives of men sufficiently to become a subject of discourse is likely to become a matter of public interest as soon as social conditions are favorable. Under such conditions myths easily replace facts, and myths as a basis for social action can be dangerous" (Montagu, 1956, p. 10).

DOES DARWINISM UNDERMINE
THE CONCEPT OF HUMAN NATURE?

Does Darwinism with its alleged antiessentialist consequences seriously undermine the validity of the concept of human nature and seriously undermine the attempt to ground morality in an understanding of the kind of creatures human beings are?

Murphy, in defending the *prima facie* plausibility of sociobiological analyses of human morality, argues that "it [is] inconceivable that there could be *no* important connections between morality and the kind of creatures we are" (Murphy, 1982, p. 96). Bernard Williams, on the other hand, holds that "[t]he project of giving to ethical life, in any determinate form, an objective grounding in considerations about human nature is not, in my view, very likely to succeed" (Williams, 1989, p. 83). Williams goes on to argue that even if it did succeed, the resulting "objective theory" would not be analogous to science insofar as the relationship between scientific principles or laws and scientific truths is not the same as the relation between visions of the good life and other ethical truths.

The argument that Darwinism undermines the concept of human nature rests on the alleged antiessentialist implications of Darwinian biology. Two points should be noted. First, many of the moral views of the seventeenth and eighteenth centuries that rest on appeals to human nature do indeed rely on what are basically essentialistic readings of the concept of human nature. Hobbes, Hume and Butler are important cases in point. Second, the essentialistic "Enlightenment" concept of human nature was challenged by Herder, Hegel and the "Romantics," who replaced it with a "contextualist" concept of human nature that varied from culture to culture (see C. J. Berry, 1982). If a culturally contextual concept of human nature can perform significant intellectual work, why not a biologically contextual concept as well?

As an example of an ethic that trades on an "essentialist" reading of human nature, consider Butler. Butler, in his *Sermons*, was concerned to establish and defend the Stoic view that "Virtue is natural, vice unnatural" (Butler, 1983, p. 28). But in what sense of *natural*? In one sense, anything we do is natural, but this sense does not support the Stoic claim because both vice and virtue are natural in this sense. In another sense, "natural" is what one does "out of character." But, again, this sense of natural will not do either, because some people's characters are wicked. There is a third sense, Butler argues, that can be invoked. The principles and propensities which motivate us can be hierarchically organized. The hierarchical ordering is based upon two criteria: 1) strength and 2) authority. Butler should be understood as postulating a hierarchical *model* of motivation which consists of two factors—benevolence and self-love in some mixture—with an appropriate strength and authority. Every individual action is presumed to be the product of a 'mixed' motivation of the same factors. We can, in principle, compare the 'motivational profile' of a given [real-world] action against the standard model. "The correspondence of actions to the nature of the agent renders them natural: their disproportion to it, unnatural" (Butler, 1983, p. 31, also cf. pp. 32f. and 39f.). Compare T. H. Huxley's argument to the point that insofar as "[b]oth the thief and the murderer follow nature as much as the saint . . . [t]he facts of evolution cannot provide a *reason* for preferring what we call good to what we call evil—both are evolutionary products" (Huxley, 1989, pp. 80f.). For the Stoics, upon whom Huxley draws, "following nature" means living in accordance with reason. One might argue that the thief and the murderer, insofar as they steal and kill, are not living in accordance with reason and not "following nature." R. J. Richards argues in this way when he attempts to show that ethical principles can be properly inferred from "nature" (Richards, 1987; see Chapter 5 later). The legitimacy of these inferences hinges on conceptions of reason as much as on the facts of biology and the facts and concepts of human nature.

The eighteenth century reaction to the philosophy of the Enlightenment included a restructuring of the concept of human nature. What counted as human nature was now seen to vary with different cultural conditions. This reaction antedated the development of evolutionary biology in the nineteenth century (see again C. J. Berry, 1982, for details).

The introduction of evolutionary considerations raises two kinds of issues with respect to the concept of human nature. First, as E. Mayr and others have forcefully pointed out, an evolutionary perspective impresses upon us the need to distinguish between phylogenetic and ontogenetic analyses of the development of organismic characteristics. The implications for our understanding of human nature are as follows. A phylogenetic analysis of the evolution of human nature implies that, far from being the same for all time and all places, our human nature has evolved and continues to evolve. This is a clear antiessentialist, anti-Humean consequence. On the other hand, focusing on the development of human nature within particular historical epochs impresses upon us the sense in which, although "natures" are historicized with respect to historical epochs, we may be said to share a certain common nature (cf. Breuer, 1982).

John Dewey, who can hardly be construed as an essentialist, argues for the derivation of the institutional structures of morality "from human nature." The difference between Dewey and an essentialist like Aquinas is that Aquinas attempts to derive specific injunctions with regard to particular practices "from human nature" in accordance with what the *telos* directs entities toward, and Dewey does not.

The Darwinian populational objection to essences has at least two components: an objection to eternal natures and an objection to natures construed as "ideal types" with the natural variety of real populations a reflection of a deviation from that type. These components are related in the Darwinian model because the variability in natural populations gives rise to the evolution of "natures" from one mean to another. The "nature" of the population can be characterized in terms of a mean and appropriate dispersion measures. Had Aquinas been a population thinker, he could not have so easily condemned homosexuality or fornication as "unnatural" such as they appear on the scale of human practice. But Aquinas had a view of what the "proper end" of these practices was as a result of his teleological approach to nature. In accordance with this ideal he could view alternative practices as "deviations."

Nevertheless, the two components of variability and appeal to an ideal type (or three, if one counts "teleological" as a separate component on the grounds that one can have a teleological view that admits alternative paths to achieve the appropriate end—teleology and variability are compatible) are independent.

The antiessentialist implications of Darwinism emerge as follows. Only essential kinds have natures, so it is said. No biological organisms are essential kinds, given the truth of Darwinism. So, no biological organisms have natures. This is the heart of the argument but, as it stands, it is too short and too swift. We need to distinguish two sources of variability for such entities. One, phylogenetic variability, is due to the contingent fact that organismic lineages evolve under the influence of natural selection and other constraints and forces. The second, developmental variability, is due more to the contingent features of ontogenetic development as particular organisms interact with their physical and social environments.

Even if we accept that phylogenetic variability is a fact of biological life, we need not conclude that organisms cannot properly be said to have natures. Consider organisms that are genetically "hard wired": ants, wasps, and so on. Although ants and wasps exhibit variability, it seems beyond dispute that ants can be said to have a nature in their present state of evolutionary development. The less plastic the development potentialities for a given species are, the more plausible attributing a nature to them seems to be. We should conclude, therefore, that *mere* phylogenetic variability does not undermine the concept of species natures nor does it undermine the concept of species essence. We have established a basis for denying phylogenetic essentialism, on the one hand, while affirming species specific natures, on the other.

Human beings are of course more plastic than ants. I take the import of this to be that human beings have more developmental flexibility than ants. The bewildering range of behaviors that humans and other primates and advanced organisms exhibit may seem to belie the claim that they have natures, but what it shows is only that the range of behaviors is more widespread. What behaviors the organisms in various populations exhibit is also going to be a function of the circumstances in which they are raised and interact. This complicates our attempts to give account of their nature. It does not mean that they do not have natures but only that their natures are developmentally variable or alterable.

What we can infer about the constraints and limitations on their behavioral repertoires is also more problematic. But as their social environment is a major contributing factor to their behavioral development and as their social environment is stable in relevant ways from generation to generation, we can expect to see a somewhat narrower range of satisfying courses of action open to them than we might be led to expect by the claim that humans have no nature and that therefore such natures cannot be appealed to in considerations of morality—which deal, in a broad sense, with appropriateness of behaviors or conduct.

Hull, who takes a dim view of the significance of the concept of human nature, argues that "if evolutionary theory has anything to teach us it is that variability is at the core of our being" (Hull, 1989, p. 16). As Hull himself points out, variability is at the core of the being of any species. Although species evolve and hence have no essences, because any characteristics that are "characteristic" of a species are liable to disappear or be modified, something is amiss. For, despite this variability and borderline cases, there are marked differences between different species. Human beings are quite different from chimpanzees in morphology and gross behavioral repertoires despite overlaps—some humans are no doubt hairier than some apes and some apes are no doubt sometimes cleverer than some human beings—but we do not find it the least bit difficult to distinguish between them.

Lineage is not the totality of what creates something and makes one species different from another. We share over 90 percent of our genome with the chimpanzees and yet the differences between chimpanzees and humans are striking. Either the behavioral differences between us and the chimpanzees are not the result of our genetics or the small genetic differences that do exist are enormously important. There is another possibility. We could share in principle 100 percent, more or less, of our genome with another species and yet—because of the relative placing of switching and developmental genes—be as different from them as we are from the chimpanzees.

Suppose we ignore humans for a moment and focus on equine nature. The same arguments about variability and change hold for horses as for humans. We are not faced with complications of culture and ambiguous construals of "equine nature" or how "unequine" some particular horse's behavior may be. We may be at a loss when forced to say which characteristics constitute the equine nature. Any list we produce will be subject to qualification and counterexample. And yet, horses are what they are in virtue of their genetic or biological endowment. That endowment serves to "constrain" the manner in which their "biological" nature is manifested.

With respect to Hull's argument that Darwinism undermines essentialism and undermines the concept of human nature, the contrast between Dewey and Aquinas is instructive. For an ethics based on a teleological, essentialistic understanding of human nature, Hull's remarks are appropriate. For a case like Dewey, not so. Dewey's appeal to human nature is not an appeal to a teleological structure, but rather to one that is endemic to the human condition. Insofar as Dewey takes these conditions to be an inevitable part of the human condition, he then may be in some sense a closet "essentialist." But for Dewey this appears to be a claim about how humans have, in fact, evolved. Given that they have so evolved, the conditions that occasion morality are part of their nature. However, should the course of evolution shift and the human lineage evolve toward asociality and presociality, then the conditions for the development of morality may cease to be part of the human condition. If these new creatures did not develop moral practices then, insofar as we would want to label them *human*, being moral would not be a part of "human nature."

The point is that we can construe "human nature" in a narrow and restricted sense—as involving some notion of "essential nature" or "teleological nature." Darwinism certainly speaks against this. But even if for Darwinians nothing is forever, this does not prevent us from looking at stretches of lineages and saying that, in the era under consideration, the organisms in question were social, presocial, language users, or whatever. Thus, we can speak of "human nature" in a wider and looser sense—which does not entail a commitment to eternal essences, teleological natures, or to essences as entailing that variation means deviation.

The second issue to consider relates to the EMM-EMT distinction. It seems disingenuous to deny that our "moralizing capacity" is part of our evolved and evolving "nature." It cannot be denied that, at some point in our phylogenetic past, proto- or pre-humans existed that evolved into human beings but lacked the necessary biological capacity to moralize. What remains problematic is the extent to which biological capacities or biological differences contribute to the emergence or "justification" of particular moral principles or practices. The EMT impact of "human nature" on ethics is not so clear.

What does the capacity to moralize amount to? The ability to make reflective evaluations of our behavior, whether separate or not from other evaluative, aesthetic, logical, and epistemological "capacities," and how these capacities evolved, is not our concern. But evolve they clearly did. And just as clearly, human beings, as far as we know, are the only creatures endowed with these capacities. Other organisms may make judgments or have a certain native intelligence or problem solving capacity or the capacity for play or "art" but again as far as we can tell human beings are the only creatures who look and reflect upon their work, their deeds, and their judgments, and deem them good (or bad or evil or wicked or beautiful, ugly, pathetic, or sublime).

In conclusion, we find that the concept of human nature plays a dual role in our conceptual scheme. On the one hand, it serves as a descriptive repository of facts about the "norms of behavior" of the human condition. In this guise, it is most vulnerable to the charge that it is an ancestral relic from the essentialist tradition. On the other hand, it provides a normative ideal that serves as a benchmark for the evaluation of human action. A good case can be made for concluding that however cautious we must be in using the concept in its former descriptive sense it is, nonetheless, an indispensable tool of conceptual analysis.

The Darwinian critique of the concept that focuses on its essentialist origins is not completely successful. One can abandon many of the more trenchant and yet undesirable versions of essentialism and still find a legitimate role for the concept of organismic nature. Phylogenetic variability implies that the nature of a species is not eternal. Ontogenetic variability implies that our concept of biological nature must be appropriately contextualized. The essentialist concept of an "ideal type" functions both descriptively and prescriptively. The prescriptive function remains even if the descriptive function has been discredited.

NOTES

1. This analogy between an organism and a society, which dates back to Plato, is alive today. See Bonner, 1988.

2. Cf. Maxwell (1984, p. 339). One of the impacts of the evolutionary perspective is that it undercuts philosophical-moral-cultural-religious systems "which are based on the premise that our mental, social or cultural qualities. . . . [are] . . . in some way *sui generis*."

3. Cf. E. O. Wilson's visionary role for human beings. "Man's destiny is to know, if only because societies with knowledge culturally dominate societies that lack it. . . . the culture of each society travels along one or the other of a set of evolutionary trajectories whose full array is constrained by the genetic rules of human nature. While broadly scattered from an anthropocentric point of view, this array still represents only a tiny subset of all the trajectories that would be possible in the absence of the genetic constraints. As our knowledge of human nature grows, and we start to elect a system of values on a more objective basis, and our minds at last align with our hearts, the set of trajectories will narrow still more. . . . As the social sciences mature into predictive disciplines, the permissible trajectories will not only diminish in number but our descendants will be able to sight farther along them. Then mankind will face the . . . perhaps final spiritual dilemma. [As our knowledge of human genetics and our understanding of the genetic foundations of social behavior matures] . . . [t]he human species . . . [will be able to] . . . change its own nature. What will it choose? . . . The true Promethean spirit of science means to liberate man by giving him knowledge and some measure of dominion over the physical environment" (Wilson, 1979, pp. 214ff.).

Chapter 5

Three Contemporary Approaches
to Evolutionary Ethics

INTRODUCTION

What is the status of evolutionary ethics today? Despite the widespread acceptance of a Darwinian perspective on human evolution, there is as yet no consensus on the relevance of that perspective for understanding human behavior and human social practices. The case for a Darwinian analysis of ethics remains problematic. In addition to the generic question of the relevance of evolutionary analyses for describing and explaining human behavior, serious questions remain about the ability of Darwinian analyses to provide a proper account of the normative dimension of ethical reasoning. In this chapter, I review three recent attempts to address these issues and provide a general theoretical foundation for ethics based upon Darwinian principles. The first section deals with the views of E. O Wilson and, more recently, Michael Ruse and E. O. Wilson. Their analysis is typical of one particular sociobiological approach to evolutionary ethics. The second section deals with the views of R. D. Alexander. Alexander's approach, which can be characterized as "sociobiological" in a broader sense, while sharing some of the features of the Wilson-Ruse approach, attempts to develop a somewhat muted genic account of the evolution and point of human morality. The third section addresses the recent attempt by Robert Richards to combine an evolutionary explanation of the origin of human morality with what he argues is an evolutionary justification of certain moral principles.

THE WISDOM OF THE GENES:
THE SOCIOBIOLOGY OF ETHICS

The last chapter of E. O. Wilson's *Sociobiology* outlines a program to apply the insights developed in the first twenty-five chapters of the book to the explanation of aspects of human behavior. This chapter provoked a storm of virulent criticism (see Caplan, 1978). Wilson was accused of a multitude of sins, including being a reductionist, an adaptationist, and a racist. While his critics loudly proclaimed his program to be both unscientific and unachievable, he went on to articulate his vision in three subsequent books, *On Human Nature* (1979) and, with coauthor Charles Lumsden, *Genes, Minds and Culture* (1981) and *Promethean Fire* (1983).

The furor of the debate of the late 1970s and early 1980s has now died down with both sides claiming victory. Although it is no doubt true that much of the program remains to be filled out, it is also true that an increasing amount of empirical research on human behavior and human institutions is being conducted and evaluated from an evolutionary point of view. In assessing the prospects and success of sociobiological analyses of human behavior, it is important to distinguish between "wide" and "narrow" construals of the field. Construed widely, sociobiology can be understood as ethology under a different description. Organisms have characteristic modes of social behavior. Sociobiology, in the wide sense, is just the investigation of the biological basis of animal social behavior. Construed in a narrow sense, sociobiology is the name of a particular genetic approach to understanding the biological basis of animal social behavior. One can very well reject some of the more radical reductionist claims made by investigators such as Wilson, Dawkins, Trivers, Hamilton, and Alexander without thereby rejecting the general program of trying to understand animal social behavior from a biological and evolutionary point of view.

With the distinction between sociobiology in a wide sense and sociobiology in a narrow sense in mind, it is fair to say that a Scot's verdict of "not proven" is an accurate reassessment of the contemporary state of sociobiology. It is not my purpose here to attempt to review or assess the vast and complex literature and debate that has been spawned by the publication of Wilson's 1975 book. Rather, I want to focus on Wilson's sociobiological analysis of morality.

At the beginning of *Sociobiology*, Wilson threw down the gauntlet in the form of a challenge to moral philosophers to stand aside and let the biologists clarify the meaning and significance of human morality (Wilson, 1975, p. 3). Wilson characterized the central theoretical problem of sociobiology to be "how can altruism, which by definition reduces personal fitness, possibly evolve by natural selection? The answer is kinship"

(Wilson, 1975, p. 3). In the light of the subsequent attempt to account for moral altruism as an enabling mechanism shaped by natural selection and of the implicit identification of the core of human morality with altruism, the stage has been set for the biologization of morality.

When Wilson comes to apply the theory to ethics in Chapter 26, he takes all philosophical analyses of ethics to be varieties of ethical intuitionism. His remarks on ethics here are only sketchy. They are more fully elaborated in *On Human Nature*. Ethical intuitionism for Wilson is the view that "the mind has a direct awareness of true right and wrong that it can formalize by logic and translate into rules of social action" (Wilson, 1979, p. 287).

Michael Ruse, in *Sociobiology: Sense or Nonsense*, argues that Wilson's critique of ethical intuitionism is both misguided and weak. It is misguided in that intuitionism is a dead horse (Ruse, 1979, p. 205). It is weak because using sociobiology to undercut ethics is circular. If sociobiology is true, then our judgments are suspect, because our organs may have evolved to deceive us. If this is so, we have no reason to believe that any scientific theory, including sociobiology, is true. One cannot argue that *only* our moral judgments are suspect because science and logic are equally adaptive. In fact, Ruse suggests, ethics is stabler than science because one can follow Socrates but not Ptolemy without derision. The sociobiological argument against intuitionism fails to distinguish *reasons* from *causes*. Just because our sense of morality is probably due to evolutionary causes is no reason to think that *reasons* for or against particular moral positions or meta-moral positions are forthcoming from evolutionary considerations. With the fullness of time, Ruse has come to recant these views and become a convert of sorts to the idea that sociobiological analyses of ethics are insightful indeed. This reversal is exemplified in a paper coauthored with Wilson (Ruse and Wilson, 1986) and in his book *Taking Darwin Seriously*.

It is a reflection of Wilson's naive reading of the philosophical literature that he sees the dominant "contractarian" tradition, exemplified by his Harvard colleague John Rawls, as the attempt to so formalize and translate the mind's "direct awareness of true right and wrong." He sees the "Achilles heel" of such approaches to consist in their appeal to "intuitions" and their reliance "on the emotive judgment of the brain, as though that origin must be treated as a black box" (Wilson, 1975, p. 287).[1] What is needed is access to the inner workings of the box. Wilson does not mean just a clearer neurophysiological understanding of how the brains of evolved primates work but also an evolutionary account of how they came to work the way they do.

The role of sociobiology as Wilson sees it is twofold. First, sociobiology has the task of reconstructing the history of the social machinery of social life (Wilson, 1975, p. 300). It is supposed to help identify the adaptive function of each of the components of social organization—some are obsolete and can be done away with; others are probably tied to traits we want to preserve and so can be tinkered with at our peril. Here the argument is that given the assumption of a genetic basis to characteristic behaviors and given the general phenomenon of gene linkage, in striving to cultivate some desirable (or desired) traits we may, with inadequate knowledge of the human genome and its import for human behavior, promote undesirable (or undesired) traits as well. This line of reasoning is put to provocative use in *On Human Nature* in an argument that could be read as cautioning against some possible perils of social reform (Wilson, 1979, Ch. 6). At the conclusion of the chapter entitled "Sex," Wilson argues that an evolutionary analysis of human sexuality reveals constraints imposed on human nature that need to be taken into account when social and political policies are formulated. These evolved constraints entail that attempts to modify social practices and institutions engender costs that are not easy to calculate. The rational design of cultures, maintained by education, reward schedules, and coercion, exacts a price "measured in the time and energy required for training and enforcement and in the less tangible currency of human happiness that must be spent to circumvent our innate predispositions" (Wilson, 1979, pp. 173ff.).

In addition, it must be recalled that Wilson's position is ultimately materialist. Sociobiology, which attempts to provide an evolutionary framework for the understanding of human sociality, is only a temporary expediency. It will be replaced, when the time comes, by an advanced neurophysiology that will allow us to calculate the social effects of our genetic endowment directly from the genes themselves. The imprecision and uncertainty that surrounds evolutionary analyses of the grounds of human behavior "means that Skinner's dream of a culture predesigned for happiness will surely have to wait for the new neurobiology. *A genetically accurate and hence completely fair code of ethics must also wait*" (Wilson, 1975, p. 300; my emphasis).

The second task of sociobiology in the reconfiguration of our understanding of human nature is to "monitor the genetic basis of social behavior. Optimum socioeconomic systems can never be perfect, because of Arrow's impossibility theorem and probably also because ethical standards are innately pluralistic" (Wilson, 1975, p. 300). Wilson expresses concern over the increased gene flow throughout the world due to its transformation into a global village. This increased gene flow, Wilson suggests, could lead to a weakening of altruistic behavior due to considerations of group bonding and hence to a less moral world (Wilson, 1975, p. 300). An uncharitable critic could be excused for reading this as an implicit argument in favor of maintaining immigration quotas and against racial mixing.

In *On Human Nature*, Wilson argues that the ultimate evolutionary function of morality is to keep the human genetic material intact (Wilson, 1979, p. 175).[2] The genes hold culture on a leash.

Three questions, which Wilson puts as dilemmas, frame the discussion in *On Human Nature*. Wilson's contention is that sociobiological arguments have a bearing on all.

1. What is the meaning of life?
2. How are we to choose between the conflicting ethical premises [= emotive strains?] in human biological nature?
3. Given the powers implicit in a biological and evolutionary understanding of human nature, how will the human species choose to change its own nature? (Wilson, 1979, p. 216).

Wilson, along with many biologists, takes the heart of morality to be altruism. He defines *altruism* as "[s]elf-destructive behavior performed for the benefit of others. Altruism may be entirely rational, or automatic and unconscious, or conscious but guided by innate emotional responses" (Wilson, 1979, pp. 221f.).[3]

The two biological questions that are central to his analysis concern the source and mode of perpetuation of altruism. Wilson considers three potential sources: (1) altruism is a divine gift (Wilson, 1979, p. 159); (2) altruism is a transcendental feature distinguishing humankind from lower animals (Wilson, 1979, p. 156, 159); and (3) altruism is a hypertrophied attribute found in nonhuman organisms (Wilson, 1979, p. 159).[4]

With respect to the maintenance of biologically altruistic behavior in a population once it has evolved, because altruists are at a selective disadvantage with respect to nonaltruists, a narrow Darwinian perspective should predict their gradual elimination from the population. How then is it maintained? For nonhuman organisms, Wilson argues that kin selection is the dominant mechanism promoting the perpetuation of such behavior. For human beings, Wilson allows that altruism has an emotional basis, perhaps promoted and sustained by kin selection given the fact that the family has been a basic unit throughout much of human history. Yet Wilson is quick to acknowledge that even if human altruism derives from "hereditary units" fixed in the past, the specific form and intensity of human altruism in different contexts are to a large extent culturally determined (Wilson, 1979, p. 160).

Wilson distinguishes between what he calls *hard core* and *soft core* altruism. Hard core altruism is unilateral. There is no anticipation of reciprocity and where it exists it is probably driven by kin selection or group selection on tribes or families (Wilson, 1979, p. 162). Soft core altruism, on the other hand, is multilateral. It is based upon anticipation of expected rewards. As such it is "reciprocal" altruism. Therefore, soft core altruism is not "true" altruism (cf. Wilson, 1979, p. 155). Soft core altruism is also ultimately "selfish," because a soft core altruist acts in anticipation of rewards that will benefit self. As far as the case can be made for reducing human morality to altruism and in particular to what Wilson calls soft core altruism, the groundwork has been laid for claiming a "scientific" foundation for a Hobbesian conception of human nature. For a positive analysis along these lines, see Ghiselin (1974); for a negative appraisal, see Lewontin, Rose, and Kamin (1984). Finally, soft core altruism promotes lying, deceit, and self-deceit. This theme is central to Alexander's analysis of the biological basis of morality.

Is hard core altruism the foundation of soft core altruism? What is the relative mix between the two? Wilson's optimistic appraisal is that selfishness, and hence, soft core altruism, is the key to a more nearly perfect social contract and global harmony.

Hard core altruism, he argues, leads to tribalism and no hope for a global society because it is routinized and inflexible: hard core altruism is the enemy of civilization (Wilson, 1979, p. 164). Hard core altruism in humans is directed toward close relatives; all the rest is soft core. This claim draws support from a subtle ambiguity in the terms *hard core* and *soft core*. Wilson seems to be assuming that the mechanisms that produce and maintain the alternative forms of altruism are universally correlated with their effects. How else could he think that one would not behave in a unilateral manner with no expectation of reciprocity towards nonrelatives? Unless the critics are right and far from supporting a Hobbesian picture of humankind, this view presupposes one. The conflicts engendered by the opposing tugs of hard core altruistic impulses and soft core altruistic impulses predict the "melange of ambivalence, deceit, and guilt that continuously troubles the individual mind" (Wilson, 1979, p. 166).

Even though most of human altruism is "soft," "all human altruism is shaped by powerful emotional controls of the kind intuitively expected to occur in its hardest forms" (Wilson, 1979, p. 169). Wilson speculates that "the deep structure of altruistic behavior, based on learning rules and emotional safeguards, is rigid and universal" (Wilson, 1979, p. 170). This point is developed further in Lumsden and Wilson (1981), where a theory of epigenetic rules is deployed to account for the supposed "hard-wired" link between inherited genetic bases and their behavioral manifestations. For Wilson, even soft core altruism is "hard wired."

"The true humanization of altruism, in the sense of adding wisdom and insight to the social contract, can come only through a deeper scientific examination of morality" (Wilson, 1979, p. 173). Wilson cites, with approval, Kohlberg's work on the ethical stages of individual development

(Kohlberg, 1981, 1984). If verified, it would support the view that the ontogeny of moral development has been "genetically assimilated" and is also under the direction of appropriate epigenetic rules.

Everything considered, Wilson denies that "the cultural evolution of higher ethical values [can] gain a direction and momentum of its own and completely replace genetic evolution" (Wilson, 1979, p. 175). Again, the genes hold culture on a leash. Nonetheless, Wilson neither supports nor suggests the view that there might be genes for altruism. As Sober's critique of "evolutionary altruism" makes clear, the altruistic-selfish distinction from a populational biological perspective is a relational notion dependent upon the structure of the population. What is "altruistic" in one setting may be "selfish" in another. It all depends on whose fitness is being enhanced at the price of decreased fitness for others. To put it another way, to be a biological altruist is not to behave in a particular kind of way as, for example, being a hunter as opposed to being a farmer. Of course, to be a moral altruist *is* to behave in a particular kind of way. Morally altruistic individuals exhibit a behavioral repertoire different from that of a morally selfish individual in a way that biologically altruistic individuals do not exhibit a behavioral repertoire different from that of a biologically selfish individual. One more reason to be suspicious of any glib attempt to identify or reduce the one concept to the other.

The preceding remarks can be construed as an attempt to derive a meta-ethical position from biological considerations. But, in addition, Wilson, in *On Human Nature*, argues that some substantive moral principles can be derived from these reflections on the evolutionary sources of human morality. In particular, he argues that three new cardinal virtues emerge in the light of our biological understanding.

1. The survival of the human gene pool emerges as a "higher" value than individual human lives (Wilson, 1979, p. 204). The human gene line is potentially immortal, discounting the fact that the ultimate long-run fate of all species appears to be extinction. An individual, on the other hand, is only an evanescent combination of genes.
2. We ought to favor diversity in the gene pool (Wilson, 1979, p. 205). For one thing, human genius is a function of rare combinations that wink on and off through the course of time. The continuous appearance of men and women of genius contributes to the maintenance of the species. Gene pool diversity enhances the possibilities that these rare combinations will be formed.
3. The message of the genes is to plump for universal human rights (Wilson, 1979, p. 206). This is a function of the mammalian

order of things. Each individual has a unique genome and hence a unique individual stake in the perpetuation of its gene line. Basically, this is a result of our diploid sexual natures.[5]

Little attempt has been made by Wilson to provide a philosophically tight argument for any of these claimed virtues, and it is easy to see how critics might conclude that these values tell us more about E. O. Wilson than they do about the ethical implications of evolution by natural selection. The ethical position developed in *On Human Nature* can be summarized as follows.

The meaning of life for the individual turns out to depend on a recognition that human beings as individuals are merely transient beings whose ultimate or evolutionary significance turns out to be to promote the continuation of the human gene pool. This is not to say that all human values can be reduced in any simpleminded way to directives of the genes but rather that all human values need to be reevaluated in the light of how well they are consistent with and promote what Wilson takes as our genetic heritage. With respect to choosing between the conflicting inherited impulses, Wilson does not allege that sociobiological analyses will provide principles of choice (cf. Murphy, 1982, p. 99). Rather, the function of sociobiology is to provide information about the biological bases of these impulses, which in turn are supposed to allow human beings more information about how to deal with those we may want to enhance and those we may wish to modify.[6] The further information about our biological nature will, if the sociobiological program is successful, provide us the needed tools to be in a position to shape our future destinies. This presents an awesome challenge and is the basis of the third dilemma: how are we to decide to change our nature? Again, the function of the sociobiological analysis does not seem to provide information on which way we should want to do this but rather information on how we might accomplish this once we have chosen one path over another.

Philip Kitcher (1985) argues that E. O. Wilson is committed to the plausibility of each of the following theses about the relevance of evolutionary biology for ethics: (1) appeals to evolutionary biology may account for the evolution of our capacity to be moral; (2) biology may serve as a source of relevant facts to be used in conjunction with moral principles to guide actions; (3) evolutionary biology might be construed as the key to meta-ethics, explaining the nature of moral obligation and the status of moral principles; (4) evolutionary considerations may serve as a source of moral principles (Kitcher, 1985, pp. 417ff.). Kitcher thinks only the first two are legitimate. He sees Alexander, who endorses only the first and second theses, as a more reasonable spokesman for a restrained sociobiological approach to human morality.

With respect to (3), Kitcher argues that "[j]ust as a detailed history of arithmetical concepts and counting practices might show us a succession of myths and errors . . . [yet not lead us to conclude that arithmetical truths are nonobjective] . . . so too reconstructions of the historical development of ethical ideas and practices do not preclude the possibility that we have now achieved a justified system of moral precepts" (Kitcher, 1985, p. 418). Even if, as Lumsden and Wilson maintain, we would be hard pressed to recognize these alleged objective truths, Kitcher denies that this bolsters the evidence from the natural history argument to the nonobjectivity of ethics. No doubt Kitcher is right that evolutionary considerations do not rule out the possibility of justified systems of moral precepts. Lumsden, Wilson, and Ruse are wrong to think that they do, if the question is whether there is an entailment from the facts of biological evolution to the nonultimacy of ethical systems. The point of the appeal to evolution is not to produce a knock-down–drag-out argument but rather to insinuate that moral systems are both less (absolute) and more (possibly serving some reproductive ends) than they appear to be. The appeal to mathematics is not decisive because, even if we were to accept Kitcher's analysis of the structure of mathematics, there are any number of other cases of the historical development of disciplines, some of which support Kitcher's point and others of which do not.

To take just two cases in point consider the evolution of modern science. Different aspects of that development can be used to bolster Kitcher's position or the position of Wilson, Lumsden, and Ruse. The development of modern science from the seventeenth century to the present has seen the continual erosion of the need to appeal to divinities to explain physical phenomena. This may have been taken by some to be a proof that God does not exist. It is not. It does serve to undermine one's confidence in the existence of God. Or it should unless one takes the tack that it was a mistake to think that explanations in science ever had anything to do with our confidence in the existence of God. That line, however, is a mistake on several grounds. First, it is an historical error. Second, it leaves the Theist open to say what phenomena do support our confidence in the existence of God, and once that is out on the table, these phenomena are liable to be accounted for in alternative ways. If, as a measure of last resort, one tries to argue that the concept of God is a construct that serves some spiritual needs, then the case is conceded to the Lumsden, Wilson, and Ruse camp.

The second case from the history of science is the development of the human capacity to do science in the first place. Presumably, from the Lumsden, Wilson, and Ruse point of view, this is an adaptation as well, but people do not argue from this fact to the nonjustifiability of scientific knowledge, do they? Of course some do just that, at least in some respects.

But even if they did not, and one took this case to support the Kitcher position, the utility of either of these cases depends on whether the evolution of the capacity to moralize is more like the one case or the other. With respect to the alleged meta-ethical implication of evolutionary biology, Kitcher sees Wilson's views as hopelessly conflicted. Wilson wants to argue both that ethical statements are emotive and that evolutionary ethics can improve ethics. Kitcher finds this conflicting because to be able to improve suggests a standard independent of the judge, a view that emotivism denies (Kitcher, 1985, p. 420).

According to Kitcher, the content of ethical statements for Wilson is "exhausted by reformulating them in terms of our emotional reactions" (Kitcher, 1985, p. 421). He has no avenue for suggesting that some ought to be improved if they conflict with the majority or are counterproductive to the maximization of fitness.

Given Wilson's emotivism, Kitcher finds it hard to understand how appeal to evolutionary considerations will result in "better" moral principles (Kitcher, 1985, p. 427). One such claim is that evolutionary considerations lead us to value human survival. Granted we are the products of earlier generations, then, how does this engender in us an obligation to preserve the species? Kitcher argues that this argument commits the naturalistic fallacy (Kitcher, 1985, pp. 428ff.). Even if it did not, the principle itself is not obviously objectively correct. "At stake are the relative values of the right to existence of future generations and the right to self-determination of those now living. The biological facts of reproduction do not give us information about that relationship" (Kitcher, 1985, p. 431).

Morality as Applied Science

It is clear that, protestations notwithstanding, Wilson's early view was that an evolutionary analysis of ethics had both meta-ethical and substantive implications. In a joint paper with Michael Ruse, converted from skeptic to partial defender of sociobiological analyses, the focus is on meta-ethics. Substantive moral principles, in the form of "epigenetic" rules, are not abandoned but the force of the evolutionary analysis is limited to *explaining* them rather than *deriving* them.

Ruse and Wilson (1986) argue that moral philosophy can be turned into an applied science. Morality, like every other human characteristic, has an ultimate biological foundation. Coming to grips with the biological basis of moral activity has four major implications. First, there are probably no extrasomatic ethical truths (Ruse and Wilson, 1986, p. 174). By this, Ruse and Wilson mean that an evolutionary analysis of the origin and function of morality undercuts the view that values exist in some "objective" sense independent of valuers. Second, there are probably no global optima for species survival, which they take to imply that there is no universal ethics (Ruse and Wilson, 1986, p. 174). Third, moral epigenetic rules exist and provide reasons for rejecting radical environmentalist analyses of variation in moral codes and behaviors (Ruse and Wilson, 1986, pp. 174, 185). Fourth, the biological basis of morality can be used to determine "generally accepted rules of conduct" (Ruse and Wilson, 1986, p. 174).

The argument rests on a number of factual assumptions about the forces of evolution. First, evolution is a universal process among all kinds of organisms (Ruse and Wilson, 1986, p. 175). Second, the dominant force in evolution is assumed to be natural selection (Ruse and Wilson, 1986, p. 175). Third, a large body of evidence supports the view that non-human behavioral traits have a genetic basis. Human evolution, they argue, appears to be no exception to the general rule. Many human genes have been identified that affect behavioral traits (Ruse and Wilson, 1986, p. 177). They deem the prospects for the future "genetic dissection of human behavior" to be good. However, this should not be construed as support for a simpleminded genetic reductionism or as denying the possibility of behavioral flexibility.

In what sense is human morality a biological phenomenon? Evidence suggests that kin selection and reciprocal altruism can lead to the kind of cooperative behavior associated with morality (Ruse and Wilson, 1986, p. 179). The empirical evidence suggests that the evolution of human cooperation was brought about by the same mechanisms as those that have produced "biological altruism" in nonhuman animals (Ruse and Wilson, 1986, p. 179). Human beings are neither robots nor conscious deceivers, "rather, human beings function better if they are deceived by their genes into thinking that there is a disinterested objective morality binding upon them, which all should obey" (Ruse and Wilson, 1986, p. 179; Alexander, 1987). The human brain is not a tabula rasa nor is it rigidly programmed for certain obligate repertoires (Ruse and Wilson, 1986, p. 180). Our moral sentiments are, like other aspects of human thought, directed by epigenetic rules. "The full sequence in the origin of morality is therefore evidently the following: ensembles of genes have evolved through mutation and selection within an intensely social existence over tens of thousands of years; they prescribe epigenetic rules of mental development peculiar to the human species; under the influence of the rules certain choices are made from among those conceivable and available to the culture; and finally the choices are narrowed and hardened through contractual agreements and sanctification" (Ruse and Wilson, 1986, pp. 180ff.).

The epigenetic "rules" are not rules in any normative sense. They are specifications of the biochemical pathways allegedly leading from genes to behavior. Nonetheless, Wilson and Ruse argue, "[s]urely some of the

moral premises articulated through ethical inquiry lie close to real epigenetic rules. For instance, the contractarians' emphasis on fairness and justice looks much like the result of rules brought about by reciprocal altruism" (Ruse and Wilson, 1986, p. 185; cf. Rawls, 1971, pp. 502f.).

These biological considerations lead to the conclusion "that there
can be no genuinely objective external ethical premises" (Ruse and Wilson, 1986, p. 186). By this, the authors appear to mean that ethical
premises or principles are not like laws of nature in being true independent of the whims or predilections of scientific investigators. The conclusion is supposed to follow from the fact that "ethical premises are the
peculiar products of genetic history, and they can be understood solely as
mechanisms that are adaptive for the species that possess them" (Ruse
and Wilson, 1986, p. 185). Because the evolutionary histories of different
species either on earth or elsewhere are not likely to duplicate our own,
we must infer that it is likely that the ethical premises or principles
adopted by such species that are capable of so doing are likely to be other
than our own.

Whatever force this argument may have seems to derive from a systematic ambiguity in the use of the term *ethical premise*. Those ethical
"premises" that are the products of genetic history have descriptive force
only. The ethical premises that function as moral principles and the
assumptions in practical reasoning have prescriptive force but are not, in
any obvious sense, the products of genetic history. The continued reference
to "premises" suggests that what are being explained are the motivations
individuals have that lead them to behave in an ethical manner. These no
doubt are cross-specific, but it does not follow that *standards* that are not
species specific cannot or should not be articulated. Also, what are we to
make of the "solely" understood in the light of the obvious objection articulated by Kitcher that we cannot argue from the fact that our perceptual and
rational powers are species specific and subjective to the conclusion that
what we use those powers to discern must be subjective as well?

We must, therefore, be suspicious of the conclusions drawn by the
authors to the effect that "[i]t follows that the ethical code of one species
cannot be translated into that of another" and that "[n]o abstract moral
principles exist outside the particular nature of individual species" (Ruse
and Wilson, 1986, p. 186). The latter conclusion trades on another ambiguity between two senses of *abstract moral principles exist*. It may well be
true that an evolutionary perspective provides a healthy antidote to
"objectivist" moral theories postulating the existence of moral premises
that provide directives for action independent of anyone's awareness of
them, as an analogue to laws of nature, for example. Nevertheless, such
considerations neither establish that there are no such principles nor do
they preclude moral beings from different species formulating principles

that are normative for both. One can imagine that meeting intelligent extraterrestrials with whom we manage to establish communications will resemble the encounters between Europeans and the people of the New World and that the effects on moral thinking will be similar. The argument from evolution does not rule this out.

Nor does it follow that "ethical laws can be changed, at the deepest level, by genetic evolution" (Ruse and Wilson, 1986, p. 186). What presumably can be changed are moral motivators. If the epigenetic account turns out to be correct and applicable to moral behavior, it seems reasonable that the "deep-seated" ethical motivators are subject to slow evolution by natural selection, drift, or the like. But, the "laws" of ethics are not obviously subject to such evolution unless the argument is that under certain conditions we may come to feel so uncomfortable in performing certain kinds of action that we abandon certain ways of behaving, respecting the rights of others for example, and come up with rationales for so doing.

To Nozick's argument that the epigenetic rules mirror an objective code, Ruse and Wilson argue that the evolutionary explanation renders the objective code redundant, because even if the code did not exist, we would still think as we do (Ruse and Wilson, 1986, p. 187). To the argument that this view leads to moral relativism, they respond that moral relativism is not a haunting specter. "The epigenetic rules of mental development are relative only to the species" (Ruse and Wilson, 1986, p. 188). This does not clearly preclude anyone from formulating an ethical code for a class of moral agents or patients that includes members of different species. We are not so precluded unless the epigenetic rules serve as constraints on moral maxims. Neither Ruse nor Wilson has offered any convincing arguments for this strong claim.

RICHARD ALEXANDER AND THE BIOLOGICAL BASIS OF MORALITY

In his recent book, *The Biology of Moral Systems*, R. D. Alexander seeks to carefully circumscribe what biology can and cannot tell us about the nature of morality. He suggests that one cannot derive substantive moral principles from the facts and theory of evolution. However, he believes one can both explain the causal origins of certain principles and explain the evolution of the human capacity to be moral from the facts and theories of evolution. In addition, biological insights provide an empirical basis for successfully altering human social behavior and institutions in ways that will promote the aims and goals of humans. The biological point of view also enables us to come to a better understanding of basic social concepts such as altruism, rationality, and interests.

Alexander's fundamental thesis is that, whereas philosophical analyses of morality recognize that moral and ethical issues arise out of conflicts of interest, such analyses fail to clarify the true nature of human interests. Considerations from evolutionary biology, Alexander argues, show that human interests are ultimately reproductive. A corollary of this thesis is the claim that by exploiting kin selection theory one can show that all forms of sociality, including morality, can be understood in terms of extensions of biological nepotism and indirect reciprocity.

The central task of Alexander's analysis is to relate the way people talk about morality to human evolutionary history (Alexander, 1987, pp. 12f.). His motivation is the perception that the world is in a state of crisis, which he shares with other scientific social reformers such as E. O. Wilson and B. F. Skinner. Civilization as we know it and the continued existence of the human species are imperiled by potential and actual dangers such as ecological disasters, dwindling resources, overpopulation, changing social structures, and the ever present threat of nuclear annihilation posed by the escalating arms race. To avert disaster, Alexander believes we need to come to a better degree of self-understanding than we now possess. Coming to grips with our biological nature and our biological heritage is a crucial stage in the process of increasing our self-awareness. Moral concepts and moral practices have biological underpinnings that, although unknown to us, are capable of leading us to self-destruction. Once exposed, these biological springs and our understanding of how they work will put us in a better position to deal with the pressing social and political questions of our age (Alexander, 1987, pp. 32ff.). Becoming more biologically literate about ourselves is not, in Alexander's view, a trivial task because human beings have evolved a resistance to self-understanding that must be overcome if we are to deal successfully with these social and political problems.

Alexander is no vulgar biological determinist. We are not destined by our biology to behave in rigid and unshakable patterns. Facing the biological basis of our behavior is not the grim prospect of realizing that we are trapped by forces beyond our control. On the contrary, uncovering the biological basis of morality is, he argues, a liberating task because with the knowledge we so gain we will be in a better position to reshape our moral institutions to suit our own desires.

Alexander argues that there are two basic perspectives on the question of how biology might contribute to an understanding of human social behavior. The one, which might be labeled the *determinist view*, holds that biology can be used to identify a core set of essential or unalterable human behaviors. Writers adopting this view tend to see "specific physiological and genetic mechanisms as the link between the biological and social sciences." Those whom Kitcher, in *Vaulting Ambition*, called the *vulgar socio-*

biologists tend to hold this view. E. O. Wilson sometimes sounds as if he holds this view but his considered opinion, as we have seen, is not quite so rigid. The second perspective, which might be labeled the *engineering view*, holds that the primary use of biological information in the social sciences is as the empirical basis for altering human social behavior. Alexander locates his own view here. The function of biology vis à vis the social sciences is to provide predictive and explanatory subtheories from general evolutionary theory, which can then be used to reshape social institutions (Alexander, 1987, pp. 8f.).

Two questions naturally arise: What is a moral system? What does biology tell us about moral systems?

The Nature of Morality

Morality, according to Alexander, arises out of conflicts of interest. Moral systems are practices or institutions, defining right and wrong, that have evolved, or have been designed, to resolve or reduce these conflicts. As such, and in view of the fact that the interests of individual humans are irreducibly in conflict with those of their fellow humans, moral systems are created and sustained by agreements and contracts. "Moral systems are systems of indirect reciprocity" (Alexander, 1987, p. 78).

Morality is, in effect, a constraint on behavior in accordance with which an individual acts and that in the long run promotes the interests of that individual. Human beings accept these constraints in part because they are social creatures and in part because of their pattern of evolutionary development. Not all social animals have moral systems. In fact, as far as we know, human beings are the only animals that exhibit moral behavior. The evolution of morality in humans is associated with the evolution of higher brain functions such as intelligence and self-consciousness.

Philosophers tend to falsely assume that "morality inevitably involves some self-sacrifice" (Alexander, 1987, p. 161). Being moral for Alexander involves behaving altruistically. He reads philosophers as typically assuming that altruistic behavior involves self-sacrifice on the part of the altruist. This view fails to take into consideration two facts. First, altruism directed toward relatives is beneficial to the altruist. The result is that philosophical analyses of self-interest, uninformed by biology, tend to be impoverished and treat self-interest as pertaining primarily to the survival of individual organisms and pleasures enjoyed by the individual. The interests of the self, in Alexander's view, are reproductive interests. Even so, an agent's interest is not so much in the proliferation of one's own offspring but in the proliferation of offspring closely related to one. Actions phenotypically self-sacrificing may be at the same time genetically beneficial. I martyr myself for the cause. A collection is taken up for my widow and offspring. My siblings and close relatives are singled out for admiration. As time passes, they are pointed to with awe: There goes the daughter, or son, or brother, or sister, or cousin of a hero. The group I belonged to confers advantages on my kin, and although I do not survive, my genetic prospects are enhanced.

Second, Alexander alleges philosophers tend to underestimate the complexity of indirect reciprocity. I may genetically profit by trading a short-term sacrifice for a long-term benefit, if my actions are observed by others who will interact with me in the future and are favorably disposed toward me on the basis of their observations.

Finally, the philosophic view fails to take into account both within-group and between-group benefits that redound to individuals who apparently sacrifice their interests for the interests of others (Alexander, 1987, p. 161).

Alexander's view of morality is group centered. It is because humans exist in groups that the possibility of morality exists. If humans were solitary or asexual organisms with no need for companionship and support, then human morality would not have evolved and would not be a factor in human existence. But our sexual natures that make us competitors also force us to be cooperators. Parents must subsume their conflicts of interest to their shared interest in seeing their offspring survive and prosper. Threats from other humans lead families to band together into larger groups, and from such seeds as these complex societies emerge (Alexander, 1987, p. 78).[7]

The theory of morality advanced by Alexander contains the following key elements:

1. Individuals seek their own interests.
2. These interests are ultimately reproductive.
3. The ultimate interests of human individuals are in conflict with the interests of their conspecifics.
4. Cooperation furthers the interests of individuals.
5. Social cooperation is engendered through mechanisms of nepotism and direct and indirect reciprocity.
6. Rules are restraints.

What is new about all of this? Alexander concedes that tracing morality to the need to deal with conflicts of interest is not new. The distinctive biological contribution lies in theses 2 and 3 as well as an emphasis on the centrality of indirect reciprocity as a means of promoting social institutions (Alexander, 1987, pp. 80ff.). We turn now to a more detailed examination of the role of biology in understanding morality.

The Contribution of Biology

Alexander rejects the view that biology offers "easy or direct" answers to moral questions. Evolutionary insights do not lead to moral principles. Particular moral systems or moral principles are not genetically determined nor are they tied to particular genetic endowments. Like all plastic phenotypic traits, they can be altered by suitably manipulating the social environment (Alexander, 1987, p. 11). "To say we are *evolved* to serve the interests of our genes in no way suggests that we are *obliged* to serve them" (Alexander, 1987, p. 40). Our evolved plasticity enables us to both recognize the historical evolution of our social practices and at the same time to change them should we so desire.

According to Alexander, the major contribution of contemporary evolutionary theory to our understanding of the evolution and nature of morality lies in the focus on genic interests, or what Alexander dubs *the mission of the genes.*

For Darwin, who knew nothing of genes, natural selection operated at either the level of the individual organism or at some group level. The modern synthetic theory, grounded as it is in genetics, raises the possibility of levels of opportunity for natural selection to operate that are below the level of the individual organism. Most contemporary sociobiologists, if not all, are so-called genic selectionists. Alexander, although he prefers to distance himself from the label of *sociobiologist,* is no exception.

[N]atural selection has apparently been maximizing the survival by reproduction of genes, as they have been defined by evolutionists, and that, with respect to the activities of individuals, this includes effects on copies of their genes, even copies located in other individuals. In other words, we are evidently evolved not only to aid the genetic materials in our own bodies, by creating and assisting descendants, but also to assist, by nepotism, copies of our genes that reside in collateral (non-descendant) relatives. (Alexander, 1987, pp. 2f.)

Lifetimes have evolved so as to promote survival of the individuals' genetic materials, through individuals producing and aiding offspring and, in some species, aiding other descendants and some non-descendant relatives as well. (Alexander, 1987, p. 37)

Organisms spend varying amounts of time and energy in various stages of their development such as youth, adulthood, and old age, in various activities such as reproduction, foraging, somatic maintenance, and senescing. The division into life stages and effort expenditure varies from species to species. The study of this phenomena is called the *theory of life history strategies*. There is no consensus on the details of the processes involved but, according to Alexander: "The theory of lifetimes most widely accepted among biologists is that individuals have evolved to maximize the likelihood of survival of not themselves, but their genes, and that they do this by reproducing and tending in various ways offspring and other carriers of their own genes—descendant and non-descendant relatives" (Alexander, 1987, p. 38).[8]

The focal points of the evolutionary drama are the genes. Organisms and phenotypes in general exist because they enable genes to deal more successfully with their environment (Alexander, 1987, p. 21). Human organisms are no exception to the rule. As such, human interests are ultimately reproductive regardless of whether they are consciously so or not (Alexander, 1987, p. 139).

Why is this not obvious to everyone? Certainly, although most people would admit to having reproductive interests, they would also maintain that some of their interests are not reproductive even derivatively or indirectly. In this instance, Alexander argues, people's intuitions about their interests are misleading. Human consciousness and intelligence have evolved in complex and subtle ways to facilitate our interactions with others. In Alexander's view, consciousness is an adaptation for competing with other humans for reproductive success.

Consciousness . . . is a game of life in which the participants are trying to comprehend what is in one another's minds before, and more effectively than, it can be done in reverse. (Alexander, 1987, p. 133)

[C]onsciousness and self-awareness are systems designed largely for seeing ourselves as others see us and then altering others' views of ourselves so as to serve our own rather than their interests when there are conflicts. (Alexander, 1987, p. 253)

Consciousness has evolved not only to enable us to outguess others but also to behave in ways that cannot be guessed by others. The techniques and strategies we develop in so doing are often suppressed when, if they were to become known by others, they would be detrimental to us. We are, in effect, self-deceptive about our practices of deceit. The subconscious or unconscious is a storage area for rules that, when followed automatically, are so socially beneficial that it is in our interests to appear to be absolutely committed to them. For example, if we consider honesty a virtue, then we are more likely to trust someone who appears transparently honest than someone who appears honest but only after some deliberation or calculation, however slight. In this way, Alexander argues, we "internalize" the most basic social rights and wrongs and develop a conscience. What has evolved, presumably, is the ability to internalize rules and not the rules themselves, because no particular genetic endowment is associated with any particular moral rule or practice. Thus, honesty is not inherited even though the disposition to be *transparently* honest as opposed to *calculatingly* honest might very well be. The difference between the two is a reflection of different abilities to internalize social norms.

Why should we internalize the rules whereby we live? Alexander conjectures that it is not always in our interests, either proximate or ultimate, for them to be known either by ourself or others (Alexander, 1987, p. 121). If our social practices are based upon deceit, then it is clearly in our interests not to let those with whom we interact in on it. It is also not in our interests for us to know about it. First, self-consciousness makes us uneasy game players and hence less effective. Second, we have evolved a resistance to the discovery of "the genes and their mission" because "bringing genes into our consciousness makes them seem like alien manipulators (which we are evolved to resist)." Finally, "talking directly about our evolutionary background and the mission of the genes and our phenotypes is like making public our most important secret. . . . Each individual has a sphere of secrecy about him, small or large" (Alexander, 1987, p. 121).

Because of our fundamentally diverse genetic interests, which are a result of our sexual natures, our fundamental, genetic, interests are in conflict with the genetic interests of everyone else. Hence, the sphere of secrecy and consequently the sphere of deceit is absolute and irreducible. Understanding our biological nature affords one of the best routes for shrinking these spheres to a minimum, a condition Alexander thinks is essential if any progress is to be made in making the world a safe and sane place for humans by forging effective agreements on long-term international cooperation (Alexander, 1987, pp. 253ff.).

Interests that serve the *needs* of *everyone* or that *everyone disapproves* of are not moral issues, according to Alexander, because they do not involve conflicts of interest. Thus, ridding the world of smallpox is not morally good, although it may be a good thing, because no human wants to defend the interests of smallpox viruses. Actually, it should not matter what anyone *wants*, it is not in any human's genetic interests to defend the interests of smallpox viruses.[9] If, however, the "moral circle" is expanded to include all life forms, then the eradication of smallpox does become a moral issue, because the interests of the viruses themselves become a relevant factor (Alexander, 1987, p. 178).

In like fashion, the survival of the human species is not a moral issue unless someone can be found who thinks that it should not survive (cf. Wilson, 1979, p. 185). "What is a moral issue is whether or not we ought to be allowed to carry out, in our own individual or subgroup interests, behavior that to this or that degree *threatens* everyone's (or for that matter, anyone else's) survival" (Alexander, 1987, p. 180).

Note that Alexander seems to vacillate between the view that moral issues turn on conflicts of interest that are ultimately genetic and the view that moral issues turn on what individuals take to be their interests, as in the smallpox case and the human survival case. If moral issues can arise because of what people take their interests to be, then the link connecting all interests to reproductive interests is considerably weakened.[10] This would appear to be in line with the general sense of Alexander's claim that evolutionary knowledge has no moral content. "The reason that evolutionary knowledge has no moral content is . . . [that] . . . morality is a matter of whose interests one should, by conscious and willful behavior, serve, and how much: evolutionary knowledge contains no messages on this issue. The most it can do is provide information about the reasons for current conditions and predict some consequences of alternative courses of action" (Alexander, 1987, p. 222).

Given this, it should come as no surprise that, when Alexander gets down to the discussion of specific moral issues such as defining acceptable levels of pollution, articulating children's rights and the rights of embryos and the moribund, the distribution of scarce resources, and the arms race, his suggestions are, as he says, "disappointingly nonradical" and commonsensical, "distinguished only by some aspects of attitude in no way restricted to biologists, and by the weighing in of certain kinds of information, especially about conflicts of interest, that are usually not considered" (Alexander, 1987, p. 208).

The fact remains, however, that there is a general resistance by biologists and nonbiologists alike to the suggestion that biology has anything significant to contribute to our understanding of human social behavior. One of the reasons Alexander cites for the current tendency to resist the rapprochement of the biological and the social sciences is the failure of workers in both fields to distinguish between two forms of biological reduction (Alexander, 1987, pp. 20f.). The one, which Alexander terms *proximate reduction*, involves the reduction of biological features to biologically proximate mechanisms. Thus, a biologist who identifies a trait as genetically determined or identifies the genes responsible for a trait is affecting a proximate reduction of the phenomenon in question to its genetic basis: Those vulgar sociobiologists who espouse genetic determinism are practicing a form of this reductionist technique. Alexander does not endorse this approach to the biological analysis of morality although the general technique is a perfectly respectable biological practice and forms the basis of controlled laboratory experiments in behavior and population genetics. The other, which Alexander terms *ultimate reduction*, seeks instead to explain phenomena in terms of their evolutionary origin. Thus, a biologist who explains why certain organisms possess a certain trait by appealing to the selective advantage the possession of that trait conferred on their ancestors is providing an ultimate explanation of the trait in question. This is the approach Alexander endorses with respect to the biological analysis of morality. It is, he says, a theoretical and philosophical approach rather than an experimental one (Alexander, 1987, pp. 17f.). As such, this approach is untouched by the criticisms directed against the vulgar sociobiologist's attempts to extrapolate conclusions derived experimentally or derived from controlled observations on nonhuman populations to the human case where such procedures are either impossible or unsanctioned. Nevertheless, Alexander's position is still open to the charge that it is unwarrantedly reductionistic in certain respects.

Critical Assessment

Despite Alexander's attempt to distance his view from certain illegitimate reductionistic theses, his position displays other reductionist tendencies that are equally questionable.

To begin with, let us examine more carefully the alleged connection between the biological theory of conflicts of interest and the biological theory of moral systems. Alexander contends that the need for and practice of morality arises from the existence of conflicts of interest. For humans, and other sexual organisms, biology tells us that these interests are basically reproductive. "The longer the usual lives of individuals, and the longer individuals continue to interact significantly with one another, the greater will be their adeptness at assessing and acting appropriately with respect to partial confluences of interest, as well as conflicts of interest, and the more complex will be society. This, then, is the basic biological theory of conflicts of interest and therefore of moral systems" (Alexander, 1987, p. 64).

But, even if we concede that conflicts of interest are a necessary condition for the existence of moral systems, it is clear that they are not sufficient. All sexual organisms, in Alexander's view, evince conflicts of interest but only humans have moral systems (see Alexander, 1987, p. 78). All sexual organisms, who must at least cooperate minimally during reproductive acts, have evolved systems and mechanisms for overcoming these conflicts to a certain extent. None of these systems, except certain human systems, are moral systems. A biological theory of conflicts of interest, at best, is a *partial* theory of moral systems.

The sense in which a biological theory of conflicting interests can be only a partial theory of moral systems is as follows. All sexual organisms exhibit inherent conflicts of interest due to their biological natures, but only humans exhibit or display moral systems. In organisms that do not exhibit moral behavior, their conflicts and the resulting behavioral syndromes are, at least in principle, explainable on the basis of evolutionary theory, including kin-selection theory and other physical theories, and genetic, physiological, and ecological information alone. In 'hard-wired' organisms, such as the Hymenoptera, where behavioral plasticity is at a minimum, the behavioral syndromes are more liable to be explained and predicted on the basis of genetic and physiological information alone. In more complicated social organisms such as the primates, birds, and ungulates, where more behavioral plasticity is apparent, the prediction and explanation of typical behavioral patterns is likely to be more complicated and more problematic. These behavioral patterns *can* be understood in terms of the principles of evolution and relevant organismic and ecological data. Such organisms are simply not capable of the reflective, rational, and intentional deliberation characteristic of moral agents. As such, their behavioral activity cannot be said to constitute a true "moral system."

When we get to human beings, however, that is another story. Human beings are capable of reflective rational and intentional deliberation, and because of this they are capable of being moral agents and constructing moral systems. Knowing the relevant organismic and ecological data *plus* the principles of evolution is *not sufficient* to explain *either* why human beings act in the specific ways they do *or* why they adopt or formulate the kinds of moral systems that they do.[11] We cannot explain such behavior or such principles, at least not completely, just because other considerations and reasons can be and are brought into play by these agents. To the extent that they cannot or are not brought into play by such agents, we tend to consider them as less than or other than moral agents.

Three qualifying observations are in order. First, the difference between the human-nonhuman case is very likely to turn out to be a matter of degree rather than a reflection of some difference in kind. I think this is the best reading of the legacy of Darwin on this, although it is not the only one. If the ability to reason, the power of deliberation, and the acquisition of a moral sense, in either the intuitive or judgmental versions, could be plausibly construed as "saltative" evolutionary developments, then one could accept both the Darwinian story that humans and nonhumans are all part of one big biological family and *also* that morality is a phenomenon peculiar to *Homo sapiens*. But, it is not plausible to construe the evolution of reasoning, of deliberation, and of the moral sense as "saltative." These abilities are more than likely complex and composite powers rather than simple powers.[12] Adumbrations of various aspects of these powers are to be found all over the biological map, and it is not in the spirit of Darwinism, as it were, to deny the attribution of proto-rational and proto-moral behavior to nonhumans. Second, we must be prepared to admit with Alexander, Wilson, and others that much of what makes up human moral systems and many moral practices and moral rules may very well be capable of being understood in terms of genetic, physiological, and nonsocial ecological considerations. In this regard, we may well want to adopt some principle of parsimony and explain as much as we can without appealing to the peculiarly human powers of rational deliberation, reflection, and moral choice. Third, there is a "wider" sense of the term *biological*, which includes what is narrowly biological (genetical, physiological, and nonsocial ecological factors) *plus* social and cultural artefacts as well. Moral phenomena, which are brought into being by the activity of biological organisms, may have a "biological" explanation in this wider sense where, in contrast to the Socrates case, relevant "biological" considerations include the giving of reasons, reflecting on reasons, deliberating about actions, and acting in intentional ways. This way of putting the issue *obscures* the real difference between those organisms that have moral systems like ourselves and all other groups of organisms that do not. The difference, even if it is only one of degree, is that human beings are capable of reflecting on what they do and by so doing render themselves capable of acting in ways that those who are cognizant only of the genetic, physiological, and physical factors underlying human activity could neither adequately predict nor adequately comprehend. This ability is what allows us to consciously subvert "the mission of the genes" if we so choose. No other organisms as far as we know have this ability.

The biological theory of conflicts of interest that is endorsed by Alexander treats these conflicts as ultimately reproductive. Indeed, as we have seen, it is not the reproductive interests of organisms that are alleged to be paramount but those of their genes. Natural selection, Alexander noted, "has apparently been maximizing the survival by reproduction of genes" (Alexander, 1987, p. 2). Now there is no doubt that natural selection has the aforementioned effects. The controversial aspect of this position is the further claim that there is selection *for* particular genes or genic combinations (cf. n. 10). That is, are the genes the primary targets or are the gene frequency changes one sometimes observes where selection is present mere *byproducts* of selection *for other* traits or characters? In the former case, talk of the "mission of the genes" is appropriate; in the latter case, it is not.[13] In particular, if changes in gene frequencies are mere byproducts of selection *for* something else, then one can hardly claim that the "interests" of the genes are in any sense paramount.

A further consideration is this. Genic selectionists tend to be arch-reductionists who see only the genic level as of importance for selection.[14] It is conceivable, however, that selection operates at several levels of biological organization and that these levels may then interact with one another in complex ways. If this scenario is correct, then again any attempt to see the significance of all biological activities in terms of a single level or a single process will be woefully inadequate. The debate between these two perspectives is ongoing and unresolved.[15]

Can organisms have proximate interests that are not ultimately reproductive? Alexander's view seems to be that they cannot (cf. n. 7). Most philosophers, he claims, untutored in biology as they are, assume that the proximate and ultimate springs of action can be treated on a par. That is, they tend to talk indifferently of somatic or phenotypic (proximate) and genetic (ultimate) interests. But, this point of view, he alleges, betrays "a failure to understand that proximate causes are evolved because of ultimate causes, and *therefore may be expected to serve them*, while the reverse is not true" (Alexander, 1987, p. 161; emphasis added).

First, note that the emphasized passage does not follow from what comes before. It is quite plausible, especially given Alexander's insistence upon the wonderful plasticity of human beings, that some interests may have evolved that need not in any sense be expected to serve the interests of what brought them about in the first place. One need but recall the dispute between Darwin and Wallace over the evolution of higher mental powers. Wallace resolutely refused to accept that such powers could have evolved by natural selection because they did not serve the reproductive interests of those who possessed them. Darwin was more willing to countenance the evolution of phenotypic traits that could take on a life of their own and thereby free themselves from the leash of their origin.[16]

Second, human beings are hierarchical systems. If there is any truth to hierarchical interaction, the conclusion that proximate causes may be expected to serve ultimate causes must be denied. The interests of human beings need not, indeed *cannot*, be reduced to or explained in terms of the "interests" or the evolution of the "interests" of their genes. Alexander, at times, seems to endorse the prima facie false view that human beings are "one-way" systems; but not always. Higher level interests *can* feed back on lower level processes—a view Alexander endorses when he argues that increased knowledge of our biological natures can be used to reshape our moral systems.

In effect, Alexander's account fails to take seriously the distinction between genetic and phenotypic self-interest. Such interests may or may not be on a par, but they are surely neither identical nor can the one be explained by or reduced to the other. Even if we were to agree that phenotypic self-interests have evolved or exist because of the evolution of ultimate or genetic self-interests, it does not follow that all phenotypic self-interests serve, or even were designed to serve, genetic self-interests.[17] The early evolution of human interests may well have been dominated by the evolution of genetic interests, but this does not rule out the development of interests independent of them.

Finally, Alexander is usually quite careful about distancing himself from those who seek to read political and moral truths in the panorama of evolutionary history and theory, but not always. One of two allegedly evolutionary insights cited by Alexander at the beginning of his study is "[T]he realization that ethics, morality, human conduct, and the human psyche are to be understood only if societies are seen as collections of individuals seeking their own self interests" (Alexander, 1987, p. 3).

If correct, this is a major "insight," insofar as it appears to rule out, on biological grounds, any holistic social, political, and moral theories. But this cannot be right even on Alexander's own terms. If we are *not obliged* to serve the interests of *our genes* surely we are not obliged to serve the interests of our phenotypic selves. And if we are not so obliged then it need not be the case that we can understand the full complexity of our social institutions by focusing on those interests.

Conclusion

John Dewey, in a famous essay, "The Implications of Darwinism for Philosophy," saw Darwinism as a major force in the dismantling of the essentialistic and idealistic modes of thought that have dominated Western philosophy since Plato. In the field of ethics, Dewey argued that Darwinism ruled out a supernaturalistic basis for ethics and shifted the burden of formulating the basis of ethics to human beings who would now have to take responsibility themselves for their values.

Darwin himself saw evolutionary theory as a means for explaining the origin of the moral sense. His own account contains traces of a "group selectionist" point of view, but kin selection theory and the theory of reciprocal altruism have suggested how socially beneficial behaviors, which include moral behavior, can be explained in terms of individual selection at the genic level. This is illuminating insofar as it shows how much of moral behavior *might* be explained in terms of evolution by natural selection. However, showing that a particular scenario is *possible* does not show that it is actually the way things occurred. And here lies the rub for the minimalist claim that evolutionary theory, or the theory of natural selection, explains at least the evolution of the moral sense or the evolution of the capacity to be moral. The sticky point in all causal analyses of phylogenetic change is the question of evidence. It is hard enough to reconstruct the causal forces behind phylogenetic changes using geological and paleontological evidence, but at least there is *some* physical evidence upon which we can build a theoretical reconstruction. In the case of the evolution of morality, and the evolution of cultural phenomena in general, there is little physical evidence at best. We cannot even say with any degree of certainty whether morality is an adaptation or not. It would probably be conceded by most that being moral confers selective advantage on those individuals who *today* possess it, although even here I suspect the evidence is at best anecdotal and hypothetical, but we have no idea what proto-moral behavior was like or whether it conferred any selective advantage on those who practiced it. Thus, even in the least controversial case for the significance of evolutionary thinking about moral phenomena, the case is still rather weak.

When we move to more controversial theses, the case gets weaker still. There is no need to rehearse here all the arguments offered for and against the view that specific systems of values are encoded in or entailed by our evolutionary heritage. Suffice it to say that the injunction, "Follow nature," leaves us unmoved because, as many have pointed out, both self-centered and cooperative behavior are "sanctioned" by natural selection.

However, although we may not expect any moral guidance from evolutionary biology, can we not, at least, expect some insight about what makes us tick? This of course is the brunt of Alexander's thesis. Such information would specifically help us to understand how we have come to be the way we are and also help us shape the way we would like to go in the future, not by providing guidelines, but by providing parameters and predictions that might serve as potential checks on proposed courses of action.

Reservations about phylogenetic reconstructions should give us pause with regard to the biological basis of the *historical* origin of morality. Alexander's biological theory of interests purports to explain *all* moral systems and it may be construed as providing a biological basis of the *conceptual* content of moral systems as well.[18] It is not clear to me whether this is part of Alexander's program. If it is, we should be chary of it as well, if the considerations raised in the last section have any merit.

This leaves for biology the role of providing an empirical basis for future policy considerations. Here, one would think, there should be a role for biology to play. After all, we are biological creatures. Of course, we are physical creatures as well but no one suggests that understanding quantum mechanics is a sine qua non for understanding human nature or as a guard against rash and ill-conceived social policies. Why is that? What is so special about our biological natures?[19] The answer seems to be that, in some sense, our biological natures are "closer" to moral and social phenomena than our quantum mechanical natures. Biological factors are more relevant. Considerations from chemistry, which are more or less intermediate between quantum mechanics and biology, show why this is the case. Our chemical nature, we are prepared to believe, is relevant to understanding our social and moral behavior. The reason is that we are witnesses every day to the effects of such things as diet and drugs on human behavior. We can also use our chemical understanding of human beings to manipulate their behaviors. Our quantum mechanical natures, so far, are inaccessible to human intervention and manipulation. In the future, should such intervention and manipulation become possible, I dare say quantum mechanical considerations would become relevant to morality as well.

Our biological systems work, for the most part, through chemical agents. Our proximate biological natures are relevant to understanding our moral and social behavior, at least insofar as they determine the limits of such behaviors. Hidden, but equally relevant, at least as far as our understanding of the proximate biological mechanisms that produce our behavior is immature, are considerations about our ultimate biological natures that evolutionary analysis reveals.[20] This is the rationale for promoting biological understanding as a component of the formulation of social policy.

There is, no doubt, something to this. The question is, how much? The problem is that we do not know, for complex human social behaviors, how to distinguish biological from cultural factors. The relevant experimental data are unavailable and probably unattainable, even if we could figure out how to identify the relevant social or biological components of particular behavior patterns. As was noted earlier, cultural factors are biological as well, in an extended sense of biological. The point of the remark is this. The phenotypic traits of organisms are an interactive product of genetic and environmental factors. This is often expressed in the equation

$$P = G + E + G{\cdot}E + \text{Higher Order Terms}$$

where P is a phenotypic character trait, G represents the relevant genetic factors, E represents the relevant environmental factors and $G{\cdot}E$ represents the contribution due to interaction between genes and the environment. For traits that can be quantified, this formula provides a convenient tool for partitioning the variance due to genetic, environmental, and interaction components. For laboratory organisms, such as *Drosophila* or *Tribolium*, it is relatively easy to control the physical environmental factors and thereby to measure the extent to which variation in particular organismic traits is a function of differences in media concentration, moisture content, alcohol presence, temperature differences, and lighting conditions. Not all traits are so analyzable, but many are. Given the evolutionary continuity between humans and other organisms, it is reasonable to assume that a similar formula holds for human traits as well. Because moral and social behaviors are appropriate aspects of Ps, the formula suggests that such behaviors have genetic and environmental components. So far so good. The problem arises when one tries to establish specific results based on the formula. For complex social traits, such as moral characteristics and behaviors, the problems are severe.

The obvious criticism, which has been leveled by many critics of human sociobiology, is that the experimental conditions under which the formula is valid have not and are not likely to be realized in the study of humans. The obvious point is that researchers are precluded, on moral grounds, from treating human beings as experimental subjects in a way that would be needed to factor traits into relevant genetic and environmental contributions. Twin studies have been urged as a method of avoiding this problem. But twin studies in the past have been shown, on reflection, to be seriously flawed in a number of respects. Currently, a new series of long-term studies on twins is being conducted at the University of Minnesota, which are claimed to be as flawless as possible under the circumstances. The final results are not in and definitive judgment on their validity and reliability will have to be deferred. Even if these studies should succeed where other studies have failed, there is reason to suspect that there is an inherent flaw in any methodology that relies on the formula for human studies at this time. Even if, for example, we overcame our scruples and permitted controlled experiments on cloned embryos and even if we had the wherewithal (in terms of patience, money, and human resources) to complete the study, a formidable problem would still remain. It is this: We have every reason to suspect that the relevant environmental factors that significantly influence the development of complex social and moral traits are not going to be simple factors like temperature, humidity, and food concentration. Rather, the relevant factors are liable themselves to be complex moral and social traits. The simple fact is we now have no adequate or even halfway adequate theory that would give us any clue as to how to factor the complex social environments in which humans live and thrive into controllable components. Even if we permitted ourselves to perform controlled experiments on human beings we have no clue as to what we should control or how. The same goes for field studies such as the twin studies. Until we have a clearer understanding of the makeup of cultural and social environments, all such studies are going to be subject to nagging doubts concerning the validity of the controls—either imposed by experimental manipulations or as they are perceived by field investigators. Note that this is not an argument to the effect that such studies are in principle impossible—only that as presently performed they are inconclusive and potentially misleading and to be done well they would require the investment of resources that may very well be put to better use elsewhere.

Alexander's analysis was written at a time when the cold war was still raging and the threat of nuclear annihilation seemed imminent to many observers. With the collapse of the Soviet Union, tensions between East and West have eased and the imminent danger of a nuclear holocaust has considerably diminished. But the victory by default of the American way of life has not led to a *pax Americana*. Instead, the splintering of the old

Soviet Union has fostered the reemergence of old and suppressed ethnic and regional conflicts. These conflicts, although local and limited in their scope at present, are potentially destabilizing factors for world order. Negotiations to resolve these disputes will ramble on and succeed or fail independent of the considerations of evolutionary biologists; but this is a practical point. From a theoretical point of view, and in the long run perhaps from a practical point of view, studies of the biological basis of human moral behavior such as those envisioned by Alexander are of extreme importance. For one thing, and this is no mean feat, they serve to keep philosophers honest. Moral reasoning and practical rationality rest on empirical premises as well as moral principles. Alexander is quite right to suggest that philosophers often tend to overlook the implications of human biology as a source for appropriate empirical assumptions about human behavior, and that they do so at our peril.

ROBERT RICHARDS AND THE REVISED THEORY

In an appendix to his book, *Darwin and the Emergence of Evolutionary Theories of Mind and Behavior*, Robert Richards attempts to resuscitate and revitalize a version of evolutionary ethics that derives from the views of Darwin and Spencer. From a broadly naturalistic perspective, Richards defends a historiographical "natural selection model," which he labels *NSM*. The model suggests that the development of ideas be construed along the lines of the evolution of species (Richards, 1987, p. 15). The structural features of the model are analogues of the biological theory of natural selection. The analogues to biological species are conceptual systems. Conceptual change is the analogue of biological change. The analogue of the gene pool is what we might call the concept pool. The role of genetic links or ties is played by logical and historical links. Different expressions of a theory are analogous to different phenotypes (Richards, 1987, p. 15). Variation in ideas, which are the elements of scientific evolution, is generally produced by recombination not through novel "mutation." Conceptual systems "live" in three different "communities," the mind of the scientist, the scientific community, and the general culture. All "ecological" factors need to be assessed. The NSM has the virtue, Richards argues, of focusing attention on historical details that tend to be overlooked or downplayed from the perspective of other approaches to the history of science. In construing conceptual systems as analogues to biological species, the NSM emphasizes the importance of understanding the growth of ideas in terms of all the constraints of the various intellectual and social environments in which it "lives."

The NSM is a descendant of a model first proposed by Donald Campbell (Richards, 1987, p. 579). As such, it is a contribution to what has become known as *evolutionary epistemology*. Richards uses the NSM to shape a historical narrative of the evolution of evolutionary ways of thinking about mind and behavior. In so doing, he hopes to straddle a middle ground between "presentism" or "Whiggism" (the view that the events of the past are to be construed as leading up to the views of the present), on the one hand, and "blind contextualism" (the view advocated by Martin Rudwick in *The Great Devonian Controversy* and, according to Richards [n. 25, p. 18]), honored more in the breach than in the observance), on the other. The NSM model directs the historian to a sensitive consideration of what was taken to be relevant at the time of the episodes under consideration but does not deny to the historian the right to make value judgments from the perspective of the present day. In addition, the NSM directs the historian to view the events of the past from a perspective in the middle of an extreme "internalism" (which sees the evolution of scientific ideas as more or less completely independent of context) and an extreme "externalism" (which views context as everything, even for the evolution of science). Just as the evolution of biological lineages is subject to "internal" constraints due to the structural features of the organisms under consideration as well as "external" constraints due to factors in the environments in which they find themselves, so too with conceptual lineages. (For an extended discussion, see Bradie 1992a.) In the light of this broadly naturalistic outlook, Richards argues that an appropriate appeal to Darwinian principles can provide not only an explanation of the evolution of ethics but a justification of ethics as well.

Evolutionary Ethics Redux

The standard accounts suggest that one of the fruits of the Darwinian revolution was the sundering of ethics from naturalistic considerations. Those, like Spencer, who tried to read some morality from the facts of nature were accused, at the very least, of committing the "naturalistic fallacy." At the very worst, they were led, by the illogic of trying to derive "oughts" from "ises" to a defense of ruthless capitalism or racist ideologies that were construed as abetting the rise of Nazism.

Although "evolutionary theory is not compatible with every social and moral philosophy, it can accommodate a broad range of historically representative doctrines." To reach particular moral or political conclusions, one must supplement the evolutionary considerations with special premises drawn from particular political or social theories: "an evolutionary approach to the moral and social environment does not inevitably support a particular ideology" (Richards, 1987, p. 598).

This indeterminacy should not be read as the inevitable outcome of trying to utilize a theory that commits an egregious fallacy. First, moral theories should not be held accountable, in themselves, for the evils done under their names. Second, the term *evolutionary ethics* covers a number of different theories and not all of them necessarily commit the alleged fallacy. Richards proposes to develop an ethical theory that he characterizes as a modified, updated Darwinian account. This theory he calls *RV*, for "revised version." Having presented his view, he considers some pressing objections to evolutionary accounts of ethics and defends his view against these objections.

Both Ruse and Richards claim to be constructing an evolutionary account of ethics from a broadly naturalistic perspective. For Ruse, this means that one can do an end run around naturalistic fallacy objections by rejecting the claim for a justification of ethical principles in the first place. Richards, on the other hand, rejects the view that an evolutionary ethics must commit the naturalistic fallacy. In particular, he thinks RV does not commit the fallacy as it is usually understood. It does derive norms from facts but, in Richards's account, all normative theories do this. The resolution of this apparent contradiction lies in the contention that the "so-called" naturalistic fallacy is not really a "fallacy" (Richards, 1987, p. 596).

Richards summarizes Darwin's moral theory as follows. In *The Descent of Man*, Darwin construes the moral sense as a kind of social instinct. Social instincts are the factors that bind animals into social wholes. The chief mechanism for the propagation of such instincts, for Darwin, was community selection, which is Richards's term to characterize the form of "group selection" Darwin invokes to account for the differential proliferation of tribal groups (Richards, 1987, p. 599). Darwin's theory involves four overlapping stages in the evolution of the moral sense: (1) social instincts bind "proto-men" into social communities that can then serve as units of community selection; (2) with the development of memory and intelligence, organisms will be able to become aware of cases where behavior dictated by social instincts was abrogated by other needs and wants, thus, the beginning of conscience; (3) linguistic competence leads to the codification of rules and regulations; (4) individuals can then be prevailed upon to acquire socially desirable habits that in turn will direct the social instincts into appropriate behaviors (Richards, 1987, p. 599).

In the ontogenetic development of individual organisms, moral codes become "second nature," and Darwin argued that they formulated implicit rules in doing so. "Darwin, a child of his scientific time, also believed that such rational principles, first induced from instinctive reactions, might be transformed into habits, and then infiltrate the hereditary substance to augment and reform the biological legacy of succeeding generations" (Richards, 1987, p. 600).

As we noted earlier, Darwin rejected the imputation that his moral theory was just a version of Utilitarianism. He saw his theory as a refutation of Utilitarianism. Pleasure was neither the usual motive nor the standard for moral conduct. Moral acts, in Darwin's view, were intrinsically altruistic. The usual motives were evolved social instincts that placed no value on the pleasure of the actor but directed action toward social welfare, and the standard was not happiness but the general good, "the welfare and survival of the group" (Richards, 1987, p. 600). Darwin also noted that people often acted as if they were what we now call *reciprocal altruists* and would also be constrained by social pressures and not "conscience" but they recognized its force even if they did not always heed it.

Richards notes Darwin's indebtedness to Mackintosh who distinguished between the moral sense, which motivates us to action, and the moral criterion, by means of which we judge what is right and wrong. Their usual coincidence was, we have seen, one of the major problems discussed by the eighteenth century British moral theorists. In Richards's view, "Darwin believed . . . he could provide a perfectly natural explanation of the linkage. . . . Under the aegis of community selection, men in social groups evolved sets of instinctive responses to preserve the welfare of the community. This common feature of acting for the community welfare would then become, for intelligent creatures who reacted favorably to the display of such moral impulses, an inductively derived but dispositionally encouraged criterion of appropriate behavior. What served nature as the criterion of selecting behavior became the standard of choice for her creatures as well" (Richards, 1987, p. 601).

On this foundation Richards proposes to construct a revised view of Darwin's ethical theory. The revised view, RV, has two parts. First, there is a factual component, consisting of a frankly speculative theory of human evolution. Second, there is a normative component that consists of a moral theory based on the speculative theory. Richards's primary logical and conceptual aim is to defend the conditional implication from part 1 to part 2 and show that it involves or need involve no fallacy. The truth of the speculative theory of human evolution is a separate issue on which Richards does not dwell save to assure the reader that the theory is not fatally flawed.

In Richards's view, the "moral sense" is "a set of innate dispositions that in appropriate circumstances move the individual to act in specific ways for the good of the community" (Richards, 1987, pp. 603ff.). The driving mechanism for the evolution of the moral sense is kin selection "aided perhaps by group selection on small communities." Childhood associations provide the basis for discriminating blood relationship and provide cues for determining kinship: "early human societies consisted principally of extended kin groups, of clans . . . [upon which] natural selection might operate . . . to promote a great variety of altruistic impulses, all having the ultimate purpose of serving the community good." In response to Sahlins's criticism that human relationships are often calculated on the basis of cultural rather than biological kinship, Richards contends that "on average the cultural representation of kin will serve nature's ends." The breakdown of clan and kinship barriers and the promotion of universalistic ethical attitudes is a result of the evolution of intelligence and cultural traditions.

RV differs from the Wilson-Ruse view in the following respect. Wilson and Ruse consider reciprocal or contract altruism to be the highest form of morality, higher even than "authentic" altruism or that form of altruism which emerges as a result of group selection. Richards sees "authentic" altruism as the "higher" form. The argument rests on the distinction between empirical and moral justification, a distinction Ruse and Wilson reject. For Richards, an empirical justification of altruism consists in providing an empirical explanation of the evolution of altruism. The speculative theory of group selection that is the empirical component of RV provides such a theoretical explanation. To establish the normative credentials of "authentic altruism," one must provide a "moral justification" as well. This "moral justification" will show authentic altruism to be "morally superior" to reciprocal altruism. In effect, where Ruse and Wilson see the naturalistic turn as signifying the rejection of any appeals for the justification (as opposed to mere explanation) of moral principles, Richards's brand of naturalism seeks to provide a justification that has naturalistic credentials.

Richards's account rests on his analysis of the sorts of objections that can be and are raised against evolutionary ethics. A careful consideration of these kinds of objections leads him to his view that the naturalistic fallacy is not a fallacy. On that basis, he attempts to provide what he considers to be a moral justification for RV. That justification, although grounded in factual assumptions, commits no fallacy. To properly assess his attempt, we need first to examine his analysis of the potential objections to his theory.

Richards distinguishes two kinds of objections to evolutionary ethics. First, there are challenges to their biological adequacy. Second, there are challenges to their moral adequacy. Objections of the first kind are to the effect that human behaviors are too complex to be reduced to genetic factors and include suspicions about the adequacy of the "group" selection mechanisms invoked by Darwin and the adequacy of kin selection accounts to explain the extension of ethical considerations to nonrelatives. Richards gives these objections short shrift. Because no empirical consensus on these questions has yet emerged, Richards concludes that such objections are not fatal to RV.

The second group of objections is to the moral adequacy of evolutionary ethics. Richards, following Carnap (1956), distinguishes between *framework* questions that challenge the fundamental principles common to all evolutionary theories and *internal* questions that challenge the structural relations internal to different versions of evolutionary theories of ethics. Framework objections amount to challenges to the very idea of an evolutionary ethics. Internal objections are objections to particular formulations of evolutionary ethics. Richards also distinguishes between ethics as a descriptive discipline (where claims require empirical justification) and ethics as an imperative discipline (where claims require moral justification). Thus, one can argue that, as a matter of fact, human beings regard altruistic behavior as moral. An empirical justification of this claim would consist in an evolutionary explanation of the origin of such sentiments. But, the mere fact that humans have been selected to think that altruistic acts are moral does not justify our belief that they are so. For this, we need another independent justificatory argument.

With these distinctions in mind, Richards goes on to consider three objections to evolutionary ethics. The first objection rests on the observation that "moral altruism" has a different meaning from "biological altruism." Hence, the former cannot be explained in terms of the latter. Richards acknowledges the differences but contends that there is a common core meaning to both usages, which he labels *action altruism*. The key idea is that an action is altruistic in this sense if the actor is motivated by altruistic motives. It is an empirical assumption of RV that organisms have evolved to act on altruistic motives through the action of kin and community selection. This is the core that human altruism and animal altruism share. For humans, "an action is good only if it is intentionally performed from a certain kind of motive and can be justified by that motive." Richards thus sees his view as in the nonconsequentialist tradition of Aristotle, Aquinas, and Kant (Richards, 1987, pp. 608f.).

This leads to a second objection. Given that to be moral means to act from altruistic motives, this raises the problem that either animals are moral creatures (because they have the same kinds of motives) or animal altruism does not arise from altruistic motives. If the latter, then the evolutionary explanation of human morality in terms of animal altruism is deficient (Richards, 1987, p. 609). This objection is defused by invoking a distinction between motives and intentions. Moral acts must be motivated by altruistic motives and the agent must intend to act from that motive. Animals can act on the basis of altruistic motives but they do not and cannot form intentions to so act. From the point of view of RV, nonhuman animals are not moral creatures. As will be made evident in the next chapter, which discusses some recent attempts to invoke Darwinism to extend the moral mantle to nonhuman animals, the notion of a "moral creature" is complex. Animals can be moral creatures in one of two senses. They may be moral agents or moral patients deserving of moral consideration.

From the perspective of RV, which requires intentionality as a condition of agency, nonhuman animals are not moral agents. Given the nonconsequentialist character of RV, I suspect that they are not due moral consideration either. We are not required to take their possible suffering into account when coming to decide what is the moral thing to do. So, animals are not moral creatures in RV in either of these two senses.

The third objection is a framework objection that calls into question the very idea of an evolutionary account of morality. Moral activity presupposes the possibility of free action. Evolutionary accounts seem to preclude this possibility. Therefore, evolutionary accounts are deficient. There are four responses to this charge. First, as Richards rightly points out, the problem of free will is not unique to evolutionary theories of ethics. Second, "an evolutionary account of why men generally act for the community good does not invalidate a logically autonomous argument that concludes this same standard is the ultimate moral standard" (Richards, 1987, p. 611). Third, even if evolution dictates that the community good is the highest good, how this is realized in particular circumstances requires the use of "improvable reason" (Richards, 1987, p. 612). Finally, "the evolutionary perspective indicates that external forces do not conspire to wrench moral acts from a person. Rather, man is ineluctably a moral being" (Richards, 1987, p. 612).

So much for the empirical justification of RV. It remains to see whether Richards can make good on his claim that it is possible to construct a validating moral justification for RV which, although rooted in empirical assumptions, commits no fallacy. The defense is in two parts. First, Richards tries to establish that the "naturalistic fallacy" is not, or rather, need not be fallacious. Second, he constructs a justificatory argument to establish the moral credentials of RV. Let us examine the claim that the naturalistic fallacy is no fallacy.

The naturalistic fallacy, classically understood, involves the derivation of ethical imperatives from evolutionary facts. Understood this way, it is thought to arise in systems like Haeckel's, which argue that evolutionary considerations show the present state of society to be morally best, or in systems such as Julian Huxley's, which argue that evolutionary considerations point out trends that indicate tendencies that are good (Richards, 1987, p. 613). It may be surprising not to see Herbert Spencer on this list. After all, the very term *the naturalistic fallacy* was applied to Spencer's evolutionary ethics by its inventor, G. E. Moore. But Richards thinks not. As we have seen in Chapter 3, Mill, in *Utilitarianism*, characterized Spencer as an anti-Utilitarian. Spencer replied with two correctives. First, he argued that "the greatest happiness" was the moral end not the proximate end of human conduct. Humans had evolved in such a way that they behave in accordance with the principle of utility, but they do not make proximate self-interested calculations using the principle as Bentham seemed to suggest. Richards comments that, for Spencer, "the evolutionary perspective demonstrates that moral judgments are not vitiated by calculations of individual gain" (Richards, 1987, p. 301). Second, Spencer distinguished between the evolutionary psychology of moral sentiment and the logically autonomous moral science of norms, deriving from this sentiment. As Spencer put it in his letter to Mill, empirical laws based on planetary observations stand to theoretical astronomical laws as calculations of utility stand to moral science as the ethics of the Utilitarians stands to the ethics of Spencer. Spencer writes:

> Morality properly so called—the science of right conduct—has for its object to determine *how* and *why* certain modes of conduct are detrimental, and certain other modes beneficial . . . I conceive it to be the business of Moral Science to deduce, from the laws of life and the conditions of existence, what kinds of action necessarily tend to produce happiness, and what kinds to produce unhappiness. Having done this, its deductions are to be recognized as laws of conduct; and are to be conformed to irrespective of a direct estimation of happiness or misery. . . . Perhaps an analogy will most clearly show my meaning. During its early stages, planetary Astronomy consisted of nothing more than accumulated observations respecting the positions and motions of the sun and planets; from which accumulated observations it came by and by to be empirically predicted, with an approach to truth, that certain of the heavenly bodies would have certain positions at certain times. But the modern science of planetary Astronomy consists of deductions from the law of gravitation—deductions showing why the celestial bodies *necessarily* occupy certain places at certain times. Now, the kind of relation which thus exists between ancient and modern Astronomy, is analogous to the kind of relation which, I conceive, exists between the Expediency-Morality [of the Utilitarians], and Moral Science properly so-called. (Bain, 1884, pp. 721–722)

Spencer's objection to Utilitarianism is that, at best, it tells us which modes of conduct are beneficial or detrimental but it does not tell us why they are so.

Richards remarks: "Spencer understood the difference between an evolutionary psychology of morals and moral science proper" (Richards, 1987, p. 302). Richards then suggests that, properly understood, Spencer's ethics does not commit the naturalistic fallacy. But in the letter to Mill it seems clear that Spencer identifies laws of nature with moral laws. This is not quite the naturalistic fallacy if that fallacy is construed as taking "ises" for "oughts" or deriving moral rules from natural facts, *but* it is somewhat problematic insofar as Spencer holds that just as "natural laws" are "derived" from facts about natural bodies so "moral laws" are to be "derived" from facts about what tends to make us happy.

Richards tries to rescue Spencer by arguing that the identification involves a complex and convoluted argument. Spencer's argument as reconstructed by Richards is as follows:

1. Progressive social adaptation leads to maximizing the freedom of each individual.
2. Maximizing the freedom of each individual leads to the greatest good for the greatest number.
3. The greatest happiness produces the moral end of conduct.
4. Justice for all and maximum freedom for each produces the greatest happiness.
5. The evolutionary end of greatest happiness equals the moral end of greatest happiness.
6. Therefore, evolutionary laws are moral principles (Richards, 1987, p. 308).

This argument leaves much to be desired as Richards himself acknowledges. Nevertheless, Richards acquits Spencer of the charge of committing the naturalistic fallacy on the grounds that Spencer did not *naively* "identify the evolutionary process with the moral process." Spencer had three arguments: (1) the general end of evolution, which amounts to complete adaptation to the social state, leads to equal freedom; (2) the general moral end equals the greatest happiness (as distributive justice); and (3) end_1 of evolution = end_2 of morality. The problem with this argument is that it equivocates on the term *end*. Here end_1 = last stage; end_2 = goal. The last stage of any process could be said to be the goal as well, but then the ambiguity is transferred to *goal*. Goals involve points or purposes where mere natural ends do not.

Richards claims that "[w]hat is at stake in defending Spencer against the objections of Huxley, Sidgwick, and Moore is not that each of his individual arguments rings solid—they certainly do not—but rather that the strategy of employing arguments in this fashion is sound, or at least does not commit the putative fallacy" (Richards, 1987, p. 325).

In any case, RV does not commit the naturalistic fallacy, either by identifying the present with the good or by identifying trends as moving toward the good. Instead, RV "maintains that the criterion of morally approved behavior will remain constant [why? because we have been selected to so think by group selection forces], while the conception of what particular acts fall under the criterion will continue to change" (Richards, 1987, p. 614).

Although RV does not commit the naturalistic fallacy, it does rest on empirical assumptions, as do all ethical theories. These assumptions are of three kinds. First, there are framework assumptions about human nature (Richards, 1987, p. 614f.). We have addressed the scope and nature of such assumptions in Chapter 4. Second, there are assumptions that connect the terms of the theory with the goods and services of the particular social communities in which the systems are realized. Acts forbidden to us may be sanctioned by others, and we may agree that they are good and that those who commit them are virtuous while not relieving us "of the obligation to stay, if we could, the [Inca] priest's hand from plunging in the knife" (Richards, 1987, p. 615). Third, there are assumptions about how the highest principles are justified. One might appeal to higher principles or one might appeal to a rule of inference of the form "Conclude as sound ethical injunctions what moral leaders preach" (Richards, 1987, p. 616). One might object that such arguments do not yield moral conclusions from purely factual premises because the rule of inference is a meta-ethical proposition or the rule of inference endorses an ethical imperative. Richards rejects both objections. Arguments from factual premises to moral conclusions that rely on moral inference rules do not illegitimately derive moral conclusions from factual premises nor do they involve using inference rules that embody implicit moral imperatives. The moral rules of inference are no more premises than are logical rules of inference. Second, the moral rules of inference license the conclusion that A is good or bad, but not "Do (or avoid) A" (Richards, 1987, p. 617).

This line of reasoning works if the parties agree about the framework rules. If not, what then? Typically, according to Richards, we appeal to common sense and what people do. But, here again, the situation is no different in morals from that in logic. Modus ponens and the like rest on similar considerations.

Richards considers three potential objections to this view and seeks to defuse them. Given that the moral rules are certified by appeal to the consensus of a group of moral agents, does this not lead to moral relativism? Second, to what reference class should we appeal? Finally, there is a greater consensus about logical principles than moral ones. Does this weaken the analogy? Richards concedes the point that the appeal to logical beliefs and practices yields a greater consensus than the appeal to moral beliefs and practices but denies that this undermines the point that some such appeal is the ground for our acceptance of moral principles. From a naturalistic perspective what other appeal could there be? The proper reference class is the class of moral agents, which on evolutionary grounds we should expect to be quite high because evolution has also produced what we take to be a large class of rational agents. Why then is there so much more disagreement about moral principles? According to Richards, the disagreement is only apparent. Many cases of apparent disagreement about moral principles arise from false beliefs. In the case of the Klu Klux Klan, most are probably quite moral—they just have false beliefs about races and so forth. The same presumably holds for the Incas and the Nazis. Richards's answer to the charge of moral relativism turns on the claim that the relativism is apparent only. From the point of view of RV, moral agents have evolved, under the pressure of group selection, to accept the communal good as the highest moral virtue. The "depth" ethical perspective of all such agents is the same. The "surface" dissimilarities of apparently different moral systems are a reflection of different environmental pressures and diverse belief systems.

This does not yet provide a justification of the system, but we are faced with the following dilemma. All attempts to justify principles lead either to an infinite regress or to an appeal to human beliefs and practices. If infinite regresses are ruled out, then all that is left is an empirical appeal. "So moral principles [and logical principles as well] ultimately can be justified only by facts" (Richards, 1987, p. 619). Because every ethical system must derive its norms from facts, "either the naturalistic fallacy is no fallacy, or no ethical system is justified." If no ethical system is justified, then Hitler and St. Francis are on a par. Hence, Richards concludes the naturalistic fallacy is no fallacy (Richards, 1987, p. 620).

There seems to be a sleight of hand here. Even if we grant that all principles have empirical warrant in the sense explained by Richards, we can still go on to distinguish between those systems that derive ethical conclusions from factual premises, and that, therefore, do commit the naturalistic fallacy in a narrow sense, from those that do not. If Richards agrees, but argues that RV does not commit the naturalistic fallacy in any narrow sense, then we must press the ground upon which the troublesome alleged moral sanctions are hidden in rules of inference and not in the premises. Is there a general rule for deciding between cases, to which we can appeal before we know how the case is going to turn out? If so, then the claim that the ethics is hidden in the principles and hence no worse than the case for logical rules of inference would be more persuasive than if the banishment occurs on a case-by-case basis, in which case, special pleading may be suspected. Note that Ruse and Wilson, faced with the same dilemma, opt for the conclusion that no ethical systems *are* justified. From their point of view, the best an evolutionary ethics can do is explain the appearance and maintenance of moral principles. No justifications are forthcoming. This is not, however, Richards's view. Let us turn to his attempt to provide an evolutionary justification for RV.

For RV, "community welfare is the highest moral good" (Richards, 1987, p. 620). This is a general norm that serves to justify the particular norms and values of different societies. These norms and values are justified to the extent that it can be shown that "all things considered, following such maxims would contribute to the community welfare" (Richards, 1987, p. 620). It remains to show that RV as a whole is justified. Richards offers three arguments to establish that fact.

The first two arguments are variations on a theme borrowed from Gewirth (1982) and rest on the fact that "Evolution . . . has constituted human beings not only to be moved to act for the community good, but also to approve, endorse, and encourage others to do so" (Richards, 1987, p. 622). This first argument is open to the obvious objection that "just because evolution has outfitted men with a moral sense of commitment to the community welfare . . . does not impose any obligation" (Richards, 1987, p. 622). Recall that T. H. Huxley had earlier rejected the appeal to evolution for moral sanctions on the ground that evolution produced the thief as well as the saint. Richards acknowledges that not every tendency with which evolution has outfitted us carries with it an obligation to behave in certain ways. He tries to distance moral behavior that is grounded in altruism from the behaviors of thieves or bullies. We are obligated to be moral but have no obligation to steal or behave aggressively. What is the difference? The difference, according to Richards, rests on the fact that evolution has shaped human nature in such a way that moral behavior is altruistic. Only "oughts" that arise in contexts that "comprise the complex traits which produce altruistic behavior" will be "moral 'oughts'." The thief, insofar as his or her nature is shaped by evolution, may be said to be under an "obligation" to steal when certain opportunities arise, but this "obligation," although an "ought" of sorts, is not a "moral" obligation. The idea seems to be this. Evolution has shaped human nature in a number of ways. One of these ways is the "moral way," in which considerations of altruism and acting for the community good are relevant. Others might include the "thieving way," the "aggressive way," the "logical way," and so on. Each of these "contexts" supports a number of "ought" conditionals. Only the "moral way" supports moral "oughts."

This leads to an obvious second objection. Granted that evolution has produced in us a tendency to promote the community good or to act altruistically, why "ought" we do so? Richards responds to this objection by claiming that the justification rests on the reliance on a rule of inference of the form "From the premise that one is in a structured context, conclude that one ought to act in ways appropriate to the context" (Richards, 1987, p. 623). This trades on the parallel between logical principles and moral principles. When in a moral context, one is morally obligated to act in ways appropriate to the context. When in a logical context, one is logically obligated to act in ways appropriate to that context. The justification for the use of such principles rests on an appeal to the beliefs and practices of moral or rational agents as the case may be. No other justification is possible.

The second justifying argument is an elaboration of the first (Richards, 1987, pp. 623f.). The ultimate justification of RV rests on the facts of evolutionary theory. These facts, as stipulated by Richards, provide evidence for "man's constitution as an altruist." We are then led to identify altruism with morality. The conclusion is that "since men so constituted are moral, they morally ought to promote the community good. "

The argument may appear to beg the question but, given Richards's analysis of validating principles, he claims it does not. It is a contingent fact that humans are constituted to promote the community good. Given that they are, and given the analysis of structured contexts, it follows that they morally ought to promote that good.

Several points need to be noted before we turn to the third justifying argument. First, although Richards derives these first two arguments from some considerations drawn from Gewirth's arguments in *Human Rights*, Gewirth himself does not endorse Richards's attempt to provide an evolutionary justification for ethics. In fact, Gewirth is extremely skeptical of the attempts to derive interesting ethical conclusions from evolutionary considerations (Gewirth, 1993). Gewirth allows that evolutionary theory may contribute to what he calls the *necessary conditions* for morality but he denies that evolutionary considerations are helpful in specifying the sufficient conditions for morality. The necessary conditions for morality include the fact that we are moral beings, that is, that we are beings capable of reflective choices. No doubt we are such because we have evolved to be so. But this does not determine what choices we shall or should make. In Gewirth's analysis, the choices human beings make are a result of "habituation and reasoning." These are influenced more by cultural factors than biological or evolutionary factors.

In addition, there is what Gewirth calls the *problem of determinacy*. This problem involves two questions. The first is the question of distribution: whose interests ought to be promoted? He finds Richards's answer that the interests of the community are to be promoted wanting. It is wanting insofar as there are any number of human communities with different aims and interests. The obvious kinds of examples are the Aztecs and the Nazis. Richards, of course, tries to defuse this by arguing that we, the Aztecs, and the Nazis all share a general commitment to the community good. The problem with the morality of the Aztecs and the Nazis for Richards, recall, is that they rest on false assumptions about the nature of human beings and the means of promoting their good. Even if we accept this, there is still a problem. Each individual in fact belongs to many communities with potentially conflicting aims and interests. A typical American, for example, belongs to a local community, is a citizen of a state, has allegiance to the national state, and is a member of a global community. The interests of these different groups are often at odds with one another. Gewirth's point can be made by the following observation: evolutionary considerations do not determine how the conflicting interests of these different groups should be weighed and evaluated. This is a fundamental problem of applied ethics. It is not clear that evolutionary ethics has anything of great significance to contribute to the solution.

The problem of determinacy involves a second question. Even if we come to some agreement about whose interests are to be promoted, there is the "substantive" question of which interests are to be promoted. Just as there are groups with conflicting interests, so there are conflicting interests within groups that need to be weighed and evaluated. The same kinds of considerations raised previously apply here as well. Again, evolutionary ethics by itself does not seem capable of resolving these conflicts. Gewirth concludes that no evolutionary ethics can be expected to provide sufficient conditions for either the explanation or justification of human ethical practices.

Gewirth's critique shows that there are serious problems for anyone who claims that evolution is the be-all and end-all of human morality. To it may be added the problem involved in Richards's endorsement of the view that morality is to be identified with altruism (see Murphy, 1982). But admitting this is not a fatal objection to Richards's position. It still remains to be seen just how much of human morality can be explained and justified by appeal to evolutionary facts and theory. For Richards, that is a great deal indeed.

We turn now to Richards's third justifying argument (Richards, 1987, pp. 627ff.). This is a second order argument: RV is warranted because it "grounds other key strategies for justifying moral principles" (Richards, 1987, p. 626). As Richards sees it, moral philosophers tend to use one of three methods to justify the central tenets of their positions. The first is a G. E. Moorish appeal to intuition. These appeals are vulnerable to the "Sorry, I don't see it" objection. The second is a Kantian appeal to the nature of genuine moral experiences. These appeals are vulnerable to a similar objection based on disagreements as to which experiences are *genuine* moral experiences, if any. Finally, there are Spencerian appeals to critics to produce an alternative morality. Once a competing principle of morality is produced, one then shows that actions which both agree are moral conform to your principle but not to the objector's or one shows that the competing principle reduces to yours. This is a general Utilitarian line of argument.

As Richards sees it, "[a]ll three strategies suppose that one can find near-universal consent among men concerning what actions are moral and what principles sanction them" (Richards, 1987, p. 627). But none has any reason to expect such near universal agreement to occur. RV supplies the reason. There is such agreement because "the pith of every person's nature, the core by which he or she is constituted a social and moral being, has been created according to the same standard. Each heart must resound to the same moral cord: acting for the common good."

Buying into this version has implications for the possibilities of galactic ethics. Assuming that there is no reason to think that all evolved organisms who reach a level of moral and intellectual ability need have reached that level through the workings of community or group selection, an empirical but important point, we may predict that such organisms will have evolved moralities in ultimate conflict with ours. There are also implications for an ethics that includes artificial persons. Robots may be constructed to think and act as we do, but if they have not evolved as we have, then the possibilities of producing robots who consistently fail to "see" the moral standards that we adhere to is a distinct possibility (cf. Lloyd, 1985).

The central moral inference principle of RV is something to the effect "From sentences of the form 'Doing X promotes the community good' infer 'Moral agents ought to do X'." It is instructive here to reconsider Hume's famous injunction or caution against inferring "oughts" from "ises." How are we to construe such inferences as being justified? If we are not careful and appear to endorse a general license to infer an "ought" from an "is," then we seem to be committed to some such principle as "From 'X is the case' infer 'X ought to be the case'." But this principle is clearly suspect and runs afoul of the Huxley-Moore criticism to the effect that the workings of evolution have produced brigands as well as saints. And, of course, when we consult the appropriate moral authorities, the principle fails to command wide assent. The same is not so clearly true of the moral inference principle that lies at the heart of RV *especially if one grants Richards the empirical premises to the effect that human beings have been selected not only to be motivated to act in the community good when such actions seem appropriate but also to endorse such acts as well.*

More needs to be said to make the case convincing. But the argument is sufficiently ingenious to deserve serious consideration from those who profess to be interested in the foundations of morals. At the very least it shows that Richards is right in contending that an evolutionary based ethics *could* be "morally" justified without committing some egregious fallacy.

Having said this, let me raise two considerations that I think need to be addressed. First, with respect to whether "contract" altruism or "authentic" altruism is the "higher" form of morality, the case against the

sociobiological thesis is not so easy. Of course, most moral agents competent to judge would deem that actions done for personal gain or only
because of reciprocal altruistic considerations would not be moral, but
Wilson, Ruse, Alexander, and the others would agree—if the calculations
are conscious either to the agent or to others observing the agent. However, when they are not, then it is not so clear what most moral agents
competent to judge would say. They very well may say that if the actions
in question are motivated by self-interest then they are not moral but if
they are not motivated by self-interest, then they are. The sociobiological
thesis is that, in some sense, all actions *are* motivated by self-interest,
despite what the most well-meaning of social moralists may think or say.
This kind of argument is not new and is reminiscent of the debates
between Hobbesians and their critics on the basis of benevolence.

Similarly, such arguments remind one of objections against the material basis of mind. It is no good argument against the materialist that
because most people do not think that the mind is material, that it is not.
We now, it might be argued, have reason to suspect that it is, and the same
goes for the altruism case as a careful consideration of the arguments of
Wilson, Dawkins, and Alexander show.[21]

Second, from the claim that every ethical system must derive its
norms from facts Richards concludes that "either the naturalistic fallacy is
no fallacy, or no ethical system is justified." If no ethical system is justified
then Hitler and St. Francis are on a par. So Richards argues the naturalistic fallacy is no fallacy (Richards, 1987, p. 620). Surely this is too quick.
Even if we grant that all principles have empirical warrant in the sense
explained by Richards, we can still go on to distinguish between those systems that derive ethical conclusions from factual premises using principles
similar to the one we supposed that Hume rightly opposed and that commit the naturalistic fallacy in a narrow sense from those which do not. And
if Richards says fine but RV does not, then we must press the ground upon
which the good principles are distinguished from the bad. The appeal to
universal consent rests on our ability to *explain away* differences between
individuals who apparently hold to different moral criteria or moral
framework principles as really being differences about how a common criterion is to be understood or interpreted in particular cases. The problem
is that this defense rests on the tenability of the distinction between
framework principles and internal rules. Although the distinction has a
venerable origin in the work of Carnap (cf. Richards, 1987, n. 40, p. 616;
Carnap, 1956, pp. 205–222) and has a plausible surface sheen, I fear it will
not stand up to careful scrutiny. Is there a problem-independent method
of specifying which are the framework principles and which the internal
rules? I think not. If not, then the charge of relativism that appeared to be
defused rears its ugly head again.

Third, there is the question of the scope of morality. For Richards, "community welfare is the highest moral good" (Richards, 1987, p. 620). There are two ways in which this claim can be understood. First, it may be the claim that, although community welfare is the highest moral good, there are other moral goods that are not particularly related to the community good. If so, then we should expect there to be moral rules of inference relevant to their deployment as well, such as "From sentences of the form 'X promotes the self-esteem of individual agents' infer 'Agents ought to do X'." Here, I suspect that the universal acclaim that Richards claims underlies the community good inference rule would not be so readily forthcoming. If so, RV as it stands is incomplete, which in itself is no fatal flaw unless the incompleteness is ineradicable. The other possibility is that if community welfare is the highest moral good, we are endorsing the view that all moral goods are such, in virtue of the fact that they promote in some way or other the community good. But if this is the reading, then it remains unsubstantiated. It is, in a sense, the flip side of the Hobbesian challenge. Instead of arguing, as the Hobbesian does, that all "moral" actions are grounded in self-interest, RV would be committed to the claim that all "moral" actions are grounded in concern, conscious or not, for the community welfare. Both positions seem immodest.

GENERAL CONCLUSION

The three theories surveyed illustrate a range of what can properly be called *sociobiological* approaches to ethics. None of the attempts is completely successful in generating an evolutionary account either of the origin of moral principles or their justification. Indeed, there is no consensus among them as to whether an evolutionary "justification" of ethical principles is either possible or necessary. What these latest efforts show, along with the similar efforts of the nineteenth century theorists, is that evolutionary considerations alone are not capable of generating a foundation for ethical theory. However, they also show that evolutionary theory is capable of contributing to discussions of the foundations of ethics. They show that a Darwinian perspective on ethics and ethical theory is capable of generating potentially deep insights into the nature of our moral practices and the formulation of our moral beliefs and principles. What is needed now is neither to wrest morality from the province of the philosophers and turn it over to the evolutionary biologists nor to unceremoniously ignore the voices of empirical investigators. The time has come to mount an interdisciplinary effort drawing on the talents and expertise of philosophers, biologists, anthropologists, psychologists, and other like-minded Darwinians to explore the complicated nuances of human morality. One area in which these interdisciplinary efforts have brought together evolutionary biologists, ecologists, and philosophers is the question of the moral status of animals. We turn to a review of some recent thinking on this issue.

NOTES

1. This complaint is a reflection of a worry that is based on Wilson's social agenda. Like other visionaries, he is concerned to develop scientific theories to deal with the social ills of the age. He argues that if we do not try to understand the evolutionary underpinnings of our behavior and the workings of our brains, we are in the position of being led on by an evolutionary heritage, which, however adaptive it may have once been, is leading us on to ecological and genetic disasters.

2. It is claims of this sort that critics label as *adaptationist*. First, one cannot argue from the persistence of morality to what its ultimate function, if any, might be. Even if morality originally evolved because it was an adaptation, it need not follow that it is still adaptive or even if it is that it is adaptive for the same reasons that led to its appearance in the first place. Second, its initial appearance may not be due to selection at all. For all we know, human morality is a spandrel that through the course of history has become functional for human society. But if so, that function need not be related to any genetic function at all. Worries along these lines indicate one must be extremely cautious in inferring anything about the "ultimate" (phylogenetic) function of any evolved trait.

3. This and similar characterizations of *altruism* have been criticized for failing to clearly distinguish between two different conceptions of altruism. "Biological" altruism is behavior that decreases the relative fitness of the altruist as compared to those who benefit regardless of any intention or consciousness of consequences, or the lack thereof, on the part of the altruist. "Moral" altruism, on the other hand, is behavior in which the altruist consciously seeks to benefit another but with no necessary repercussions or consequences that affect his or her own fitness or reproductive success. An incredibly wealthy individual who donates a minuscule fraction of his wealth to the poor is acting altruistically in this sense even though his reproductive success does not decrease nor does the reproductive success of those he benefits increase. The quick argument against the sociobiological approach is that biological altruism is too weak to capture or be the basis of moral altruism, because the former does not involve intentions whereas the latter does. The quick argument on the other side is that human intentions need to be understood in an evolutionary light. Intentionality and non-fitness-enhancing "altruism" are byproducts of an enabling mechanism driven by biological altruism. For some of the debate, see Kitcher (1985), Sober (1989), Alexander (1987), Caplan (1978), and articles in a special number of the *Philosophical Forum* (*13* no. 1–2, 1981–82) devoted to the sociobiology debate. Whether altruism in either sense is the core of human morality is something else again.

4. "In this book it is suggested that most kinds of human social behavior are hypertrophic forms of original, simpler responses that were of more direct adaptive advantage in hunter-gatherer and primitive agricultural societies" (Wilson, 1979, p. 226).

5. More recently, Wilson has argued that the genetic community we share with all living things can be tapped to develop a conservation ethic. To this end, he has become actively involved in conservation projects that aim to preserve the biodiversity that is the lifeblood of the maintenance of the genetic pools of non-human organisms. See his very personal 1984 book, *Biophilia* and Wilson (1992). See also Singer (1981), Stone (1983), Rodd (1990), and Rachels (1990) for reflections on related themes. The moral standing of nonhuman organisms and nonorganisms is a complex and controversial question. One of the issues involved is discussed in Chapter 6.

6. See discussions by Singer (1981) and Kitcher (1985) that challenge the significance of such information for practical moral debates.

7. It may appear that Alexander is guilty of oversimplification in implicitly identifying morality with altruism (self-sacrificial behavior for the benefit of another) and both implicitly and explicitly with rules of social constraint (e.g., p. 88). Many philosophically inclined biologists have been charged with the same mistake. Jeffrie Murphy, for example, characterizes Darwin's view on the evolution of morality as enlightened but limited (Murphy, 1982, p. 84). It is enlightened insofar as Darwin argues that no specific moral principle was in any way biologically determined. It is limited insofar as Darwin took the scope of morality to be the set of principles, based on evolved instincts, that promote social cooperation. But, Murphy urges, the scope of morality is wider than this and includes nonsocial virtues, personal virtues such as integrity, purity of heart, and so on. Can natural selection account for the "non social dimension" of morality, he asks (Murphy, 1982, p. 85)?

I take it that Alexander's considered opinion, and the considered opinion of sociobiologists in general, is that natural selection *can* account for the evolution of such nonsocial virtues because, in fact, they promote individual genetic success. I am much more likely to elicit the cooperation of others and thereby enhance my reproductive efforts if I am known or believed to be a person with purity of heart than if I am known or believed to be a blackguard. (Compare Alexander's remarks on the evolution of conscience [Alexander, 1987, p. 102] and on the evolution of self-deception [pp. 117ff.].)

8. For an opposing view, see Russell Lande, "A Quantitative Genetic Theory of Life History Evolution" (1982, pp. 607–615). Lande argues that the quantity which is maximized is r, the intrinsic rate of increase of a *population* (see p. 611).

9. On reflection, this does not seem quite right. If every human is in reproductive conflict with every other human, then one strategy for decreasing the reproductive options of others would be to champion the interests of viruses in the hopes that the chances of oneself succumbing are small enough or outweighed by the chances of others succumbing.

10. Perhaps not. If compromises promote the well-being of some over that of others the *net effect* of the compromise may be to enhance the reproductive interests of some over others. So, regardless of what the prima facie interests under consideration are, the bottom line interests being served are the reproductive interests of some group. This is the case, even if that was not the intent of the compromising parties. If this is the view, then we need to remind ourselves of Sober's distinction between *selection for* and *selection of* (Sober, 1984). In Sober's view, there is selection

of genes whenever there is selection *for* anything. But, the resulting gene frequency changes, if any, are merely a reflection of bookkeeping and do not necessarily reflect anything important. Similarly, it may be true that whenever we compromise on interests of any kind we are, ipso facto, compromising on genetic interests as Alexander understands them. However, it does not follow that this is a reflection of anything important.

11. Recall in this context the reasoning by Socrates, in the *Phaedo*, by means of which he rejected the materialistic theory of mind defended by Anaxagoras: "I felt very much as I should feel if someone said, 'Socrates does by mind all he does'; and then, trying to tell the causes of each thing I do, if he should say first that the reason why I sit here now is, that my body consists of bones and sinews, and the bones are hard and have joints between them, and the sinews can be tightened and slackened, surrounding the bones along with flesh and the skin which holds them together; so when the bones are uplifted in their sockets, the sinews slackening and tightening make me able to bend my limbs now, and for this cause I have bent together and sit here; and if next he should give you other such causes of my conversing with you, alleging as causes voices and airs and hearings and a thousand others like that, and neglecting to give the real causes. These are that since the Athenians thought it was better to condemn me, for this very reason I have thought it better to sit here, and more just to remain and submit to any sentence they may give. For, by the dog! these bones and sinews, I think, would have been somewhere near Megara or Boeotia long ago, carried there by an opinion of what is best, if I had not believed it better and more just to submit to any sentence which my city gives than to take to my heels and run" (Plato, 1956, pp. 502f.).

12. Recall Descartes's argument, on the one hand, for the unity of the mind, and, on the other, his list, in the *Meditations*, of what strikes us today as a hodgepodge of powers, capacities and contents that he took to be encompassed by "the mental."

13. In commenting on this sentence, Alexander argues that "The mission of the genes is realized via the production of phenotypes—via ontogeny. Selection disfavors phenotypes. Differential gene loss is the (incidental) result" (private communication). There is some merit to this point. Sober's bookkeeping analogy underplays somewhat the causal relationship between genes and phenotypes— ledger balances are more or less the passive results of economic activity. They may induce activity in the firm's agents but any mission that results is the agent's not the balances'. Genic balances are more active in their role but whether they could be said to have a mission is somewhat problematic.

14. There is no necessary connection between the thesis of genic selectionism and reductionism as the analysis by K. Sterelny and P. Kitcher (1988) clearly shows.

15. For the hierarchical point of view see, e.g., Arnold and Fristrup (1982), Gould (1982), and Eldredge (1985). For the single-level point of view, see Dawkins (1976).

16. Of course, mechanisms that evolve because they are selectively advantageous in one environment may turn out to be selectively disadvantageous in other environments. This does not mean that they did not originally evolve to serve the

"interests" of the genes. Alexander (Alexander and Borgia, 1978) points out that the evolution of mechanisms in moths for finding mates, which are certainly functional for this purpose, turn out to be dysfunctional when the moths find themselves in environments with candle flames. Fair enough, but the point here is not that mechanisms can go awry in environments where they have not evolved, but that they can generate new interests that are not the genic "interests" that gave rise to them in the first place. Every *unintended* consequence of X is a *consequence* of X, but new interests are more than mere consequences—every interest of a product of X is not necessarily an interest of X.

17. Bear in mind that the *self* in these labels is not the same in the two cases. The *self* in *phenotypic self-interest* is the phenotype or organism. The *self* in *genetic self-interest* is the gene.

18. I do not intend this in the objectionable sense of trying to derive an "ought" from an "is," which Alexander rejects. Rather, the point is that Alexander appears to be claiming that, properly understood, all human interests are reproductive interests. Biological insights would then provide us with the "true" meaning of our moral concepts.

19. On this, Julian Huxley has the following to say: "I have not referred to any influence of modern physics on our problem, for I do not consider that the influence is destined to remain. . . . [Indeterminacy from quantum considerations has an apparent but no real bearing on questions of free will and morality] . . . On the contrary, it is the growth of biology which is shedding light on our problem. Modern physics is now seen to be a science of the highest degree of abstractness, abstracting from reality everything which cannot be dealt with mathematically. Biology, on the other hand, by demonstrating that man, albeit an extremely peculiar organism, has evolved from lower organisms by natural means, that all life is part of a single process, and that life must have developed from 'not-life' during a peculiar phase of our planet's history, forces us to pay attention to a great many other attributes of reality—such as sensation, perception, emotion, rational insight, and purpose. We cannot abstract these from the biological facts without sacrificing something of biological reality, for they play an important role in the later reaches of biological evolution . . . now that biology has drawn attention to their validity as attributes of reality . . . when it has attained a certain level and type of organization, the physicists must give up trying to draw ultimate and general conclusions from physics alone" (Huxley and Huxley, 1947, pp. 35f.).

20. In this regard, Alexander claims that "[a]s knowledge of the physiochemical underpinnings of human social behavior becomes extensive and detailed, the value of evolutionary theory in guiding our understanding of ourselves will necessarily diminish" (Alexander, 1987, p. 8).

21. To question the competence of most antimaterialists in an attempt to subvert the parallel will not work without further argument. Such a move appears to be too patently self-serving.

Chapter 6

Darwinism and the Moral Status
of Animals

INTRODUCTION

As noted in the last chaper, Richards sought to defuse what he saw as a potential objection to his revised version of evolutionary ethics by arguing that it did not, in fact, entail that nonhuman animals were moral agents. But, even if it is conceded that nonhuman animals do not have the "intentional capacity" that most argue to be a prerequisite of moral agency, a number of arguments still seek to establish some moral standing for animals. If they are not agents at least their pain and suffering must be reckoned into any moral calculation. Such has not always been the received wisdom. (See Singer, 1983; Turner, 1964. For a recent critique of extending moral status to animals, see Leahy, 1991.) Darwin's theory has been construed by many, including Darwin himself, as supporting the enhanced moral standing of non human animals.

In this chapter, I examine some arguments from Peter Singer, James Rachels, and Rosemary Rodd concerning the "expanding circle" and the moral status of animals. I conclude that their appeals to Darwinism are inconclusive with respect to the moral standing of animals. It would be nice if one could provide a conclusive argument against such appeals but I am not convinced that any such blanket conclusion can be reached.

SINGER'S EXPANDING CIRCLE ARGUMENT

The Expanding Circle is an assessment of the relevance of sociobiological investigations for ethics (Singer, 1981). Although rejecting any attempt to claim that ethics can be grounded in or completely accounted for by biological considerations, Singer argues that sociobiological considerations play both a negative role and a positive role in ethical deliberations. The negative contribution of sociobiology consists, in part, in undermining certain views about the nature of ethics. Two grounds for resisting the view that the core of human ethics has a biological basis include alleged differences between human behavior and animal behavior and the wide cultural variation in particular ethical systems. The first consideration is undermined by the evidence of the sort first marshalled by Darwin in *The Descent of Man*. The second consideration shows that cultural factors are an important modulating force with respect to the particular form of ethical systems, but in Singer's view sociobiological evidence suggests that there are common elements underlying all ethical systems. Although establishing that certain practices and rules have a biological basis does not establish their ethical credentials, it can undermine our confidence in the absoluteness of such rules (Singer, 1981, p. 158).

The positive role of sociobiological analyses is similarly constrained. No specific moral principles or maxims are forthcoming from biological or evolutionary considerations. Nonetheless, as a consequentialist Singer sees evolutionary biology as one more important source of information for making informed ethical judgments. The evolutionary arguments that establish the continuity between humans and nonhuman animals serve as support for the extension of the moral community to include nonhuman animals.

In addition to the biologically engendered interests human beings have, an important component of human morality is our ability to reason. It may well be true that the ability to reason evolved because it was an "enabling" mechanism that was selectively advantageous but, once evolved, rational standards for action may be established that are independent of the interests of particular individuals. In this respect, Singer endorses the importance of "impartiality" as a moral desideratum at least with respect to individual actions.

Singer distinguishes between social moralities and individual moralities in an attempt to sidestep the problem that a truly impartial morality would be a morality of saints beyond the capacities of ordinary human beings. Nevertheless, "[w]hen we think about our own individual actions, impartial reason is unimpeachable . . . when I ask myself what it would really be best for me to do—best not in terms of my own interests and desires, but best from an objective point of view—the answer must be that I ought to do what is in the interests of all, impartially considered" (Singer, 1981, p. 153). Whose interests are these? For Singer, "all beings with interests, of whatever species" (Singer, 1981, p. 170).

In *Animal Liberation*, Singer argues that all sentient creatures, insofar as they are capable of suffering, have interests that require equal consideration, although *not* equal treatment. "If a being suffers there can be no moral justification for refusing to take that suffering into consideration" (Singer, 1983, p. 9). But why not?

In Singer's view, humans are arbitrarily speciesist if they single out human beings for special consideration merely because they are human beings. When one inquires about the principle upon which such treatment is warranted, one finds, Singer alleges, either arbitrary fiat or a principle that includes nonhumans as part of the moral community as well. However, one can argue that what this shows is not that speciesism is wrong but that the proffered justifications for it are lacking. What is needed, one might argue, is not to abandon speciesism but to find another foundation for it. That foundation can also be discovered in evolutionary theory. We begin with our biological disposition to give preference to our close relatives first. We expand the moral circle by contracts or fiats—and the basis of the rights or duties owed to other individuals rests on these implicit contracts. This does not preclude expanding the moral circle to all sentient creatures but it does not enjoin us to do so either. The fact is that, from this point of view, merely having interests or the capacity to suffer is not enough. There must be some reason for us to take the suffering or interests of others into account.

Singer holds that speciesism is a form of racism. No right-minded person wants to be labeled a *racist*. Therefore, no right-minded person should want to be a speciesist. Singer concludes that "to discriminate against beings solely on account of their species is a form of prejudice, immoral and indefensible in the same way that discrimination on the basis of race is immoral and indefensible." His own view, he says, is *not* prejudiced but based on reason. I am not convinced that the parallel is apt. Racism *is* an arbitrary and prejudiced point of view. But it is such in the light of our prior commitment to a moral position in which race is an irrelevancy. What counts is rationality or the capacity to suffer or a little bit of both. If we are committed, as Singer and some Utilitarians are, to the view that moral relevancy is determined by the capacity to suffer and nothing more, then speciesism might be construed as a parallel prejudice. But again, why should the suffering or interests of others be of moral concern to us? In what sense is choosing the capacity to suffer as a mark of moral relevance any less a "prejudice" than choosing "being human," or "being white," or "being an American"? Evolutionary considerations, *per se*, do not prescribe that the capacity to suffer should be the touchstone of who does or does not belong in the moral community. Of course, Singer does not think that it does. The point, though, is that evolutionary theory and the facts of our evolutionary history cannot serve as the ground or foundation of one moral position rather than another if those facts and that theory can be used by competing theorists to come to alternative conclusions about who does or does not have moral standing. This is not to say that evolutionary theory is irrelevant to such decisions but only that, at least in Singer's argument, it plays a subsidiary role to substantial moral assumptions. Someone who did not accept those assumptions could just as easily deploy arguments based in evolutionary theory to challenge them. James Rachels is a case in point.

JAMES RACHELS ON "MORAL INDIVIDUALISM"

According to Rachels, the development of moral thought can be divided into four stages. Each stage is characterized by a factual world-view, a set of cosmological assumptions about nature, humankind's place in nature, and assumptions about what constitute adequate explanations of natural phenomena. The two cosmological stages that are relevant to Rachels are the Aristotelian world-view and the modern "naturalistic" world-view, which is the product of the several scientific revolutions that have occurred since the 1600s. Associated with each factual world view is an associated moral world-view, which is more or less loosely supported by the corresponding cosmological view.

Stage I couples the Aristotelian teleological world-view with its associated Judeo-Christian theology, a world of value-laden facts, with a moral world-view that emphasizes the sanctity of human life. The doctrine of the sanctity of human life, or the intrinsic value of human dignity, is the "matching moral idea" of what Rachels calls the "Image of God Thesis." The Image of God Thesis is the view that "[m]an is special because he alone is made in the image of God, and above all other creatures he is the object of God's love and attention. The other creatures were given by God for man's use" (Rachels, 1989, p. 308). With the secularization of the classical world-view, the uniqueness of man does not disappear but rests on a different foundation. Rachels calls the secular basis for the sanctity of human life the *Rationality Thesis*. The Rationality Thesis is the claim that "[m]an is special because he alone is rational. Nonhuman animals are not rational, and so are not to be compared, in this regard, with humans" (Rachels, 1989, p. 308).

Stage II begins with the scientific revolution of the seventeenth century, which banned teleology from the physical world, and culminates in Darwin's banishment of teleology from the biological world and the world of human beings. The Darwinian universe is a universe of populations of varying individuals in which the difference between humans and nonhuman becomes one of degree and not one of kind. This factual world-view is in tension with the traditional morality with its emphasis on the essential and sharp differences between humankind and nonhuman kind.

Stage III, which is the present, corresponds to a time when the moral implications of the Darwinian revolution are beginning to be appreciated and moral philosophers are casting about for a "matching moral idea" that will reharmonize our naturalistic world-view with an appropriate ethical stance. Peter Singer's views on the expanding circle implications of Darwinian theory, Rosemary Rodd's and Tom Regan's briefs for the rights of animals, as well as Rachels's own "moral individualism" are stabs in this direction.

Stage IV, still in the future, will be the stage at which our naturalistic world-view is reequilibrated with an appropriate "matching moral idea."

How are these factual world-views related to their moral counterparts? The relation is not one of inductive support or deductive entailment but a looser notion of rational support (Rachels, 1990, pp. 93–98; Rachels, 1989, pp. 313–316). The basic idea is that the factual world-view provides reasons for accepting or adopting particular moral beliefs. Discrediting these reasons undermines those moral beliefs. The basic structure of the line of reasoning Rachels has in mind is as follows:

1. R is a reason for B.
2. R is rejected on the basis of new evidence E.
3. We conclude that B is undermined by E.

Undermining is not the same as refuting or disproving. Rejecting a reason for holding a belief is not the same as showing the belief in question to be false. Yet as our reasons for holding B fall by the wayside, it becomes more and more unreasonable to maintain B. There is something decidedly Wittgensteinian about this approach, and perhaps Socratic as well. A favorite tool of the later Wittgenstein was to formulate a philosophical view and then undermine it by showing that the reasons one might have for holding it were weak, confused, or mistaken. Factual beliefs can undermine normative claims in just this way. One of the results of the seventeenth century scientific revolution was the shift away from theism to the deism of the eighteenth century and the atheism of the nineteenth century. How did this shift occur? The mechanical world-view did *not* entail that God did not exist, rather it provided an alternative factual world-view that undermined one of the key reasons for believing in the existence of God. This had moral implications insofar as it contributed to the unreasonableness of ethical views that relied explicitly or implicitly on assumptions about the divine source of morality. The mechanical world-view and the Darwinian revolution contributed to undermining the "Image of God Thesis" and its secular counterpart, the "Rationality Thesis." In this respect, the "shallow rhetoricians," as Rachels dubs them, were right and Thomas Henry Huxley was wrong. Darwin's theory has grave moral implications indeed.

Darwin's theory undermines the Rationality Thesis in a number of ways. First, the continuity between humans and animals calls into question the implicit assumption of the Rationality Thesis that the difference between human beings and animals is a difference in kind and not one of degree. Second, it is becoming increasingly evident that rationality is not a single trait but a complex of characteristics many of which we share to a greater or less degree with nonhuman animals. Third, species are composed of populations of individual organisms exhibiting a wide range of variability. The Darwinian world-view is antiessentialist. The Rationality Thesis is one vestigial manifestation of an essentialist world-view. With its demise comes a fatal challenge to the concept of human dignity, which is a reflection of the idea that "human beings are in a special moral category" (Rachels, 1990, p. 4). Darwinism, which promotes the importance of individual differences, requires a different matching moral idea.

Rachels proposes to replace the ethics based on human dignity by an ethics of "moral individualism." "According to moral individualism, the bare fact that one is human entitles one to no special consideration. How an individual should be treated depends on his or her own particular characteristics, rather than on whether he or she is a member of some preferred group—even the 'group' of human beings. I offer various reasons for thinking this approach is morally sound, as well as reasons for thinking it is the natural view to take if one views the world from an evolutionary perspective" (Rachels, 1990, p. 5).

Moral individualism rests on two principles, an Equality Principle and a Relevance Principle:

1. Equality Principle: Treat *relevantly* equal cases in the same way.
2. Relevance Principle: Differences are relevant or not depending on the treatment in question.

A corollary to the Relevance Principle is this: No one difference (species, gender, race, or the ability to suffer[?]) will prove to be relevant for all cases.

As Rachels points out, moral individualism has radical consequences with respect to how we think about and value the lives of animals as well as how we think about and value human lives. In a sense, human lives as such are devalued whereas animal lives as such are enhanced in value.

Two varieties of speciesism are rejected in virtue of this account. Rachels endorses Singer's view that unqualified speciesism is a form of racism. Qualified speciesism, the view that species membership is not morally relevant but that it is correlated with morally relevant features, is undermined by the Relevance Principle.

There is a "complex pattern of similarities and differences" between any two animals, conspecifics or not (Rachels, 1990, p. 194). Thus, moral individualism "goes naturally with an evolutionary perspective because an evolutionary perspective denies that humans are different in kind from other animals; and one cannot reasonably make distinctions in morals where none exist in fact" (Rachels, 1990, p. 174). Darwinism "supports" but does not entail moral individualism.

However, even if we accept the doctrine of moral individualism as "supported" by Darwinism, then the question of how equals should be equally treated, once they have been determined to be equal, remains open. No specific injunctions regarding abortion, infanticide, euthanasia, homosexuality, suicide, and so forth, follow, only that, whatever the situation, humans and nonhumans need to be judged by the relevance principle appropriate to the situation and appropriate action taken in the light of that determination. There is no clear mandate from evolutionary facts or theory about either (1) what the appropriate relevance principles are for particular cases or (2) what are appropriate responses, given that we have decided that two individuals are relevantly alike.

RODD ON THE RIGHTS OF ANIMALS
AND OUR DUTIES TOWARD THEM

Against certain sociobiological interpretations, Rodd seeks to defend the thesis that it is "biologically possible for us to experience a genuine moral concern about our fellow creatures' welfare." Insofar as nonhuman animals can be said to experience relevant mental states in particular and insofar as they can be said to have beliefs and desires, the foundations of interests and rights, they become subject to appropriate moral concern (Rodd, 1990, Ch. 1).

Regardless of whether the case for animal rights can be made, human beings have duties toward them not to cause unnecessary suffering or, at least, prima facie, not to eat them or raise them for food. This rests on the assumption that certain mental states are pleasant or unpleasant and consequently good and desirable or bad and undesirable. To the extent that nonhuman animals are capable of experiencing such states, and this Rodd argues rests only on their being conscious, we are enjoined from causing them to suffer, if possible, and from harming them by killing them.

Rodd sees human moral systems as devices for resolving conflicts of interests and insofar as nonhuman animals can be said to have interests, their interests have to be taken into account.

Rodd points out that the question of animal rights is not merely part of the general question of moral issues relating to the environment (Rodd, 1990, Ch. 5). Duties to species are different from duties to individual animals. The former relates to a general environmental ethic and the latter is a question of *rights*. The case of "surplus kill" in zoos is a good example of the conflicts that can arise between a concern for the species (for which killing surplus animals to maximize the effective population is a plus) and concern for individuals (where, clearly, the "interests" of the individual organisms are not best served by death).

In the case of conflicts of interest between humans and nonhuman animals, as in raising animals for food, Rodd urges that, at least in the developed countries, "the balance of interests is overwhelmingly upon the side of food animals and against humans who want to kill them in order to eat them" (Rodd, 1990, p. 139). This is not at all clear. Even if we concede that nonhuman animals have appropriate interests, morally relevant interests, it does not follow that their interests should count as much as our own. If the individual loss in interest of each slaughtered animal is sufficiently small, then even if we concede that nonhuman animals do have interests, 31 million slaughtered animals per year may not outweigh the interests of the humans who feed on them. That is so if we measure interests in terms of degrees of consciousness or prospects for the future, and so forth. A rights-based approach forces us to provide a stronger justification of the practice, especially if we assume that animals have nontrumpable rights of some magnitude, however small. But that puts a double or triple burden on the position, first, to show that such animals have rights; second, to show that they have nontrumpable rights; and third, to determine the extent of the interests on which these rights rest.

Rodd rejects the view that sociobiological analyses entail that morality is a delusion or illusion, the "error theory" of morality defended by Mackie (1978), Ruse, and E. O. Wilson (1986), among others. Human beings have evolved the capacity for making choices and reflecting on them (Rodd, 1990, Ch. 9). Once so evolved, the scope of human ethics is not constrained merely by considerations of survival and genic reproduction. Reproductive success is the ultimate value of the evolutionary game. The suffering and death of individuals, to the extent it reduces reproductive success, is a "natural evil." In the course of the development of human morality, this has been generalized to the point that the foundation of morality is the idea that all suffering is evil (Rodd, 1990, Ch. 10). Notwithstanding this, not all suffering is avoidable given the variety of interests of all the relevant parties. The net effect is a moral system that rests on precontractual considerations of right and wrong, emerging from evolved states of pleasure and pain, but that relies for its implementation on explicit and implicit contractual arrangements. Rodd suggests that a "contractual" state of some sort may be assumed to exist between humans and the animals they exploit—pets, farm animals, and so on. This being so, she finds many such contracts are "violated."

This conclusion brings out again the difficulties that beset such views. Even if we concede all that needs to be conceded in terms of animal beliefs, desires, interests, and rights to get the view off the ground, it strains credulity to assume that, given the difficulties in determining the extent of the interests, demands, and rights of animals, we can conceive of our relationship to them in any sense as contractual.

CONCLUSION

The range of moral implications for animals drawn by these authors from evolutionary arguments should give pause to those who wish to use Darwinian arguments to bolster the case for enhancing the role of nonhuman animals in the moral community. Even when we grant the biological continuity between us and the beasts, no nonproblematic moral consequences seem to follow. To illustrate this point we may reconsider Singer's argument that speciesism is a form of racism. It should be obvious that my purpose here is *not* to defend racism but to point out that neither the theory of evolution nor an understanding of the evolutionary history of human beings and other animals, in and of itself, rules out either racism or speciesism. Most of the work being done by any argument about the scope of the moral circle is being done by more basic normative presuppositions.

To see this, consider the following evolutionary case against vegetarianism. Human beings as living creatures have an affinity with plants that is no more nor no less based on our evolutionary heritage than is our affinity with other animals. If we are to include animals within the moral circle perhaps we should include plants and micro-organisms as well. A case may well be made for the moral standing of viruses too, although I shall not stop to pursue it here. One moral consequence, following both Singer and Rodd, is that if we should not eat animals because of our moral affinity to them, then we should not eat plants either. To the argument that we must eat something to survive, there is a ready reply. We currently, or will soon, possess the necessary technological knowledge to create foodstuffs directly from chemical elements. It may be expensive but perhaps no lives need be taken. It is no argument against the moral sanctity of plants that, in the past, we have been forced to eat plants through ignorance of how to do without. The moral issues that arise in medicine through technological innovation are a related case in point. One hundred years ago, the prenatal selection of more perfect children was not a moral issue because no one knew how to do anything about it. Now we know and now it is.

Another objection to extending the moral mantle to plants rests on their alleged incapacity to feel pain or suffer. Even granting that they do not feel pain or suffer, there is no evolutionary reason why the capacity to feel pain and to suffer should be singled out as especially morally significant. The argument from moral individualism advocated by Rachels establishes this point. That Utilitarians do treat the capacity to feel pain or to suffer as morally significant is already a reflection of a deep moral commitment. How deep? Suppose we were to encounter an intelligent alien species, one whose members we could communicate with, that, through reasons of time and space, could not possibly share a common evolutionary heritage with us. Suppose, in addition, that we come to accept that these creatures had the capacity to feel pain and to suffer. It is impossible to say for certain what our moral sentiments would be in such a case, but my sense is that the evolutionary affinity criterion, which acts in this instance to limit the moral circle, would be dropped in favor of a sentience and sapience criterion that would act to expand the circle.

What this shows is that evolutionary theory and evolutionary considerations are often pressed into service where and when they are convenient in furthering the antecedent moral convictions of those who appeal to them. If ethical theorists are to be expected to take evolutionary arguments for moral positions seriously, then such arguments must be capable of overriding at least some moral positions.

Chapter 7

Final Reflections

SUMMARY OF THE ARGUMENT

The final words on the scope and limits of evolutionary theory to our understanding of morality are yet to be written. In these pages, I have argued for both a historical thesis and an analytical thesis. The historical thesis concerns the place of Darwin's evolutionary analysis of the moral sense in the history of moral theory. The analytical thesis concerns the ramifications of a Darwinian analysis for our understanding of morality.

With respect to Darwin's place in the history of moral theory, I have sought to establish the sense in which Darwin's moral theory is an evolutionary contribution to the post-Hobbesian debate over the nature and role of benevolence as a moral motivator. This debate shaped the discussions of the eighteenth century British moral theorists. The argument was focused on two issues. The first concerned the relationship between benevolence and self-interest. The Hobbesian position was understood to be that benevolence or regard for the welfare of others was merely disguised self-interest. Several of the eighteenth century moral theorists disputed this on phenomenological grounds. Butler and Hume, among others, argued that introspective evidence made it clear, if not self-evident, that motives of benevolence were independent of and irreducible to motives based on self-interest. However, it was generally conceded by all that benevolent motives were considerably weaker than self-interested motives. This raised a second issue: How was it that human beings often acted benevolently in the face of strong motivations to always act in one's own self-interest? The consensus resolution was that a coincidence existed between self-interest or self regard and benevolence or regard for others. Was this coincidence accidental or essential? The eighteenth century moral theorists concluded that the coincidence was essential and derived from principles inherent in human nature. Both Hume and Butler, for

163

example, held some such view although Butler had the advantage of being able to attribute the concordance to the wisdom of the Creator.

Darwin's contribution to this discussion was to provide an evolutionary analysis of the shaping of human nature whereby the coincidence could be explained in terms of the forces of natural selection acting to determine human sociality. The independence of the springs of human motivation can be accounted for in terms of the different selective forces acting on human development. Darwin was not, however, a moral theorist, and the brief sketch of the development of the moral sense he offered in *The Descent of Man* is not and was not intended to be a complete analysis of the problem. A host of other nineteenth century analysts, in addition to T. H. Huxley, Spencer, and Kropotkin, whose views were discussed in Chapter Three, rushed in to fill the gaps. The resulting discussions were inconclusive with respect to the merit of evolutionary contributions to the understanding of morality. G. E. Moore's indictment of Spencer's evolutionary ethics and his elaboration of Sidgwick's contention that naturalistic analyses of ethics committed an egregious "naturalistic fallacy" reduced the discussion to a murmur. There it remained for the most part until the publication of E. O. Wilson's *Sociobiology*. The suggestive remarks at the end of the book about the implications of sociobiological analysis for the human sciences led to an acrimonious debate in a chorus of voices both praising and condemning the very idea of a biological analysis of human nature and human institutions. Out of this chorus emerged a new debate over the possibility of "biologizing ethics." The battle lines of the late twentieth century debate closely resemble those drawn in the eighteenth century with *altruism* standing in for *benevolence*. The selfish gene theorists are the latter-day reductionist Hobbesians. Views like those of Richards, which rely on appeals to group selection to account for the emergence of human altruism, argue for the antireductionist point of view. The evolutionary perspective has clarified and reshaped the problem but has not resolved it. More work needs to be done on both the conceptual and empirical level. At the conceptual level, the simpleminded identification of human altruism with biological altruism has been rejected but no consensus about how the two are related has yet emerged. At the empirical level, one would like to see more empirical studies to evaluate when motives of benevolence or self-interest are operative and whether they are independent of each other. The development of experimental protocols to make these determinations face a number of confounding difficulties, but some preliminary steps in this direction have been taken by Batson and his associates (Batson, 1991).

What then are we now in a position to say about the implications of evolutionary theory for ethics? The range of issues in moral philosophy is both wide and deep. I do not pretend to have plumbed them to their depths. The contribution of an evolutionary perspective varies considerably along this spectrum.

In the first place, it is important to distinguish between what I have called *EMM* (evolution of moral mechanisms) and *EMT* (evolution of moral theses) implications. An incontrovertible achievement of Darwin's theory is that it has situated humankind among the other animals. *Homo sapiens* is the result of a long evolutionary development from ancestral forms. The full range of human endowments that make up human nature—physical, intellectual, and moral—are also the result of eons of evolutionary development. The capacities for reason and making moral judgments are no exception. As such, no one seriously questions that such capacities rest on the emergence of a biological substrate that makes their exercise possible. So much is uncontroversial. This is the basis of the claims of evolutionary theory to shed light on the nature of the biological mechanisms that are the wherewithal of our capacities for moral reasoning. Nevertheless, there are still formidable difficulties in trying to advance beyond this point. For one thing, the phylogenetic reconstruction of the emergence of our capacity to be moral is no light task. For another, although it is clear that certain extant brain structures are the basis of our moral natures, no one really knows which structures these are or how they work. Much work needs to be done here. Fruitful research in this area will require the collaboration of evolutionary biologists with psychologists, neurophysiologists, cognitive scientists, and philosophers. The contribution of evolutionary biology to the discussion is to situate any "proximate" accounts of moral behavior (or any other behavior or characteristic, for that matter) in an "ultimate" or phylogenetic context. So even if cognitive psychology, broadly conceived, provided an adequate proximate account of moral reasoning and moral motivation, the phylogenetic question of what led to the evolution of these proximate mechanisms would still remain. Given the historicity of biological organisms, this is not a question that can be safely ignored.

With respect to the implications of evolutionary theories for the EMT program, the results are more problematic. Three broad areas of moral philosophy were outlined in the first chapter: normative ethics, moral theory, and meta-ethics. The impact of evolutionary considerations on these areas is not the same. To suggest that evolutionary theory is relevant to the day-to-day ethical decisions that people make in the course of a lifetime is to focus on the wrong level of analysis. So much is clear. We can also conclude that attempts to derive specific moral maxims from evolutionary history or evolutionary theory are fraught with difficulty. Nevertheless, it does seem as if an appeal to evolutionary arguments can help explain the general shape of our moral principles. Certainly Spencer thought that his evolutionary gloss provided a foundation for Utilitarianism. Similarly, Richards's Revised Version of Darwinian ethics seeks to account for the emergence of general ethical principles in terms of selectionist pressures. In all of these cases, however, it would be premature to say that an evolutionary explanation has brought the debate over the nature and adoption of moral principles to an end.

One area where we can be more positive is the negative ruling out of certain possibilities as live options. Given that we can say, with some confidence, that morality is an "enabling mechanism" produced through evolution because (at least initially) it is fitness enhancing, certain options are ruled out or seem less plausible. Any version of moral realism that holds that moral "facts" exist independent of the constitution of human nature is suspect. This includes any moral theory that holds the source of moral value to be a divine will. At a recent conference held at the University of Pittsburgh on the philosophy of biology, there was a murmuring in the crowd when this was advanced as a virtue of an evolutionary analysis. The general sentiment was that no one holds such views seriously in our modern age. The very next day saw the announcement of the publication of *Veritatis Splendor*, an encyclical by Pope John Paul II addressing, among other things, the status of moral truths. Such truths are held to be based on human nature and not based on individual and subjective convictions. This nature, however, is not one shaped by evolutionary forces but rather by God as understood in the Christian Bible.

The import of Darwin for religion is a complex and controversial issue that I do not propose to deal with in depth. However, I think it is fair to say that the general effect of Darwin on moral issues should be construed as roughly equivalent to the general effect of Newton on physical issues, at least with respect to questions of the relevance of God or religion on them. Both Newtonian mechanics and Darwinian evolutionary theory have the general effect of marginalizing the need for and significance of appeals to religion or to divinities. With respect to our understanding of the physical world, God as creator became a "God-of-the-gaps," invoked only as a last resort when our physical explanations failed.[1] Appeals to God to account for the constitution of human nature on which our moral nature rests should be viewed in the same light.

Are we then condemned to moral relativism as the Pope fears? Well, yes and no. We can no longer appeal to an objective world of moral facts or principles independent of human nature to ground our moral deliberations. But we can, and do, appeal to a shared human nature to conclude that our moral deliberations rest on an objective, intersubjective shared human heritage as shaped by the forces of evolution. The question of the moral standing of nonhuman animals, which was briefly addressed in the last chapter, remains an open one. In addition, we can safely conjecture that any alien species that has evolved to the point of having moral sensibilities is liable to have sensibilities very different from our own. Thus, Darwinism would seem to commit us to an interspecific relativism, at least with respect to species that have evolved completely separately from any lineages on earth.

What then of justification? Can we not hope for such in a moral system shaped by natural forces? The ethical naturalists, as we have seen, are divided on this issue. Richards argues that evolutionary theory can be used both to explain moral behavior and to justify moral principles. Ruse and Wilson argue that justification, in the sense that Richards and the traditionalists require, is neither possible nor necessary. I do not think that this dispute can be simply resolved one way or the other; however, it illustrates the manner in which traditional problems in moral theory need to be rethought in the light of an evolutionary view of human nature.

The bottom line is that an evolutionary perspective on human nature provides a factual *and* normative background in terms of which the moral dimension of human beings needs to be explored. The dual dimension of claims resting on appeals to human nature was defended in Chapter 4.

THE BIOLOGICAL ROOTS OF MORALITY

We have come to the end of our investigation. The issues that have arisen are complex and thorny and, at best, some of the central features of the problems have been somewhat illuminated. Is there a "secret chain" that links evolution, biology, and morality? Unequivocally, yes. If human beings are moral creatures at all, it is as a result of evolution. This is not to say, however, that one should look to human biology or evolutionary history for the answer to all our questions about the nature of morality. What is needed to produce an integrated picture of moral behavior, moral reasoning, and moral rules are cooperative coordinative studies by biologists, neurophysiologists, evolutionary theorists, psychologists, and moral philosophers.

Given our evolutionary point of view, it is indisputable that the human capacity to be moral is an evolutionary product. The capacity to be moral, to engage in moral reasoning, to make moral judgments, and to formulate moral rules, rests on a number of other more fundamental capacities. Among these we can single out the fact that we have needs or interests, that we are sensitive, that we have the capacity to suffer, and that we are reflective. There may be other indispensable capacities as well but if any of these is missing then no moral behavior seems possible. The capacity to reflect is a function of the development of our brains. We do not know and perhaps may never know exactly when, in the course of human evolution, we first became moral creatures. Even if we assume that the structure of our brain has remained more or less unchanged from the time of the first appearance of *Homo sapiens*, it need not be the case that the earliest *Homo sapiens* were moral creatures in any way that we would understand today. Even given that the earliest humans were in some sense social creatures, we cannot conclude that morality, which today serves such an important role in the maintenance and regulation of human social structures, served such a function then. There are social organisms without the capacity for morality. Nonetheless, the evolution of human social structures seems hardly possible without the development of rule systems which are characteristic of moral systems.

We would not be what we are today were it not for the evolutionary development of the human lineage. But so what? To say that the products of evolution would not be what they are were it not for that evolution is not to say much. Not nothing but not much. Given that human beings have developed moral systems and given that, had we not evolved in the ways that we did, we might not have developed such systems, can we learn anything of importance about those systems from an investigation into the evolutionary history of humankind and a biological assessment of human organisms? Again, I think that the answer is "yes," but we have to be careful about what we conclude can be learned about these systems. There are two extreme points of view on this, both of which are probably mistaken.

On the one hand, one might think that a proper understanding of human evolutionary history and human biological nature will prove to be the be-all and end-all of human morality. To believe this is to believe that, in some sense, morality can be "reduced" to biology. It is not clear that anyone has ever held this extreme view, although the charge that sociobiologists are "biological determinists" indicates that some have thought so. Responsible sociobiologists such as Wilson and Alexander, even though they think much is to be gained from an evolutionary perspective on ethics, do not endorse this extreme reductionist point of view. The simple observation that groups of humans who share a general and specific evolutionary history may yet construct different social and moral systems is enough to put the lie to any simpleminded biological or evolutionary reductionism.

On the other hand, one might argue that our evolutionary history and biological nature have nothing to say about our moral systems. That we are creatures who construct and employ standards is one thing, but which standards and how we should employ them is another. In this view, evolutionary and biological information about how humans evolve or behave is a contribution to a descriptive understanding of human nature. Questions of morality are prescriptive and evolutionary and biological considerations are irrelevant to them. Now if this is construed to mean that we cannot simply "read off" norms and practical imperatives from biological and evolutionary descriptions, the point is well taken. But factual assumptions are relevant to moral considerations in several ways. First, the applicability of moral injunctions is constrained by factual considerations and scientific models. The debate over the rights of nonhuman animals and human obligations toward them, in large part, turns upon alleged facts about the differing capacities of humans and nonhumans. These differing capacities are rooted in biological similarities and differences. In the nineteenth century, a debate raged over human origins with some arguing for a monophyletic origin and others arguing for a polyphyletic origin. The monophyleticists won out, although the debate continues after a fashion in the dispute between those who hold for a common human ancestry evolving from African roots and others who hold out for multiple ancestries from Africa and Asia. Had the polyphyleticists won, grounds for discrimination and differential treatment would have existed. The fact that biological differences or similarities between populations exist does not in itself dictate what anyone is to make of them. But considerations of which factors to deem relevant for differentiation of moral treatments are implicit or explicit reflections of theories of human nature, and biological and evolutionary information is surely relevant to the construction of such models. Second, some strong psychological evidence suggests that constructing norms and applying standards is a trait that appears fairly consistently across cultures at around the ages of two or three. The specific norms and standards that children develop are culturally contingent, but the general rule, invariant across cultures, is that humans begin naturally to assess and evaluate their actions and the actions of others at a relatively young age. Why? Morality, or the assessment and evaluation of actions, is such a central aspect of our lives that it is hard to believe that it does not serve some important function. How and why did such a capacity evolve? It is clearly not selectively disadvantageous. Is there any way in which we might formulate and test hypotheses concerning the evolution of such innate capacities? The most immediate and accessible aspect of such phenomena, beyond psychological investigations, is the study of the neural structures that make such capacities possible. Here is a task for future evolutionary neuropsychologists that will require the cooperation of neurophysiologists, developmental psychologists, evolutionary biologists, and philosophers. The first task would seem to be the identification of the neural structures that make such behavior possible. Once they are identified, then evolutionary psychobiologists can construct informed speculations about how and why these structures might have evolved. Third, some such as Wilson and Richards, we have seen, have argued that moral imperatives themselves can be derived from and justified in the light of evolutionary fact and theory. These claims I have argued are much more problematic. Still, they are not completely wrongheaded. Ghiselin (1974) argues that the human brain evolved, as did other human attributes, primarily to serve "in the interests of our gonads." The human intellect does much more, of course, but the point of the life of the intellect is not at all clear beyond this basic reproductive facilitating point. "Nevertheless, an ability to come to grips with the world as it really is can hardly be dismissed as maladaptive. Above all else, the truth has ethical significance. . . . If, as we have some reason to think, selection within the context of society has somewhat elevated our baser sentiments, and if, as the facts suggest, self-interest and common welfare are not fundamentally beyond reconciliation, we can reasonably hope to develop ethical standards consistent with biological reality" (Ghiselin, 1974, p. 263). I take the reflections of Alexander to be in the same direction. In the wide sense in which human morality is a function of and reflection of our social and psychological nature, several recent attempts to treat such issues from an evolutionary point of view merit some mention.

Fox (1983) offers a provocative attempt to reorient the social sciences within an evolutionary framework. He argues that the correct framework within which we should analyze and understand anthropological information is a framework that puts such information into its evolutionary context. From an evolutionary point of view, the key considerations are fitness and reproductive success. Lineages evolve by accumulating traits that confer differential fitness and enhance reproductive success. Insofar as natural selection is a dominant factor in the evolution of such lineages, these traits and characters will be adaptations that serve as (what Wilson has called) enabling mechanisms—mechanisms that appear and become fixed because they contribute to the differential reproductive success of individuals. This applies to both physical and behavioral traits. Both the human mind and human sociality are evolutionary products. What then are their evolutionary functions? Why did the human mind evolve? And why did it evolve in the specific way that it did? Why did human societies evolve? Do they exhibit general features that are common to all? Do they serve an evolutionary function and, if so, what is it?

Even though Fox holds that the general shape of human mentation and human social life is fixed by inherited tendencies and propensities, he is sensitive to the fact that the details of the social life of human beings cannot be read off from the biological features of individual organisms. Cultural and social factors play a major role. However, social and cultural factors are ultimately evolved biological adaptations. Chomsky's innate grammar model is paradigmatic of this approach. When Chomsky argues that human linguistic capacities are innate and inherited, he is not claiming that a knowledge of the genetical and biological structures of the developing fetal brain would ever be sufficient to predict what specific language a given infant would learn. But, whatever language that infant would learn, it would be a human language. In Chomsky's view, all human languages possess certain characteristic, fixed, general features that serve as a framework within which the diversity of different human languages develop. So, the human child is born with a certain range of capacities and the specific development of these capacities is a function of the environment within which it develops. This kind of analysis has a point only to the extent that it provides an exclusionary set of bounds. If everything is possible, then the biological basis of human behavior becomes a truism—human behavior has a biological basis because human beings are biological organisms. This latter point is the thesis of the so-called environmentalists, who hold that all human behavior is cultural, where *cultural* has to be construed as an alternative to "biological".

Fox's thesis is a (less provocative) variation on the Wilsonian point that the genes hold culture on a leash. Human nature, the human mind, and human society can be construed as evolutionarily constrained within the same sort of broad limits. This is no crude biological or genetic determinism, although it may be deterministic nonetheless (cf. Fox, 1983, pp. 197f.). Is biology destiny? It depends on the level of analysis. The general shape of behavioral repertoires—what constitutes our nature, as it were—is inherited from our evolutionary past. The specific forms these shapes assume cannot be predicted from our evolutionary heritage but are subject to the whims and fancies of environmental fortune.

The debate between the biological determinists and the cultural determinists and all the gradations between is, of course, just one more variation on the "nature-nurture" debate of bygone days. The simple and to an extent simpleminded resolution is to argue that the distinction is bogus. Every aspect of animate development is partially natural and partially nurtural. This will not do to dampen the debate, however, because once acknowledged, the question of how much nature and how much nurture is bound to rekindle the argument. For the specific problem at hand, we can put the issue as follows. Let us limit the "biological" to the structure and behavior of the human brain. Everything else is "cultural." So, if we examine Baby Doe's brain and find in her architecture a fixed pathway to Japanese grammar, then we will say that her development as a Japanese speaker is dominated by biological influences. On the other hand, if her birth or nutritive parents are Japanese speakers, this counts as a cultural factor with respect to her acquisition of linguistic skills. This way of drawing the distinction, albeit crude, is fine enough for our purposes and should suffice to slow down the opposition to drawing any distinction at all.

Given this, we can pose the "how much?" question in the following way. All human behavioral attributes, traits, or characteristics exhibit variation. Part of this variation is due to underlying differences in brain structure and part of it is due to underlying differences in culture. One way to put the issue between cultural and biological determinists is to ask, for a given trait, how much of the variation is due to variation in brain structure and how much of it is due to variation in culture. In the case of the native Japanese speakers, my guess is that most, if not virtually all, of the variation is due to variation in culture—what language one speaks as a native is a function of the linguistic community one is brought up in. In fact, for most "cultural" traits, this should be the case. The biological basis has become "fixed" through evolution. It is virtually universal and, as such, does not vary in the population.

If we stop here, the environmentalist comes back with the retort of "I told you so! Biological pedigrees are no predictors of the specific differences between human social groups which are the meat and drink of anthropologists, sociologists and psychologists. Biology, far from being destiny, drops out of the human behavioral equation. All, or virtually all, of the variation in human behavior is due to cultural differences." This is right but misses the point. Biology is still destiny because, at least in Fox's view, the environmentalist is focusing on the wrong level of analysis. Where biology has its punch is in the variation between humans and other species. What gets washed out in the intraspecific variation is the core of human nature such as it is—the characteristic shape we possess that distinguishes us as human. Several points emerge. First, it behooves us to support interspecific comparative studies as crucial for delimiting the scope of the human spirit. These studies, though difficult, will help to establish what, if any, boundaries to the development of the human potential exist. Second, is there any reason for social scientists to take this approach seriously given the variational argument rehearsed previously? The answer to this hinges on a question we posed earlier. Are there significant boundaries to the range of the development of the human behavioral potential or cultural universals or inherited generic propensities? If the answer to this is yes, then an evolutionary analysis will be able to contribute in a meaningful way to an analysis of the human condition. If the answer is no, then perhaps not. The nonhuman animal evidence suggests the answer is yes. No one doubts that chimpanzees, seals, cats, dogs, iguanas, snakes, and butterflies have natures imprinted by their evolutionary history. Can human beings be the only exception? The argument that they are rests on arguments about the power of the human brain and mind. These capacities are no doubt great, but are they sufficient to "free" human beings from the constraints of their inherited capacities?[2]

So much for abstract intellectual considerations. Another factor remains that needs to be taken into account. What is the relative cost effectiveness of pursuing various lines of research? Scientific knowledge costs money. Given the difficulties, both conceptual and experimental, in doing and interpreting sociobiological research on humans, can we expect the return to be worth the investment? In the short term, I suspect not.

The value of more information, under the circumstances, is something that needs careful consideration. Insofar as no scientific theory is going to be able to completely explain or justify any moral system, the effect of introducing evolutionary considerations into the discussion is going to be indeterminate. That is, unless one argues that particular moral practices or codes can be "read off" from the facts and theory of evolution, those facts and that theory are going to underdetermine any particular moral system. A similar point applies to the policy considerations which play so large a role, for example, in Alexander's thinking. Including biological or specifically evolutionary considerations in our deliberations is not going to lead to the adoption or justification of particular policies. It is to Alexander's credit that he does not think they will. To think otherwise is to treat moral issues as primarily "technical" problems, to borrow a felicitous phrase from Putnam who used it in connection with his criticism of B. F. Skinner's analysis of human happiness. All relevant information is potentially useful in producing explanations, providing justifications, and reaching policy decisions. This provides a *weak* justification for the deployment of resources to garner further biological data that may be relevant to the construction of moral systems. It is weak insofar as it equally justifies the collection of *any* information that might prove useful in this endeavor. What is needed, however, is some sense that the biological data and biological theories will be or are *more* relevant to reaching appropriate policy decisions than some other data or other theories. This *strong* justification for the relevance of biology to morality is what is so far lacking in Alexander's and other sociobiological analyses of moral phenomena.

THE RELEVANCE OF DARWIN FOR MORAL PHILOSOPHY

Darwin's relevance for philosophy is still a matter of dispute. John Dewey and Josiah Royce, among many, felt that one of the achievements of Darwin's theory of evolution would be to bring about a revolution in philosophy. Therefore, Dewey, writing fifty years after the publication of the *Origin*, described what he took to be Darwin's philosophical contribution in the following words:

> Old ideas give way slowly; for they are more than abstract logical forms and categories. They are habits, predispositions, deeply ingrained attitudes of aversion and preference. Moreover, the conviction persists—though history shows it to be a hallucination—that all the questions that the human mind has asked are questions that can be answered in terms of the alternatives that

the questions themselves present. But in fact intellectual progress usually occurs through sheer abandonment of questions together with both of the alternatives they assume—an abandonment that results from their decreasing vitality and a change of urgent interest. We do not solve them: we get over them. Old questions are solved by disappearing, evaporating, while new questions corresponding to the changed attitude of endeavor and preference take their place. Doubtless the greatest dissolvent in contemporary thought of old questions, the greatest precipitant of new methods, new intentions, new problems, is the one effected by the scientific revolution that found its climax in the "Origin of Species." (Dewey, 1910)

Josiah Royce, around the same period, expressed similar sentiments: "*The Origin of Species.* . . . With the one exception of Newton's *Principia* no single book of empirical science has ever been of more importance to philosophy than this work of Darwin" (cited by Flew, 1984, p. 3). On the other side, we have the epigram from Wittgenstein, that "Darwin's theory has no more to do with philosophy than any other hypothesis in natural science" (*Tractatus*, 4. 1122).

Flew attributes the conflict to a difference in what one takes "philosophy" to be—in either a strict and technical sense or a loose and popular sense. No doubt this is true, to an extent: one can construe philosophy in such a way that no scientific evidence or theories are relevant to it. But, so much the worse for narrow and technical senses of philosophy. On the other hand, the prospects for an interdisciplinary attack upon the problems of the human condition from an evolutionary point of view are very exciting. Philosophers would do well to consider how they may contribute constructively to what promises to be a difficult but potentially very rewarding series of investigations.

NOTES

1. We see a contemporary version of this phenomenon in the rush by some contemporary physicists to invoke the divine to explain phenomena at or around the Big Bang that, for the moment at least, lie beyond the explanatory scope of current physical theory.

2. This again is an echo of a Wilsonian theme. But, one difference between Fox and Wilson is that, whereas for Fox the important biological differences are between human and nonhuman, for Wilson there is a suggestion that even at the level of intrahuman differences, biological differences may be a factor. Wilson does not, of course, think that human beings are born with a special propensity to learn Japanese as opposed to any other human language, but he has suggested that specific genetic differences between Japanese and occidental populations may be

implicated in differences between the drinking behavior of Japanese and non-Japanese populations. Whether this thesis or similar claims are sustainable is, in large part, an empirical issue. The point is we do not need to endorse them to endorse the view that an evolutionary perspective is the proper approach to the study of human behavior.

Bibliography

Alexander, Richard. 1987. *The Biology of Moral Systems*. New York: Aldine De Gruyter.

———— and G. Borgia. 1978. "On the Origin and Basis of the Male-Female Phenomenon." In *Sexual Selection and Reproductive Competition in Insects*, ed. M. F. Blum and N. Blum, pp. 417–440. New York: Academic Press.

Alexander, S. 1892. "Natural Selection in Morals." *International Journal of Ethics*, 2, no. 4 : 411–439.

Appleman, Philip, ed. 1959. *Darwin: A Norton Critical Edition*. New York: W. W. Norton and Company.

Arnold, A. J., and K. Fristrup. 1982. "The Theory of Evolution by Natural Selection: A Hierarchical Expansion." *Paleobiology* 8: 113–129.

Axelrod, Robert. 1984. *The Evolution of Cooperation*. New York: Basic Books.

Bachem, A. 1958. "Ethics and Esthetics on a Biological Basis." *Philosophy of Science* 25: 169–175.

Badcock, C. 1990. *Oedipus in Evolution: A New Theory of Sex*. Oxford: Basil Blackwell.

————. 1986. *The Problem of Altruism*. Oxford: Basil Blackwell.

Bagehot, Walter. 1956. *Physics and Politics: Or Thoughts on the Application of the Principles of "Natural Selection" and "Inheritance" to Political Society*. Boston: Beacon Press.

Bain, Alexander. 1884. *Mental and Moral Science*. Vol. 2. London: Longmans, Green and Co.

Baldwin, James M. 1909. *Darwin and the Humanities*. Baltimore: Review Publishing Company.

Balguy, John. 1976. *The Foundations of Moral Goodness: Or a Further Inquiry into the Original of Our Idea of Virtue*. New York: Garland Publishing.

Ball, Stephen W. 1988. "Evolution, Explanation, and the Fact/Value Distinction." *Biology and Philosophy* 3: 317–348.

Bartley III, W. W. 1987. "Philosophy of Biology versus Philosophy of Physics." In *Evolutionary Epistemology, Theory of Rationality and the Sociology of Knowledge*, ed. G. Radnitsky and W. W. Bartley III, pp. 7–45. La Salle, IL: Open Court.

Batson, C. Daniel. 1991. *The Altruism Question: Toward a Social-Psychological Answer*. Hillsdale, NJ: Lawrence Erlbaum Associates.

Beatty, John. 1981. "Hopes, Fears, and Sociobiology." *Queens Quarterly* 88 (Winter): 607–619.

Berry, Christopher J. 1982. *Hume, Hegel and Human Nature*. The Hague: Martinus Nijhoff.

———. 1986. *Human Nature*. Atlantic Highlands, NJ: Humanities Press International.

Bonner, John Tyler. 1988. *The Evolution of Complexity by Means of Natural Selection*. Princeton, NJ: Princeton University Press.

Boring, E. G. 1950. *The Influence of Evolutionary Theory Upon American Psychological Thought*. London: Yale University Press.

Bowler, Peter. 1988. *The Non-Darwinian Revolution*. Baltimore: Johns Hopkins University Press.

Boyd, Robert, and Peter Richerson. 1985. *Culture and the Evolutionary Process*. Chicago: University of Chicago Press.

Bradie, M. 1986. "Assessing Evolutionary Epistemology." *Biology and Philosophy* 4: 401–459.

———. 1989a. "Evolutionary Epistemology as Naturalized Epistemology." In *Issues in Evolutionary Epistemology*, ed. K. Hahlweg and C. A. Hooker, pp. 393–412. Albany: State University of New York Press.

———. 1989b. "The Implications of Evolutionary Biology for Ethics." In *Akten des 13, Internationalen Wittgenstein Symposiums*, ed. R. Weingartner and G. Schwarz. Vienna: Holder-Pichler-Temsky.

———. 1990. "Should Epistemologists Take Darwin Seriously?" In *Evolution, Cognition and Realism: Studies in Evolutionary Epistemology*, ed. N. Rescher, pp. 33–38. Lanham, MD: University Press of America.

———. 1991. "The Evolution of Scientific Lineages." In *PSA 1990*, vol. 2, ed. L. Wessels, A. Fine, and M. Forbes, pp. 245–254. Lansing, MI: The Philosophy of Science Association.

———. 1992a. "Darwin's Legacy." *Biology and Philosophy* 7: 111–126.

———. 1992b. "Ethics and Evolution: The Biological Basis of Morality." *Inquiry* 36: 199–217.

Breuer, George. 1982. *Sociobiology and the Human Dimension*. Cambridge: Cambridge University Press.

Brewer, Marilynn B., and Linnda R. Caporael. 1990. "Selfish Genes vs. Selfish People: Sociobiology as Origin Myth." *Motivation and Emotion* 14, no. 4: 237–243.

Broad, C. D. 1949. "Review of Julian S. Huxley's *Evolutionary Ethics*." In *Readings in Philosophical Analysis*, ed. H. Feigl and W. Sellars, pp. 564–586. New York: Appleton-Century-Crofts.

Bryson, Gladys. 1945. *Man and Society: The Scottish Inquiry of the Eighteenth Century*. Princeton, NJ: Princeton University Press.

Buss, David M. 1983. "Evolutionary Biology and Personality Psychology: Implications of Genetic Variability." *Personality and Individual Differences* 4: 51–63.

———. 1984. "Evolutionary Biology and Personality Psychology: Toward a Conception of Human Nature and Individual Differences." *American Psychologist* 39: 1135–1147.

———. 1990a. "Evolutionary Social Psychology: Prospects and Pitfalls." *Motivation and Emotion* 14, no. 4: 265–286.

————. 1990b. "Toward a Biologically Informed Psychology of Personality." *Journal of Personality* 55: 1–16.

————. 1991. "Evolutionary Personality Psychology." In *Annual Review of Psychology*, ed. Mark R. Rosenzweig and Lyman W. Porter, pp. 459–91. Palo Alto, CA: Annual Reviews.

Butler, Joseph. 1983. *Five Sermons*. Indianapolis: Hackett.

Callebaut, W., and R. Pinxton, ed. 1987. *Evolutionary Epistemology*. Dordrecht: Kluwer Academic.

Campbell, D. T. 1960. "Blind Variation and Selective Retention in Creative Thought and in Other Knowledge Processes." *Psychological Review* 67: 380–400.

————. 1974a. "Evolutionary Epistemology." In *The Philosophy of Karl Popper*, ed. P. A. Schilpp, pp. 413–463. LaSalle, IL: Open Court.

————. 1974b. "Unjustified Variation and Selective Retention in Scientific Discovery." In *Studies in the Philosophy of Biology*, ed. F. J. Ayala and T. Dobzhansky, pp. 139–161. London: MacMillan.

Campbell, Richmond. 1984. "Sociobiology and the Possibility of Ethical Naturalism." In *Morality, Reason and Truth*, ed. David Copp and David Zimmerman, pp. 270–285. Totowa, NJ: Rowman and Allanheld.

————. 1988. "Gauthier's Theory of Morals by Agreement." *Philosophical Quarterly* 38: 343–364.

Campbell, T. D. 1971. *Adam Smith's Science of Morals*. London: George Allen and Unwin.

————. 1975. "Scientific Explanation and Ethical Justification in the *Moral Sentiments*." In *Essays on Adam Smith*, ed. Andrew S. Skinner and Thomas Wilson, pp. 68–82. Oxford: Clarendon Press.

Cantor, Nancy. 1990. "Social Psychology and Sociobiology: What Can We Leave to Evolution?" *Motivation and Emotion* 14, no. 4: 245–254.

Caplan, Arthur ed. 1978. *The Sociobiology Debate*. New York: Harper and Row.

———— and Bruce Jennings, ed. 1984. *Darwin, Marx, and Freud: Their Influence on Moral Theory*. The Hastings Center Series in Ethics. New York and London: Plenum Press.

Caporael, Linda, and Marilynn Brewer. 1990. "We ARE Darwinians, and This Is What the Fuss Is All About." *Motivation and Emotion* 14, no. 4: 287–293.

Carnap, Rudolf. 1956. *Meaning and Necessity*. Chicago: University of Chicago Press.

Cela-Conde, C. J. 1986. "The Challenge of Evolutionary Ethics." *Biology and Philosophy* 1, no. 3: 293–297.

Chamley, P. E. 1975. "The Conflict Between Montesquieu and Hume: A Study of the Origins of Adam Smith's Universalism." In *Essays on Adam Smith*, ed. Andrew S. Skinner and Thomas Wilson, pp. 274–305. Oxford: Clarendon Press.

Cherry, Christopher. 1975. "Nature Artiface and Moral Approbation." *Proceedings of the Aristotelian Society* 76: 264–282.

Churchland, P. M. 1989. *A Neurocomputational Perspective: The Nature of Mind and the Structure of Science*. Cambridge, Mass.: The MIT Press.

Clark, Stephen R. L. 1976–1977. "God, Good and Evil." *Proceedings of the Aristotelian Society* 77: 246–264.

Connon, R. W. 1979. "The Naturalism of Hume Revisited." In *McGill Hume Studies*, ed. David Fate Norton, Nicholas Capaldi, and Wade Robison, pp. 121–145. San Diego: Austin Hill Press.

Cooley, Charles H. 1956. *The Two Major Works of Charles H. Cooley: Social Organization and; Human Nature and the Social Order.* Glencoe, IL: The Free Press.

Cooper, David E. 1979. "The Argument from Evolution." *Proceedings of the Aristotelian Society* Supplementary Volume 53: 223–237.

Cosmides, Leda, and John Tooby. 1987. "From Evolution to Behavior: Evolutionary Psychology as the Missing Link." In *The Latest on the Best: Essays on Evolution and Optimality,* ed. John Dupre, pp. 277–307. Cambridge, Mass.: The MIT Press.

Cronin, Helena. 1991. *The Ant and the Peacock.* Cambridge: Cambridge University Press.

Danto, A. C. 1967. "Naturalism." In *Encyclopedia of Philosophy,* vol. 5, ed. Paul Edwards. New York: Macmillan.

Darley, John M., and Thomas R. Shultz. 1990. "Moral Judgments: Their Content and Acquisition." In *Annual Review of Psychology,* ed. Mark R. Rosenzweig and Lyman W. Porter, pp. 525–556. Palo Alto, CA: Annual Reviews.

Darwin, Charles. 1936. *The Origin of Species.* New York: The Modern Library.

———. 1981. *The Descent of Man, and Selection in Relation to Sex.* Princeton, NJ: Princeton University Press.

Davis, Bernard. 1982. "Alleged Threats from Genetics." In *Logic, Methodology and Philosophy of Science VI: Proceedings of the Sixth International Congress of Logic, Methodology and Philosophy of Science,* ed. L. J. Cohen, pp. 835–842. Amsterdam: North-Holland Publishing Company.

Dawkins, Richard. 1976. *The Selfish Gene.* Oxford: Oxford University Press.

Dewey, John. 1910. *The Influence of Darwin on Philosophy and Other Essays in Contemporary Thought.* New York: Henry Holt and Co.

———. 1938. *Logic: The Theory of Inquiry.* New York: Henry Holt and Company.

———. 1957. *Human Nature and Conduct.* New York: The Modern Library.

———. 1972. "Evolution and Ethics." In *Early Works of John Dewey 1882–1898,* pp. 34–53. Carbondale: Southern Illinois University Press.

Edel, Abraham. 1955. *Ethical Judgment: The Use of Science in Ethics.* Glencoe, IL: The Free Press.

Eldredge, Niles. 1985. *Unfinished Synthesis: Biological Hierarchies and Modern Evolutionary Thought.* Oxford: Oxford University Press.

Emerson, Roger L. 1990. "Science and Moral Philosophy in the Scottish Enlightenment." In *Studies in the Philosophy of the Scottish Enlightenment,* ed. M. A. Stewart, pp. 11–36. Oxford: Clarendon Press.

Flanagan, Owen. 1986. *The Science of the Mind.* Cambridge, MA: The MIT Press.

Flanagan, Owen J. 1981. "Is Morality Epiphenomenal? The Failure of the Sociobiological Reduction of Ethics." *Philosophical Forum* XIII: 207–225.

Flew, Antony. 1967. *Evolutionary Ethics.* London: Macmillan.

———. 1984. *Darwinian Evolution.* London: Paladin.

Flohr, Heiner. 1986. "The Importance of Biology for the Social Sciences." *Ratio* 28: 1–19.

Foley, Vernard. 1976. *The Social Physics of Adam Smith*. West Lafayette, IN: Purdue University Press.

Foot, Philippa. 1963. "Hume on Moral Judgment." In *David Hume: A Symposium*, ed. D. F. Pears, pp. 67–76. London: Macmillan and Co.

Fox, Robin. 1983. *The Red Lamp of Incest: An Inquiry into the Origin of Mind and Society*. Notre Dame, IN: Notre Dame Press.

Frank, Robert H. 1988. *Passions Within Reason*. New York: W. W. Norton and Company.

Gardiner, P. L. 1963. "Hume's Theory of the Passions." In *David Hume: A Symposium*, ed. D. F. Pears, pp. 31–42. London: Macmillan and Co.

Gewirth, Alan. 1982. *Human Rights: Essays on Justification and Applications*. Chicago: University of Chicago Press.

———. 1986. "The Problem of Specificity in Evolutionary Ethics." *Biology and Philosophy* 1, no. 3: 297–305.

———. 1993. "How Ethical is Evolutionary Ethics?" In *Evolutionary Ethics*, ed. Matthew N. Nitecki and Doris V. Nitecki, pp. 241–256. Albany: State University of New York Press.

Ghiselin, Michael T. 1974. *The Economy of Nature and the Evolution of Sex*. Berkeley: University of California.

Gibbard, Alan. 1990. *Wise Choices, Apt Feelings: A Theory of Normative Judgment*. Cambridge, MA: Harvard University Press.

Gilligan, C. 1982. *In a Different Voice: Psychological Theory and Women's Development*. Cambridge, MA: Harvard University Press.

Goldman, Allan. 1987. "Red and Right." *Journal of Philosophy* 84: 349–362.

Goldman, Alvin. 1992. "Empathy, Mind and Morals." *Proceedings and Addresses of the American Philosophical Association* 66, no. 3: 17–41.

Goldsmith, Timothy H. 1991. *The Biological Roots of Human Behavior: Forging Links between Evolution and Behavior*. Oxford: Oxford University Press.

Gould, Stephen. 1983. "Nature Holds No Moral Message." *Bostonia* (August): 36–41.

Gould, S. J. 1982. "Darwinism and the Expansion of Evolutionary Theory." *Science* 216: 380–387.

Grave, S. A. 1960. *The Scottish Philosophy of Common Sense*. Oxford, England: Clarendon Press.

Grean, Stanley. 1967. *Shaftesbury's Philosophy of Religion and Ethics: A Study in Enthusiasm*. Athens: Ohio University Press.

Grice, G. R. 1970. "Hume's Law." *Proceedings of the Aristotelian Society* Supplementary Volume 44: 89–104.

———. 1978. "Moral Theories and Received Opinions." *Proceedings of the Aristotelian Society* Supplementary Volume 52: 1–12.

Gruber, Howard E. 1974. *Darwin on Man: A Psychological Study of Scientific Creativity*. London: Wildwood House.

Guttenplan, Samuel. 1979. "Moral Realism and Moral Dilemmas." *Proceedings of the Aristotelian Society* 80: 61–80.

Guyau, J. M. 1909. *Education and Heredity*. New York: Walter Scott Publishing Company.

Haeckel, Ernst. 1977. "Last Words on Evolution." In *Comparative Psychology*, ed. Daniel R. Robinson, reprinted from the 1906 ed., vol. 3. Washington, DC: University Publications of America.

Hardin, Garrett. 1961. *Nature and Man's Fate*. New York: New American Library.

Hare, R. M. 1989. *Essays in Ethical Theory*. Oxford: Clarendon Press.

Harrison, Ross. 1976. "The Only Possible Morality." *Proceedings of the Aristotelian Society* Supplementary Volume 50: 21–42.

Hempel, C. G. 1949. "Geometry and Empirical Science." In *Readings in Philosophical Analysis*, ed. H. Feigl and W. Sellars, pp. 238–249. New York: Appleton-Century-Crofts.

Hinde, R. A. 1987. *Individuals, Relationships, and Culture: Links Between Ethology and the Social Sciences*. Cambridge: Cambridge University Press.

Hirschman, Albert O. 1977. *The Passions and the Interests*. Princeton, NJ: Princeton University Press.

Hirshleifer, Jack. 1982. *Evolutionary Models In Economics and Law*, vol. 4. Research in Law and Economics, ed. Richard O. Zerbe, Jr. Greenwich, CT: Aijai Press.

————. 1987. "On the Emotions as Guarantors of Threats and Promises." In *The Latest on the Best: Essays on Evolution and Optimality*, ed. John Dupre. Cambridge, MA: The MIT Press.

Hobbes, Thomas. 1972. *De Homine*. Garden City, NY: Anchor Books.

Höffding, Harald. 1909. "The Influence of the Conception of Evolution on Modern Philosophy." In *Darwin and Modern Science*, ed. A. C. Seward, pp. 446–464. Cambridge: Cambridge University Press.

————. 1912. *A Brief History of Modern Philosophy*, trans. Charles Finley Sanders. New York: Macmillan.

Holland, R. F. 1967. "Moral Scepticism." *Proceedings of the Aristotelian Society* Supplementary Volume 41: 185–198.

Home, Henry. 1976. *Essays in the Principle of Morality and Natural Religion*. New York: Garland Publishing.

Hrdy, S. B., and G. Hausfater. 1984. "Comparative and Evolutionary Perspectives on Infanticide: Introduction and Overview." In *Infanticides: Comparative and Evolutionary Perspectives*, ed. Glenn Hausfater and Sarah Blaffer Hrdy, pp. xii–xxxv. New York: Aldine Books.

Hughes, William. 1986. "Richards' Defense of Evolutionary Ethics." *Biology and Philosophy* 1, no. 3: 306–315.

Hull, David. 1988. *Science as a Process: An Evolutionary Account of the Social and Conceptual Development of Science*. Chicago: University of Chicago Press.

————. 1989. *The Metaphysics of Evolution*. SUNY Series in Philosophy and Biology, ed. David Shaner. Albany: State University of New York Press.

Hume, David. 1825. "Of the Standards of Taste." In *Essays and Treatises on Several Subjects*, pp. 221–248, vol. 1. Edinburgh: Bell and Bradfute, and W. Blackwood.

————. 1946. *An Enquiry Concerning the Principles of Morals*, reprinted from the 1777 edition ed. La Salle, IL: Open Court.

———. 1957. *An Inquiry Concerning Human Understanding.* New York: Liberal Arts Press.

———. 1978. *A Treatise of Human Nature*, edited with an analytical index by L. A. Selby-Bigge with text revised and variant readings by P. H. Nidditch, 2d ed. Oxford: Clarendon Press.

Hutcheson, Francis. 1969. *An Inquiry Concerning the Original of Our Ideas of Virtue or Moral Good.* New York: Gregg International Publishers.

———. 1971. "A System of Moral Philosophy." In *Four Early Works on Motivation*, ed. Paul McReynolds. Gainesville, FL: Scholars Facsimiles and Reprints.

Huxley, Julian. 1926. "The Case For Eugenics." *Sociological Review* 18: 279–290.

———. 1960. *Knowledge, Morality and Destiny.* New York: Mentor Books.

———. 1942. *Evolution: The Modern Synthesis.* London: Allen and Unwin.

Huxley, T. H. 1888. "The Struggle for Existence in Human Society," *The Nineteenth Century.* Reprinted in P. Kropotkin, *Mutual Aid*, pp. 329–341. Boston: Extending Horizon Books, 1955.

———. 1989. "Evolution and Ethics." In *Evolution and Ethics*, ed. James Paradis and George Williams. Princeton, NJ: Princeton University Press.

——— and Julian Huxley. 1947. *Touchstone for Ethics: 1893–1943.* New York: Harper.

Isen, Alice M. 1990. "Adaptation: Sociobiology, Evolutionary Psychology, and the Variety of Lessons to Be Learned." *Motivation and Emotion* 14, no. 4: 295–302.

Jacquette, Dale. 1988. "Explanatory Limitations of Sociobiology." *Journal of Social Philosophy* 19: 56–62.

Kagan, Jerome. 1984. *The Nature of the Child.* New York: Basic Books.

Kahane, Howard. 1989. "Making the World Safe for Reciprocity." In *Reason and Responsibility*, ed. Joel Feinberg, pp. 511–519, 7th ed. Belmont, CA: Wadsworth Publishing.

Kant, Immanuel. 1978. *Anthropology from a Pragmatic Point of View.* Carbondale, IL: Southern Illinois University Press.

———. 1989. *Foundations of the Metaphysics of Morals*, trans. Lewis White Beck. New York: Macmillan.

Katz, J. 1990. *The Metaphysics of Meaning.* Cambridge, MA: The MIT Press.

Kemp, J. 1970. *Ethical Naturalism: Hobbes and Hume.* New York: Macmillan.

Kitcher, Philip. 1985. *Vaulting Ambition.* Cambridge, MA: The MIT Press.

———. 1988. "Imitating Selection." In *Evolutionary Processes and Metaphors*, ed. Mae-Wan Ho and Sidney W. Fox. New York: John Wiley and Sons.

Kohlberg, L. 1981. *The Philosophy of Moral Development: Moral Stages and the Idea of Justice.* San Francisco: Harper and Row.

———. 1984. *The Psychology of Moral Development: The Nature and Validity of Moral Stages.* San Francisco: Harper and Row.

Kropotkin, P. 1947. *Ethics: Origins and Development*, trans. Louis S. Friedland and Joseph R. Piroshnikoff. New York: Tudor Publishing Company.

———. 1955. *Mutual Aid: A Factor of Evolution.* Boston: Extending Horizon Books.

Landau, Misia. 1978. "Human Evolution as Narrative." *American Scientist* 72: 262–268.

Lande, Russell. 1982. "A Quantitative Genetic Theory of Life History Evolution." *Ecology* 63, no. 3: 607–615.

Laudan, L. 1984. *Science and Values*. Berkeley: University of California Press.

———. 1990. "Normative Naturalism." *Philosophy of Science* 57: 44–59.

Leahy, Michael P. T. 1991. *Against Liberation: Putting Animals in Perspective*. London: Routledge.

Lewis, H. A. 1979. "The Argument From Evolution." *Proceedings of the Aristotelian Society* Supplementary Volume 53: 207–221.

Lewontin, R. C., Steven Rose, and Leon J. Kamin. 1984. *Not in Our Genes: Biology, Ideology, and Human Nature*. New York: Pantheon Books.

Lloyd, Daniel. 1985. "Frankenstein's Children: Artificial Intelligence and Human Value." *Metaphilosophy* 16: 307–318.

Long, James. 1969. "An Inquiry into the Origin of the Human Appetites and Affections." In *Four Early Works on Motivation*, ed. Paul McReynolds. 3rd ed. Gainesville, FL: Scholars Facsimiles and Reprints.

Lorenz, Konrad. 1977. *Behind the Mirror*. London: Methuen.

———. 1982. "Kant's Doctrine of the *a priori* in the Light of Contemporary Biology." In *Learning, Development, and Culture: Essays in Evolutionary Epistemology*, ed. H. C. Plotkin, pp. 121–142. New York: John Wiley and Sons.

Lumsden, C., and E. O. Wilson. 1981. *Genes, Mind and Culture*. Cambridge, MA: Harvard University Press.

———. 1983. *Promethean Fire*. Cambridge, MA: Harvard University Press.

MacIntyre, Alasdair. 1979. "Why is the Search for the Foundations of Ethics So Frustrating?" *Hastings Center Report*: 16–22.

Mackie, J. L. 1977. *Ethics: Inventing Right and Wrong*. New York: Penguin.

———. 1978. "The Law of the Jungle: Moral Alternatives and Principles of Evolution." *Philosophy* 53: 455–464.

Mackintosh, Robert. 1899. *From Comte to Benjamin Kidd: The Appeal to Biology or Evolution for Human Guidance*. New York: Macmillan.

Mackintosh, Sir James. 1834. *A General View of the Progress of Ethical Philosophy*. Philadelphia: Carey, Lea and Blanchard.

Manier, Edward. 1978. *The Young Darwin and His Cultural Circle*. Boston: D. Reidel Publishing Company.

Masters, Roger D. 1989. "Obligation and the New Naturalism." *Biology and Philosophy* 4: 17–32.

Maxwell, Mary. 1984. *Human Evolution: A Philosophical Anthropology*. New York: Columbia University Press.

———. 1990. *Morality Among Nations: An Evolutionary View*. Albany, NY: State University of New York Press.

Mayr, Ernst. 1978. "Evolution." *Scientific American* 239 (September): 46–56.

———. 1988. "The Origin of Human Ethics." In *Towards a New Philosophy of Biology*, Cambridge, MA: Harvard University Press.

McConnaughey, G. 1950. "Darwin and Social Darwinism." *Osiris* 9: 397–413.

McCown, Theodore D., and Kenneth Kennedy, ed. 1972. *Climbing Man's Family Tree*. Englewood Cliffs, NJ: Prentice-Hall.

McDowell, John, and I. G. McFetridge. 1978. "Are Moral Requirements Hypothetical Imperatives?" *Proceedings of the Aristotelian Society* Supplementary Volume 52: 13–42.

McGinn, Colin. 1979. "Evolution, Animals, and the Basis of Morality." *Inquiry* 22: 82–99.

McNaughton, David. 1988. *Moral Vision*. Oxford: Basil Blackwell.

Michod, Richard E. 1984. "The Theory of Kin Selection." In *Genes, Organisms, Populations: Controversies over the Units of Selection*, ed. R. N. Brandon and R. M. Burian, pp. 203–237. Cambridge, MA: MIT Press.

Midgley, Mary. 1979a. *Beast and Man: The Roots of Human Nature*. New York: Harvester Press.

———. 1979b. "Gene-Juggling." *Philosophy* 54: 439–458.

———. 1973–74. "The Neutrality of the Moral Philosopher." *Proceedings of the Aristotelian Society* 74: 211–229.

———. 1984. *Wickedness: A Philosophical Essay*. London: Routledge and Kegan Paul.

Monro, D. H. 1953. *Godwin's Moral Philosophy*. Westport, CT: Greenwood Press.

Montague, Ashley. 1956. *The Biosocial Nature of Man*. New York: Grove Press.

Monteiro, Joao-Paulo. 1976. "Hume, Induction, and Natural Selection." In *McGill Hume Studies*, ed. David Fate Norton, pp. 291–308. San Diego: Austin Hill Press.

Moore, G. E. 1962. *Principia Ethica*. London: Cambridge University Press.

Moore, James. 1976. "The Social Background of Hume's Science of Human Nature." In *McGill Hume Studies*, ed. David Fate Norton, pp. 23–42. San Diego: Austin Hill Press.

———. 1990. "The Two Systems of Francis Hutcheson: On the Origins of the Scottish Enlightenment." In *Studies in the Philosophy of the Scottish Enlightenment*, ed. M. A. Stewart, pp. 37–59. Oxford: Clarendon Press.

Mossner, E. C., and I. S. Ross, ed. 1987. *The Correspondence of Adam Smith*, 2d ed. Oxford: Clarendon Press.

Munz, Peter. 1985. *Our Knowledge of the Growth of Knowledge: Popper or Wittgenstein*. London: Routledge and Kegan Paul.

Murphy, Jeffrie. 1982. *Evolution, Morality, and the Meaning of Life*. Totowa, NJ: Rowman and Littlefield.

Nagel, T. 1978. "Ethics as an Autonomous Theoretical Subject." In *Morality as a Biological Phenomenon*, ed. Gunther S. Stent, pp. 198–205. Berkeley: University of California Press.

———. 1986. "Review of B. Williams' *Ethics and the Limits of Philosophy*." *Journal of Philosophy* 83: 351–360.

Nisbett, Richard E. 1990. "Evolutionary Psychology, Biology, and Cultural Evolution." *Motivation and Emotion* 14, no. 4: 255–263.

Nordau, Max. 1922. *Morals and the Evolution of Man*. New York: Funk and Wagnalls.

Norton, David Fate. 1982. *David Hume: Common-Sense Moralist, Sceptical Metaphysician*. Princeton, NJ: Princeton University Press.

——— Nicholas Capaldi, and Wade L. Robison, ed. 1976. *Studies In Hume and Scottish Philosophy*. McGill Hume Studies. San Diego: Austin Hill Press.

Nowak, Martin A., and Karl Sigmund. 1992. "Tit for Tat in Heterogeneous Populations." *Nature* 355 (January 16): 250–252.

Nunner-Winkler, Gertrude. 1984. "Two Moralities? A Critical Discussion of an Ethic of Care and Responsibility versus an Ethic of Rights and Justice." In *Morality, Moral Behavior, and Moral Development*, ed. William Kurtines and Jacob Gewirtz, pp. 348–361. New York: John Wiley and Sons.

O'Hear, Anthony. 1987. "Has the Theory of Evolution Any Relevance to Philosophy?" *Ratio* 29 (June): 16–35.

Osofsky, Stephen. 1979. *Peter Kropotkin*. Boston: Twayne.

Paley, W. 1785. *Principles of Moral and Political Philosophy*. London: R. Faulder.

Panksepp, Jack. 1989. "Altruism, Neurobiology Of." In *Neuroscience Year: Supplement 1 to the Encyclopedia of Neuroscience*, ed. George Adelman, pp. 7–10. Boston: Birkhauser.

Passmore, John. 1970. *The Perfectability of Man*. New York: Charles Scribner's Sons.

———. 1974. *Man's Responsibility for Nature*. New York: Charles Scribner's Sons.

Peach, Bernard, ed. 1971. *Francis Hutcheson's "Illustrations on the Moral Sense."* Cambridge, MA: The Belknap Press of Harvard University Press.

Plato. 1956. *Great Dialogues of Plato*, trans. W. H. D. Rouse. New York: Mentor Books.

Popper, K. R. 1968. *The Logic of Scientific Knowledge*. New York: Harper Books.

———. 1972. *Objective Knowledge: An Evolutionary Approach*. Oxford: Clarendon Press.

———. 1976. "Darwinism as a Metaphysical Research Programme." *Methodology and Science* 9: 103–119.

———. 1978. "Natural Selection and the Emergence of Mind." *Dialectica* 32: 339–355.

———. 1984. "Evolutionary Epistemology." In *Evolutionary Theory: Paths into the Future*, ed. J. W. Pollard, pp. 239–255. London: John Wiley and Sons.

Potts, Richard. 1991. "Untying the Knot: Evolution of Early Human Behavior." In *Man and Beast Revisited*, ed. Michael H. Robinson and Lionel Tiger, pp. 41–59. Washington, DC: Smithsonian Institute Press.

Putnam, Hilary. 1987. *The Many Faces of Realism*. LaSalle, IL: Open Court.

Quillian, William F., Jr. 1945. *The Moral Theory of Evolutionary Naturalism*. New Haven, CT: Yale University Press.

Quine, W. V. O. 1975. "The Nature of Natural Knowledge." In *Mind and Language*, ed. S. Guttenplan, pp. 67–81. Oxford: Oxford University Press.

———. 1990. *Pursuit of Truth*. Cambridge, MA: Harvard University Press.

Rachels, James. 1987. "Darwin, Species, and Morality." *Monist* 70: 98–113.

———. 1989. "Why Darwin is Important for Ethics." In *Mind, Value and Culture: Essays in Honor of E. M. Adams*, ed. David Weissbord. Atascadero, CA: Ridgeview Publishing.

———. 1990. *Created from Animals: The Moral Implications of Darwinism*. Oxford: Oxford University Press.

Railton, Peter. 1986. "Moral Realism." *Philosophical Review* 95 (April): 163–207.

Raphael, D. Daiches. 1947. *The Moral Sense*. London: Oxford University Press.

————. 1958. "Darwinism and Ethics." In *A Century of Darwin*, ed. S. A. Barnett. Cambridge, MA: Harvard University Press.

————. 1972–1973. "Hume and Adam Smith on Justice and Utility." *Proceedings of the Aristotelian Society* 73: 87–103.

————. 1975. "The Impartial Spectator." In *Essays on Adam Smith*, ed. Andrew S. Skinner and Thomas Wilson, pp. 83–99. Oxford: Clarendon Press.

————. 1985. *Adam Smith*. Past Masters, ed. Keith Thomas. Oxford: Oxford University Press.

———— ed. 1991. *British Moralists 1650–1800*, vol. 1. Hobbes–Gay; vol. 2. Hume–Bentham. Indianapolis: Hackett.

Rawls, John. 1971. *A Theory of Justice*. Cambridge, MA: Belknap Press of Harvard University Press.

Regan, Tom. 1983. *The Case for Animal Rights*. Berkeley: University of California Press.

Rescher, N. 1977. *Methodological Pragmatism*. Oxford: Basil Blackwell.

————. ed., 1990a. *Evolution, Cognition, and Realism*. Lanham, MD: University Press of America.

————. 1990b. *A Useful Inheritance: Evolutionary Aspects of the Theory of Knowledge*. Savage, MD: Rowman and Littlefield.

Richards, Robert J. 1986. "Justification Through Biological Faith." *Biology and Philosophy* 1, no. 3: 337–354.

————. 1987. *Darwin and the Emergence of Evolutionary Theories of Mind and Behavior*. Chicago: University of Chicago Press.

Ritchie, A. D. 1948. *Essays In Philosophy and Other Pieces*. New York: Longmans, Green and Co.

Ritchie, David G. 1890. "Darwinism and Politics." *The Humboldt Library*, no. 125: 5–36.

————. 1893. *Darwin and Hegel with Other Philosophical Studies*. London: Swan Sonnenschein and Co.

Roberts, T. A. 1973. *The Concept of Benevolence*. London: Macmillan.

Robinson, Michael H., and Lionel Tiger, ed. 1991. *Man and Beast Revisited*. Washington, DC: Smithsonian Institution Press.

Rodd, Rosemary. 1990. *Biology, Ethics and Animals*. Oxford: Clarendon Press.

Rorty, Richard. 1989. "Solidarity or Objectivity." In *Anti-Theory in Ethics and Moral Conservatism*, ed. S. G. Charles and E. Simpson. Albany: State University of New York Press.

Rosenberg, Alexander. 1990. "The Political Philosophy of Biological Endowments: Some Considerations." *Social Philosophy and Policy* 5, no. 1: 1–31.

Rottschaefer, William A. 1990. "Really Taking Darwin Seriously: An Alternative to Michael Ruse's Darwinian Metaethics." *Biology and Philosophy* 5, no. 2: 149–173.

Rudwick, M. J. S. 1985. *The Great Devonian Controversy: The Shaping of Scientific Knowledge Among Gentlemanly Specialists*. Chicago: University of Chicago Press.

Ruse, Michael. 1979. *Sociobiology: Sense or Nonsense?* Dordrecht: Reidel.

————. 1985. "Is Rape Wrong on Andromeda? An Introduction to Extraterrestrial

Evolution, Science, and Morality." In *Extraterrestrials*, ed. E. Regis, Jr., pp. 43–78. Cambridge: Cambridge University Press.

———. 1986. *Taking Darwin Seriously: A Naturalistic Approach to Philosophy.* New York: Basil Blackwell.

——— and E. O. Wilson. 1986. "Moral Philosophy as Applied Science." *Philosophy* 61: 173–192.

Russett, Cynthia Eagle. 1976. *Darwin In America: The Intellectual Response 1865–1912.* San Francisco: W. H. Freeman and Company.

Sanderson, J. R. 1912. *The Relation of Evolutionary Theory to Ethical Problems.* Toronto: Toronto University Press.

Saunders, Peter T. 1988. "Sociobiology: A House Built on Sand." In *Evolutionary Processes and Metaphors*, ed. Mae-Wan Ho and Sidney W. Fox. New York: John Wiley and Sons.

Scheffler, S. 1987. "Morality Through Thick and Thin." *Philosophical Review* 96 (July): 411–435.

Schilpp, Paul Arthur. 1977. *Kant's Pre-Critical Ethics.* Reprint of the 2d ed. published by Northwestern University Press, Evanston, IL. New York: Garland Publishing Co.

Schneewind, J. B., ed. 1990. *Moral Philosophy from Montaigne to Kant*, vols. 1 and 2. Cambridge: Cambridge University Press.

Schoeman, F. 1987. *Responsiblity, Character and the Emotions.* New York: Cambridge University Press.

Schurman, J. G. 1888. *The Ethical Import of Darwinism.* New York: Charles Scribner's Sons.

Schwartz, Barry. 1986. *The Battle for Human Nature: Science, Morality and Modern Life.* New York: W. W. Norton and Company.

Scoccia, Danny. 1990. "Utilitarianism, Sociobiology, and the Limits of Benevolence." *Journal of Philosophy* 87 (July): 329–345.

Sidgwick, Henry. 1981. *The Methods of Ethics.* 7th ed. Indianapolis: Hackett.

Singer, Peter. 1981. *The Expanding Circle: Ethics and Sociobiology.* New York: Farrar, Straus and Giroux.

———. 1983. *Animal Liberation.* Wellingborough: Thorsons.

———. 1984. "Ethics and Sociobiology." *Zygon* 19 (June): 141–158.

———. 1987. "Animal Liberation or Animal Rights." *Monist* 70: 3–14.

Skinner, Andrew S. 1972. "Adam Smith: Philosophy and Science." *Scottish Journal of Political Economy* 19: 307–319.

———. 1974. "Adam Smith, Science and the Role of the Imagination." In *Hume and the Enlightenment: Essays presented to Ernest Campbell Mossner*, ed. William B. Todd, pp. 164–188. Edinburgh: University of Edinburgh Press.

——— and T. Wilson, ed. 1975. *Essays on Adam Smith.* Oxford: Clarendon Press.

Skinner, B. F. 1953. *Science and Human Behavior.* New York: Macmillan.

Smith, Adam. 1980. *Essays on Philosophical Topics.* Oxford: Clarendon Press.

———. 1982. *The Theory of Moral Sentiments.* Indianapolis: Liberty Classics.

Smith, Norman Kemp. 1960. *The Philosophy of David Hume: A Critical Study of Its Origins and Central Doctrines.* London: Macmillan and Co.

Sober, Elliott. 1984. *The Nature of Selection: Evolutionary Theory in Philosophical Focus.* Cambridge, MA: The MIT Press.

———. 1988a. "Apportioning Causal Responsibility." *Journal of Philosophy* 85 (June): 303–318.

———. 1988b. "What is Evolutionary Altruism?" *Canadian Journal of Philosophy* 14: 75–99.

———. 1989. "What Is Psychological Egoism?" *Behaviorism* 17: 89–102.

———. 1993. "Evolutionary Altruism, Psychological Egoism, and Morality: Disentangling the Phenotypes." In *Evolutionary Ethics*, ed. Matthew N. Nitecki and Doris V. Nitecki, pp. 199–216. Albany: State University of New York Press.

Sorley, W. R. 1904. *Recent Tendencies in Ethics*. London: William Blackwood and Sons.

———. 1969. *The Ethics of Naturalism: A Criticism*. Freeport, NY: Books for Libraries Press.

Spencer, Herbert. 1852. "A Theory of Population, Deduced from the General Law of Animal Fertility." *Westminster Review* 57: 468–501.

———. 1966. *The Principles of Ethics*, reprint of the 1879 edition, vol. 1. Osnabrück: Otto Zeller.

Sperber, Dan. 1984. "Anthropology and Psychology: Towards an Epidemiology of Representations." *MAN* 20: 73–89.

Stanley, G. Clark, and Even Simpson, ed. 1989. *Anti-Theory in Ethics and Moral Conservatism*. Albany: State University of New York Press.

Stearns, Stephen. 1992. *The Evolution of Life Histories*. Oxford: Oxford University Press.

Stephen, Leslie. 1907. *The Science of Ethics*. London: J. Murray Publishing Company.

———. 1949. *English Thought in the Eighteenth Century*. 3rd ed. New York: Perter Smith.

——— and Frederick Pollock, ed. 1879. *Lectures and Essays by the Late William Kingdon Clifford, F. R. S.*, vol. 2. London: Macmillan and Co.

Sterelny, K., and P. Kitcher. 1988. "The Return of the Gene." *Journal of Philosophy* 85, no. 7: 339–361.

Stewart, M. A., ed. 1990. *Studies in the Philosophy of the Scottish Enlightenment*. Oxford: Clarendon Press.

Stone, Christopher D. 1983. "On the Moral and Legal Rights of Nature." *Bostonia* (July–August): 29–35.

Stroup, Timothy. 1984. "Westermarck's Ethical Methodology." In *Man, Law and Modern Forms of Life*, ed. Eugenio Bulygin, Jean-Louis Gardies, and Ilkka Niiniluoto, pp. 85–95. Dordrecht: Reidel.

Taylor, W. L. 1965. *Francis Hutcheson and David Hume as Predecessors of Adam Smith*. Durham, NC: Duke University Press.

Tennant, Neil. 1988. "Two Problems For Evolutionary Epistemology: Psychic Reality and the Emergence of Norms." *Ratio* 1: 47–63.

Thomas, Laurence. 1986. "Biological Moralism." *Biology and Philosophy* 1, no. 3: 316–325.

Tinbergen, N. 1989. *The Study of Instinct*. Oxford: Clarendon Press.

Tooby, J., and L. Cosmides. 1990. "On the Universality of Human Nature and the Uniqueness of the Individual: The Role of Genetics and Adaptation." *Journal of Personality* 58, no. 1: 18–67.

Toulmin, Stephen. 1967. "The Evolutionary Development of Natural Science." *American Scientist* 55, no. 4: 456–467.

———. 1972. *Human Understanding: The Collective Use and Evolution of Concepts*. Princeton, NJ: Princeton University Press.

———. 1974. "Rationality and Scientific Discovery." In *Boston Studies in the Philosophy of Science*, ed. K. Schaffner and R. Cohen, vol. 20, pp. 387–406. Dordrecht: Reidel.

———. 1981. "Evolution, Adaptation, and Human Understanding." In *Scientific Inquiry and the Social Sciences: A Volume in Honor of Donald T. Campbell*, ed. M. B. Brewer and B. E. Collins, pp. 18–36. San Francisco: Jossey-Bass.

Trigg, Roger. 1986. "Evolutionary Ethics." *Biology and Philosophy* 1, no. 3: 325–335.

Trivers, Robert. 1985. *Social Evolution*. Menlo Park, CA: Benjamin/Cummings.

Turner, E. S. 1964. *All Heaven in a Rage*. London: Quality Book Club.

Vollmer, G. 1987. "On Supposed Circularities in an Empirically Oriented Epistemology." In *Evolutionary Epistemology, Theory of Rationality and the Sociology of Knowledge*, ed. G. Radnitzky and W. W. Bartley III, pp. 163–200. LaSalle, IL: Open Court.

von Schilcher, F., and N. Tennant. 1984. *Philosophy, Evolution and Human Nature*. London: Routledge and Kegan Paul.

Wake, C. Staniland. 1878. *The Evolution of Morality. Being a History of the Development of Moral Culture*. London: Trubner and Co., Ludgate Hill.

Westermarck, Edward. 1932. *Ethical Relativity*. New York: Harcourt, Brace and Company.

Wiles, Anne M. 1989. "Harman and Others on Moral Relativism." *Review of Metaphysics* 42: 783–795.

Williams, B. J. 1989. "The Scientific and the Ethical." In *Anti-Theory in Ethics and Moral Conservatism*, ed. S. G. Clarke and E. Simpson. Albany: State University of New York.

Williams, G. C. 1989. "A Sociobiological Expansion of Evolution and Ethics." In *Evolution and Ethics*, ed. J. Paradis and G. C. Williams. Princeton, NJ: Princeton University Press.

Williams, Thomas Rhys. 1959. "The Evolution of A Human Nature." *Philosophy of Science* 26: 1–13.

Wilson, E. O. 1975. *Sociobiology*. Cambridge, MA: Harvard University Press.

———. 1979. *On Human Nature*. New York: Bantam Books.

———. 1980. *Sociobiology* abridged edition. Cambridge, MA: The Bellknap Press.

———. 1984. *Biophilia*. Cambridge, MA: Harvard University Press.

———. 1992. *The Diversity of Life*. Cambridge, MA: Belknap Press.

Wittgenstein, L. 1988. *Tractatus Logico-Philosophicus*, trans. D. F. Pears and B. F. McGuinness. London: Routledge.

Wren, Thomas E., ed. 1990. *The Moral Domain: Essays in the Ongoing Discussion Between Philosophy and the Social Sciences*. Cambridge, MA: MIT Press.

———. 1991. *Caring about Morality: Philosophical Perspectives in Moral Psychology*. Cambridge, MA: The MIT Press.

Wuketits, Franz. 1990. *Evolutionary Epistemology and Its Implications for Humankind*. Albany, NY: State University of New York Press.

Index

191

AHM 778
MN-51